Classic Car
Electrical
Systems
Repair Manual

Dave Pollard

Haynes Publishing

First published in 1999

© Dave Pollard 1999

Dave Pollard has asserted his right to be identified as the author of this work.

British Library cataloguing-in-publication data:
A catalogue record for this book is available from the British Library.

ISBN 1 85960 433 1

Library of Congress Catalog Card Number 98-74167

Haynes North America Inc.
861 Lawrence Drive, Newbury Park,
California 91320, USA

Published by Haynes Publishing, Sparkford,
Nr Yeovil, Somerset BA22 7JJ, UK

Tel: 01963 440635 Fax: 01963 440001
Int. tel: +44 1963 440635 Fax: +44 1963 440001

E-mail: sales@haynes-manuals.co.uk
Web site: http://www.haynes.com

Printed and bound in Great Britain by J. H. Haynes & Co. Ltd

Jurisdictions which have strict emission control laws may consider any modification to a vehicle to be an infringement of those laws. You are advised to check with the appropriate body or authority whether your proposed modification complies fully with the law. The publishers accept no liability in this regard.

While every effort is taken to ensure the accuracy of the information given in this book, no liability can be accepted by the author or publishers for any loss, damage or injury caused by errors in, or omissions from, the information given.

Contents

Acknowledgements

My thanks go to the following, who were instrumental in providing information, photography or technology at the right time; Mr M. A. Ford (Autocar Electrical), Roger Davis and Martin Ethelston (Auto Sparks), Claire Newman (Bosch), Phil Blundell (Capri Care MK), Nigel Hedges (Fluke), Granville Unsworth (Gunson Limited), Frank Harper-Jones (Lunken Security), Lucas Automotive, Nick Bundy (Metabo), Sara Lamper (Ring, Cibié), Christine Whitworth (Sykes Pickavant/ITT), M. R. Pindard (Vehicle Wiring Products).

Peter and Jim at P & J Autos provided a wealth of classic car electrical information and did the step-by-step strip and rebuild sections for the dynamo, alternator and two types of starter motor. From Pilots to Pintos there's nothing they don't have, can't get or won't try to fix.

Jeremy Holden and his team at Holden Vintage & Classic opened up their not inconsiderable stores and wealth of knowledge. Not least of this related to distributors, for which they are probably the largest single source in the country.

Thanks, as ever, to my wife Ann for proofing, checking and researching.

Introduction

In the happy world of Haynes restoration manuals I have met numerous 'amateur' (i.e. unpaid) car restorers, whose skill and ingenuity leave me speechless with admiration. In some cases these qualities also extend to the electrical system, but often it is shunned like a politician at a classic car rally (David Steel and Alan Clark excepted). And this is often by owners who think nothing of stripping and rebuilding their dohc engines, making up new panels from scraps of steel and alloy, and welding a complete chassis to Formula 1 standard.

Some areas of a car's electrical system can be a little tricky to grasp, but as long as you have a good understanding of the basics you, at least, will be able to pinpoint a problem and, even if you can't solve it yourself, you'll know how to accurately identify it when directing someone else to solve it for you. Remember that 'electrics' on classic cars have become 'electronics' on today's automobiles – a different *word* altogether as befits a different *world* altogether from that of the classic, where complex electrics were all but non-existent until well into the '70s.

The theory

For most of us, the theory behind electricity is likely to bring back hazy memories of endless physics lessons, seemingly designed just to clutter up the day with talk of amps, ohms and watts – and lots of other things you thought you would never need. I'm sure that if someone had had the wit

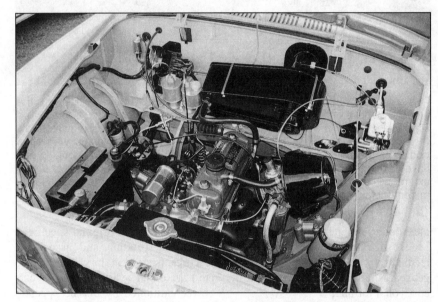

Compare this wonderfully simple engine bay scene with that which confronts you when you open the bonnet of a modern car. For many tasks, you can work on classic car electrics with little more than a test light and a logical approach. Add in a multimeter and a few tools and you have just about everything you need to sort out what's watt.

to link such a 'dry' subject to that of motor cars or, better still, motorcycles, there would have been considerably more interest taken! As it was, for most of us it couldn't compete with the highlights of the previous night's *Goon Show* or getting black-market tickets to see the Beatles live.

Nevertheless, it's important to have at least *some* grasp of the fundamentals before you delve deep into your car's wiring loom. We're not talking rocket science – just as long as you understand the basics of your car's electrical system, you'll be OK. After all, you don't need to know how your TV or video works in order to use them, but you do need to know

what is likely to wreck rather than repair, or kill rather than cure!

Though 'official' wiring diagrams and symbols are covered, most of the diagrams shown in this book are of the schematic type, which are much simpler to understand.

Practical proposition?

Since most of us classic owners also drive a 'modern', we can compare the spares situation quite easily. Want an interior light lens for your Vauxhall Astra? It's sitting on the shelf at your local dealers. Friends and neighbours will quote this sort of thing as they watch you struggling to solve a com-

This glorious Coventry Climax engine with its twin Webers is a sight to stir the blood and make grown men ponder giving up an eye tooth or two. It retains the simple electrics of the time, but because the Lotus Elite has a fibreglass body, there are a set of unique problems that don't beset those of us with steel bodied cars. Most of these relate to earthing problems, where earth connections have to be made to the chassis. All fibreglass cars suffer to a greater or lesser extent, with occasional flickering lights, interesting ignition problems and intermittent fuel pump operation being typical.

plex loom problem on your 1966 MGB, sucking loudly through their teeth as they predict that 'you'll never get spares for that – and if you do it'll cost you a fortune!'

They're only partly right. It's true that cars such as Ferraris, Duesenburgs and Bugattis will present their own specific and very expensive problems, but these cars are in the stratosphere of classic ownership rather than the down to earth practical classics that this book concerns itself with – the sort of classic car that can be owned and driven on a daily basis without the need for a special arrangement with the Old Lady of Threadneedle Street. Getting most electrical items for popular cars like Hillman, MG, Morris, Rover, Triumph, *et al*, is surprisingly easy, with plenty of mail order companies (such as Holdens, Rimmer Bros, Vehicle Wiring Products, Auto Sparks and Moss) servicing a massive market for older cars. In addition, many owner clubs (particularly the larger ones) take the trouble to source parts or even have them

remanufactured to original specification. Even rotating and associated electrics (starter motors, generators, etc.) are either available new or can be reconditioned by classic specialists such as P & J Autos.

The concours connection

As the owner of two classic cars (and a classic bike), I fall into that category of drivers who want to be able to use their classics on a regular basis without having to memorise the RAC's number and who aren't likely to get over-excited if some mud gets on the paintwork. Also, when it comes to maintenance and occasional uprating, practicality wins every time. When the Imp's awful pressure windscreen wash system got the better of me, it was a half-hour job, involving less than £10 from the piggy bank, to wire in an electric thumb, which works just as well as any 'modern'. Equally, when electronic ignition promised better starting, performance, fuel economy and reliability, I had no hesitation in popping the old points into my 'box of things that might eventually come in useful' tucked away at the back of my increasingly crowded garage.

This book reflects a practical way of thinking and driving – after all, few '60s cars were driven for long before they had been doctored in some way or other by a first or second owner. It's in the nature of the motorist to try to improve what the manufacturer has spent millions developing in the first place.

A summer's day, beautiful sunshine and an atmosphere of classic car enthusiasm engenders a heady feeling of 'must buy', which is not always a good thing.

A typical 'electrical' layout, with all sorts of interesting electronic bits and pieces. Items such as rear lamp clusters (top left) are fairly safe buys; you should be able to recognise the part you need and you can check it physically for cracks and splits. Other items are not so easy to check – those radios look wonderfully period late '60s and early '70s and would be the ideal addition to your classic, but do they work? Thoughtful stall holders bring along 12V batteries to show whether or not electrical products still work. Some products can be checked to some extent (resistance for example) by taking along your multimeter.

Second-hand

However, it's almost inevitable that you'll eventually need something that isn't so readily available. Again, your first port of call should be your club – advertise your requirements and you'll probably find that an enthusiast somewhere has just what you need in an oily

Rotating electrics are often on display, like this MGB starter motor for 'just' £25. But, at the time of writing, P & J Autos can supply a fully reconditioned and guaranteed unit for little more than that, which shows the wisdom in knowing how much something costs new (or reconditioned) before you buy used. Their advice is to make sure that at least the motor spins when a 12V power source is applied. Checking the operation of the inertia gear is not possible in situations like this.

A whole pile of accessory lamps, highly tempting for that period look. Check that the lens is not cracked or damaged (not an MoT problem, just a practical one) and that the reflector – the shiny bit behind the lens – is mirror-like with no signs of rusty discoloration.

cardboard box at the back of his garage. It may be possible to do a swap in order to allay the onset of financial embar-

rassment. There are such things as classic scrapyards, but they're few and far between. The next line of defence is the public show or autojumble. The key here is to know exactly what you want; take a part number if possible, the exact model of your car with engine/chassis number or the old unit for comparison, especially where the manufacturers changed the design several times during the life span of your car.

If you're buying something that can't actually be seen to be working (such as a starter motor), then tread with care and follow the rules suggested by P & J Autos in the rotating electrics chapters; the essence being that, unless you're searching for a real rarity, an item that doesn't work is virtually worthless.

General hints and tips

Substitute
There's no substitute for substitution. Sometimes you can face an electrical problem which defies logic, despite your best efforts and patience. You can console yourself to some extent with

the knowledge that if you were working on a 'modern', you'd probably have ten times the trouble!

Often, one of the simplest ways around this kind of difficulty is to replace a suspect part with one that is known to be good, and this is where the classic car owner scores, as he is more likely to know someone with the same or similar car – or knows a man who does, not least through club membership. Moreover, lots of club members have workshops full of odds and sods that 'might come in handy one day' and, being fellow classic car owners, are more than likely to lend you something to see if it solves the problem.

Meter checks

Wherever possible, checking procedures using a multimeter have been shown. It's important that resistance checks (ohms) are NEVER made on a circuit with power in it. At the least it could blow a fuse in your meter, and at worst it could damage the meter and/or the component being tested.

Chapter 1

Preparations and safety

Working on your classic car's electrics, whether it's simple maintenance or complete component restoration, will give you immense satisfaction. However, it's important to stay safe long enough to enjoy the fruits of your labours. Cars, no matter how old and (apparently) friendly, are inherently dangerous. So, your personal safety – and that of those around you – should always be your primary concern. Here are a few basic guidelines.

Preparations

When you're working on your car, always make sure that someone knows where you are and ask them to check up on you on a regular basis – it could be your life-saver.

Wear overalls, not least because there are less likely to be loose items of clothing to get caught in moving parts.

Impose a NO SMOKING rule in your workshop at all times.

Remove watches and jewellery where possible.

Hand care

It's always wise to protect your hands, not least from the unpleasant effects of oil and grease which are now known to be carcinogenic.

General safety tips

● Make sure that the gearbox is in

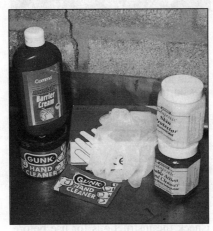

Use a quality barrier cream before you dirty your hands so that any dirt/oil you get on them will simply wash off. Better still, wear vinyl or latex gloves to keep dirt and oil off your skin altogether. When you wash your hands, use a purpose-made cleaner which will pull off the dirt without removing your skin's natural oils.

neutral ('park' on auto 'boxes) before starting the engine.
● Don't leave the key in the ignition while you're working on the car unless it's required for a specific electrical test. Remove it again once you've finished testing.
● Keep things tidy – a workshop with cables and pipes running all over the floor is a recipe for disaster.
● When fitting something new, READ the instructions! It's best to do this in the warmth of your living room, as you'll be prone to skip bits out in a cold workshop.

● When cleaning components DON'T use petrol (gasoline). Use white (mineral) spirit, paraffin (kerosene) or purpose-made industrial cleaners.
● When using any power tools, or even hand tools, there may be a danger of flying detritus (chiselling a seized nut, for example). Always wear goggles to protect your eyes, especially when using grinders, etc.
● Use quality tools – an ill-fitting spanner could damage the component, your car and, of course, yourself!
● Time is a vital element in any workshop. Make sure you've got enough to finish a job; rushed work is rarely done right.
● Children are naturally inquisitive, but don't allow them to wander unsupervised round or in your car, especially if it is jacked up.

Picture this

For most of us, earning a living takes precedence over working on our classics, and there can often be gaps of days or weeks between, say, starting a dynamo strip-down and completing the rebuild. Don't believe that you'll be able to remember everything – it's amazing how much the memory fades. If you're working on particularly complex items, make notes and diagrams as to where the various component parts should go.

Alternatively, use a camera or even a video camera to show a dismantling procedure and replacement order. Using the latter also gives the opportunity for a running commentary.

Battery earth

It's usual practice to remove the battery earth lead when working on a car. If you need to check which wires carry power, etc., do so before removing the lead, and make sure you know any radio codes and, in extreme circumstances, that you will not 'upset' any electronic ECUs on the car. However, many of the checks and repair sequences require power to a circuit or component, so battery disconnection is clearly not always possible; in which case you must be very aware of the dangers of electric shock, particularly from ignition components, which can involve many thousands of volts. Most batteries give off a small amount of highly explosive hydrogen gas, so you should never allow a naked flame or a spark near your battery. Equally, a spark from an accidental short circuit can easily ignite fuel – or even fuel vapour from the carburettor – and, given that a full tank of fuel can be anything up to 20 gallons, it's something best avoided!

Sparks also occur outside the car – for example, two metal surfaces striking against each other, or even a central heating boiler starting up. And don't forget naked flames when using, say, a gas welder or gas soldering iron.

Fire

That said, it's foolish not to anticipate the worst. It's good practice to carry a fire extinguisher in any car, but in a classic, where the wiring has often seen better days, it is essential. Choose a carbon dioxide type or, better still, dry powder, but **never** a water type extinguisher for car/workshop use. Water conducts electricity and, in some circumstances, could actually make an oil or petrol based fire worse. Where possible, fit it on a bracket permanently in the car.

Ideally, have one in the car and a larger one for workshop use.

Always have a fire extinguisher to hand and know how it works – the Basil Fawlty school of fire fighting is not recommended! There are so many things in your workshop and on your classic that are flammable, you can't afford to be without one. Ideally, buy a smaller extinguisher to carry inside your vehicle and a larger model for workshop use.

Otherwise, take the one from the car and place it to hand on your workbench ready for use – just in case. Check the instructions for use before you need to use it, and always direct the jet at the base of the flames.

Finishing

When you've finished, clean up the workshop and clean and return to their place all your tools. You'll reap the rewards in time saved next time out and in tools that last much longer and work much better.

Mains electricity

Mains power tools should be used with special care outdoors. Use the correct type of plug with correct and tightly-made connections. Where applicable, make sure that they are earthed (grounded).

Use an RCD – a residual circuit breaker which, in the event of a short circuit cuts the power immediately to reduce the risk of electrocution.

Fumes

Never run the engine of your classic (or any car) in an enclosed space – the exhaust fumes contain deadly carbon monoxide and can kill within minutes. This also applies to catalyst-equipped cars – not so if you own a Euro classic, but American cars were commonly fitted with 'cats' 30 years before us. Treat all chemicals with great care, not least of which, petrol. Many cleaning agents and solvents contain highly toxic chemicals and should not be used in confined spaces or used for long periods without a break. Wear gloves when working with chemicals, and if any are spilled on your skin rinse off with water immediately.

High tension ignition

Touching parts of the ignition system with the engine running (or being turned over), notably the HT leads themselves, can lead to severe electric shock, especially if the vehicle is fitted with electronic ignition. Voltages produced by electronic ignition systems are much higher than normal and could prove fatal, especially to those with cardiac pacemakers.

The likelihood of an electric shock is more pronounced in wet or damp

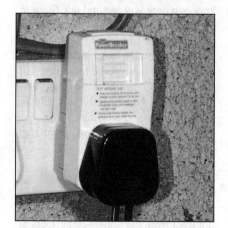

RCDs can be purchased quite cheaply from most DIY stores. Take special care when working in damp conditions, especially if you are using a mains extension lead. Wherever possible, work indoors and/or use battery powered tools.

conditions, when a spark can 'jump' to an earthing point – you! Take great care when performing a task which requires the engine to be running (setting the timing, for example) not to touch any ignition components.

Petrol safety

Petrol is a highly flammable, volatile liquid and should be treated with great respect. Even its vapour will ignite at the slightest provocation. If you work in a pit, extra care is required, as petrol vapour is heavier than air and will tend to build-up in the bottom of the pit.

Engine oils

There is some danger from contaminates that are contained in all used oil and, according to some experts, prolonged skin exposure can lead to serious skin disorders. Just about every electrical component under the bonnet is likely to have at least some oil on it (unless your classic is a top-notch concours winner), so always use barrier cream on your hands and wear plastic or rubber gloves when handling oil stained components.

Fluoroelastomers

Many items found on modern cars (e.g. oil seals, gaskets, diaphragms, and 'O' rings) appear to be rubber but, in fact, they are made from a synthetic substitute which contains fluorine. Such materials are called fluoroelastomers, and if heated to more than 315°C (600°F) they can decompose in a dangerous manner. Indeed, some decomposition can occur at temperatures of around 200°C (392°F). These temperatures would normally only be found on a car if it were to be set alight or if it were 'broken' by a vehicle dismantler using a cutting torch.

Where there is any water present, including atmospheric moisture, the heated fluoroelastomers produce extremely dangerous by-products.

The Health and Safety Executive says: 'Skin contact with this liquid or decomposition residues can cause painful and penetrating burns. Permanent irreversible skin and tissue damage can occur.' Clearly, this is important to note if your car has caught fire, even if only partially, or if it has been stolen and 'fired' by the thieves. Even more caution is required if you are searching for used parts in a vehicle dismantlers.

Observe the following safety procedures:

1 Never touch blackened or charred pieces of rubber or anything that looks like it.

2 Allow all burnt or decomposed fluoroelastomer materials to cool down before inspection, investigations, tear-down or removal.

3 Ideally, don't handle parts containing decomposed fluoroelastomers. If you have to, wear goggles and PVC protective gloves whilst doing so. Never handle them unless they are completely cool.

4 Contaminated parts, residues, materials and clothing, including protective clothing and gloves, should be disposed of by an approved contractor to landfill or by incineration according to national or local regulations. Oil seals, gaskets and 'O' rings, along with contaminated material, must not be burned locally.

Ramps are favourite for working under your car, but remember that the wheels on the ground will still need chocking, as well as leaving the handbrake on and, where applicable, the car in gear.

Raising your classic safely

For the most part, work on your classics' electrical system can be carried out with all four (or three!) wheels on the ground. However, it's sometimes necessary to raise the car – for example, when removing or checking a starter motor. You simply cannot be too careful when working under your car – 20 people die every year as a result of a car falling on them!

If you can't use ramps, use a quality trolley jack to raise the car. This is an Omega jack with a handy foot-operated lever to make initial raising easier. The Clarke axle stands can handle 3 tonnes apiece – more than enough for the largest car.

Under the car

● Never work under your classic when it is supported only by a jack. Use additional support from securely placed axle stands.
● Before you get under the car, make sure the ignition keys are in your pocket!
● Protect your eyes and hands using goggles and gloves.
● Don't attempt to loosen high-torque nuts or bolts while the car is off the ground. Torque them up when the vehicle is back on the floor.
● Never touch any part of the exhaust or manifolds before ascertaining whether or not they are hot.

First aid

General treatment rules

This being an electrical rather than a medical book, there is not room to cover all eventualities. However, one golden rule to remember is that anyone suffering injuries whilst working on the vehicle (or even out on the road) should not be moved unless there is an obvious other danger. For example, someone who has suffered a hefty electrical shock from the HT circuit should be left where they are unless the accident has also started a garage fire and they are in even more danger!

It's good practice to keep a first aid kit in your car, and when you're working on it, keep it to hand alongside the fire extinguisher. Make sure it's green with a white cross (so everyone knows what it is – it's the internationally accepted colouring) and get one produced for, or at least recommended by, the St John Ambulance Brigade.

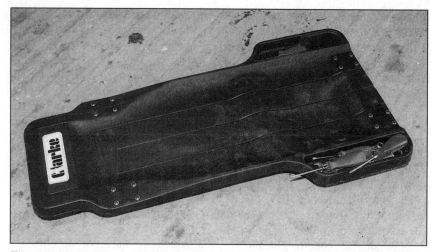

The simplest way to get around under your car is to use a wheeled crawler, like this one. Note the handy trays at either side, so you don't end up rolling around on your tools.

It's a good idea to contact the SJAB for details of first aid procedures relating specifically to motoring – there are regional centres all over the country and courses are being run for beginners throughout the year. The details of the SJAB head office are given in Appendix I.

Chapter 2
Electrical tools

Test lamps

For some electrical tasks, you'll need to know whether a specific wire is live. In many cases a good old-fashioned test lamp will prove adequate for this (notably when you're fiddling around under a dark dashboard, looking for a power source). However, test lamps have their limitations in that they give no value readings. To measure voltage, amperage and resistance a multimeter is needed.

The basic proprietary test lamp takes the form of a 'screwdriver' with a pointed end which passes through the see-through handle and makes contact with a small bulb. A length of wire is plugged into the handle (and makes contact with the other bulb terminal) end of the device and at the other end of the wire is a crocodile clip. Typically, the clip is connected to a good earth and the probe used to search for a live feed – when one is found, the bulb lights up.

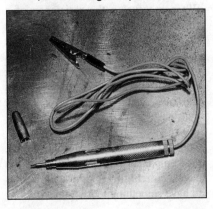

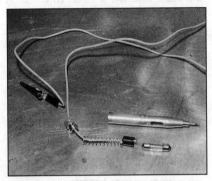

As you can see, it's a simple piece of equipment, with the light inside being a festoon type bulb held in place by a spring which also pushes the contact on to the top of it. This in turn is connected to the wire which passes out of the top of the body of the device and culminates in the crocodile clip.

However . . .

You should never use a test light on anything other than very basic electrical components. The power drain of even a small bulb could damage some ECUs (Electronic Control Units), and though they weren't commonplace on classic cars, some high-performance classics did feature fuel injection and clever electronics in the 1960s.

Multimeters

For more detailed work on your classic's electrics, a multimeter is not only useful but, in some cases, essential. And just because you have an old car, it doesn't mean you have to use old-style equipment to keep it going.

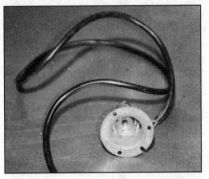

The DIY alternative is to take a bulb in a holder, attach a pair of wires with crocodile clips (available from electrical specialists such as Maplins or Tandy) to the ends, and you have a simple testing device.

The latest state-of-the-art diagnostic electronic devices will make light work (or maybe even your lights work) of problems that would have appeared much more serious 30 years ago. Prices vary considerably, though the general rule of thumb which applies to all tools applies here, in that the very best doesn't come cheap. However, there are plenty of devices around that don't cost mega-money.

A good multimeter will be an investment you'll recoup several times over. The more features it has, the better – even if you can't see a need for them now, you never know about the future, and having later to buy a new meter (or another device altogether) makes it a short-term false economy to skimp now. Typically, a good meter will show voltage readings (DC for car use and AC for mains use – ideal when you're wiring up your garage lighting/heating/electric door opener, etc.), resistance, engine rpm, points dwell angle, amps, diode checking – and the better ones have the option to test temperatures, so that you can, for example, check that a sensor designed to operate at a specific engine temperature is doing just that. If you consider that a good multimeter is an expensive toy, consider that many garages are now charging £35 an hour, and those asking £50 are not uncommon. Compare this cost to that of your meter – it doesn't have to work too hard to pay for itself, does it?

Choosing a multimeter
Always look for signs of good build quality and a long warranty. All meters should have some kind of overload protection for the inevitable occasion when you cross-hobble the connections or connect a heavy load on the wrong setting. You need to protect your financial investment and yourself.

Auto-ranging and display
It's not hard work to select, say, a specific voltage range to work in, but it's easier if the machine does it for you – that's auto-ranging. A digital meter feature worth having is dual display, where the number display is backed up by a bar graph, the latter of which can react more quickly and give an idea of what's happening in analogue form. Ideal where a reading is changing quickly and the eye couldn't possibly follow the number fluctuations (effectively, it's the digital equivalent of an analogue needle).

Beep beep
A 'beeper' which warns when there is no resistance (or *vice versa*) is ideal for in-car use, especially when you're delving deep into the darkness of your under-dash area and can't possibly see the display.

Sharp probes, clips and wiring
Look for solid, thick wires to the probes. The probes should be pointed

and easily able to be inserted through a wire's plastic sheath where it is impossible to reach a terminal to take a reading. As well as probes, it's always advisable to have crocodile clips for total versatility.

Temperature gauge
Well recommended, as it means you can relate electrical readouts to a specific temperature – water, oil or even air.

The case for a stand
Automotive meters have a hard life, so invest in some form of case right from the start. Equally, a stand (often built into the back of the meter or its case) is very useful when you run out of hands.

What can it do?
The more features a meter has, the more useful it is and (all things being equal) the more it costs. A good meter will typically be able to deal with:

Battery charge
The 'DC/Volts' setting will let you see the current state of battery charge.

Battery cranking
How well is the battery performing under the biggest load it has to handle – turning over a cold engine?

Battery leakage
A flat battery is often caused by a small drain on it over a period of time. Check whether or not there is excessive leakage and gradually pinpoint the cause.

Alternator charging
Batteries are often replaced when there's no need because it's really the alternator to blame. If you can check it beforehand, you save your time and your money.

Voltage drop
A common classic problem, where voltage loses its way between components.

Resistance
It's often necessary to know the electrical resistance of a specific component

or piece of wire. Also, it is a simple way to check for a break in a wire, especially where it disappears into the depths of a loom. A meter which 'bleeps' when the circuit is broken is particularly handy when you can't actually see the meter.

Dwell angle
The dwell angle is a very important part of setting up the contact breaker points in a distributor.

Tachometer
Many a classic won't have a tachometer (rev counter) but even when it does, it's not necessarily going to be that accurate and, regardless, it will be hard to see when you're under the bonnet. As many engine tuning and diagnostic jobs are linked to specific engine revs, having a meter which lets you know the true engine speed is very useful. Some meters give you the actual reading, whilst others are geared up to 4 cylinder cars, and for other combinations, calculations have to be made.

Lambda sensor
More comprehensive meters may have the facility to check the functioning of the lambda sensor, a device essential where a catalytic converter is fitted. Although these have only become a legal requirement in the UK since 1992 (and only common since 1990), they have been used on American cars since the 1960s – very relevant to many classic car buffs.

Measuring notes
Resistance
When measuring the resistance of a component, the meter itself provides a small voltage, so it is VITAL that resistance measurements are always made with the component being tested disconnected from your car's electrical system.

Voltage
Conversely, when measuring voltage, the component must be connected and have a current flowing through it, so as to have something to measure.

Current

When measuring current, the original circuit has to be 'broken' and the meter inserted into it.

Safety when using a meter

The following safety tips are by courtesy of Fluke (UK) Ltd.
● Avoid working alone.
● Take extreme care when working around moving parts.
● Never use a meter if it looks damaged.
● Regularly inspect the leads for damage – exposed wiring could be very dangerous.
● Disconnect the power and discharge all high-voltage capacitors before testing resistance, continuity or diodes.
● Use great caution when testing voltages above 60V DC or 25V AC, because of the shock hazard.
● Always keep your fingers well above the metal probes or clips when making measurements.
● Disconnect the live test lead before disconnecting the common test lead.
● Check the meter fuse before

If you're really taking the job seriously, a multimeter package like this ITT from Sykes-Pickavant, will handle just about everything you could ask of it this side of tuning a Formula 1 Ferrari! It comes with stand, case, long leads with hefty crocodile clips, specific current sensor and inductive pick-up which is clipped on to the number one plug lead and which allows such things as rpm to be read off directly from the display without the need to disconnect any part of the system.

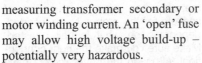

measuring transformer secondary or motor winding current. An 'open' fuse may allow high voltage build-up – potentially very hazardous.
● ALWAYS use clip-on probes when measuring current exceeding 10A.

Here, it has been connected to show that the engine is running at 797rpm – slightly high, although it was still cold and running some choke. Many tuning and maintenance operations relate directly to engine speed, so a meter with this function will soon start to earn its keep.

Of course, many owners still prefer to use an analogue, needle type meter. Though not suitable for many tasks involving ECUs and other complex electronics found on modern motors, it's just the ticket for older cars, especially as this has been specifically designed for car use by the electrical novice. It scores in simplicity by having colour-coded zones denoting whether or not a reading is good, OK or bad. In this case, it has been connected to give an indication of the alternator condition whilst the engine is running. The needle is in the green centre part of the scale, showing the alternator is charging correctly. If the needle were positioned to the red zone on the left, it would be undercharging; in the red zone to the right would indicate an overcharging situation. Simple, isn't it.

A typical selection of multimeters, ranging from those which can handle just about any electrical task there is to car-specific units, geared solely to such things as points dwell angle.

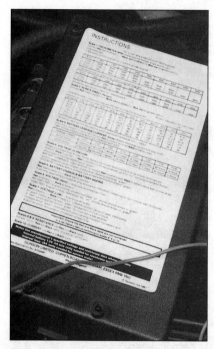

The meter's use is made simpler by having the instructions listed clearly on the underside of the unit, so saving the need to constantly refer to a manual that you know you had somewhere, but can't quite remember where you put it!

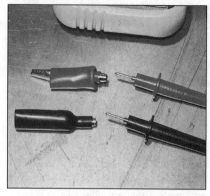

It's important to use strong probes and thick wiring – especially if you're dealing with large currents. In order to be of any use, the probes have to be needle sharp, to enable readings to be taken from lengths of wire where there are no terminals to touch on to. Make sure you keep your fingers on the right side of the probe! Crocodile clips are invaluable for some jobs, particularly when you're working on your own. Some clips push on to the probes, others screw-on. As the photo shows, modern meters often have a selection of sockets for the probes to be inserted, depending on what is being tested. Make sure you make the right connection! (Although the better meters have internal fuses to protect their innards from too much of a bad thing where they don't want it.)

Soldering irons

Once upon a time, a soldering iron was just that – a lump of iron on a long handle which was placed into a fire to heat it up. Thankfully, things have progressed since then, and there's a more convenient choice for the classic electrician.

Electrical

There are two types of electrical iron – the 240V mains type and the 12V type, both of which have their pros and cons. Mains irons are generally more powerful and don't flatten your battery. However, they do have that hefty lead on the end of them and in most cases will require the use of an extension lead if you're actually working in your car. This can be a real hassle, especially if you're working outdoors, and more still if it starts to rain. An RCD (see Chapter 1) should **always** be used with any 240V device used outside.

The 12V type is connected to the car battery, or better still, a separate 'slave' battery, using crocodile clips. It is more portable than the 240V mains style of iron, albeit not as powerful,

If you're just starting to build up your electrical tool collection, it's worth considering buying a kit containing several associated items. This one from Hella (under their Optilux branding) contains a multimeter, strobe light with inductive pick-up and a compression tester, all of which are useful when you're engine tuning or fault-finding. Again, this is aimed specifically at the automotive market.

Many meters come complete with a temperature probe (in some cases, it may be available as an optional extra). This can be very useful – for example, when 'boiling up' a thermostat to make sure it's opening and closing at the right temperature. Most temperature probes can be used to test ambient air as well as most liquids, including water and oil. Make sure you know whether your meter reads in Fahrenheit or Celsius – some can toggle between the two – otherwise you'll get some very confusing results!

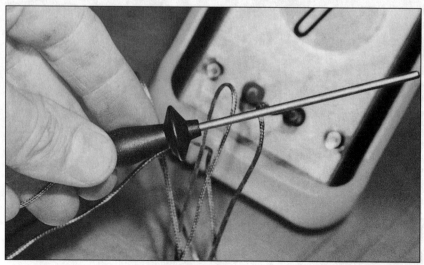

Seen here is a 12V iron on the left, a conventional 240V iron in the centre and on the right is a more expensive trigger-type 240V iron.

and it takes longer to warm up. Moreover, it can soon flatten a battery that isn't quite up to the mark. It is limited in range by the length of the cable, and care has to be taken to avoid trapping it (say, in the door) otherwise a short circuit/fire could occur.

Whatever your choice, your iron should be capable of handling the tasks you have in mind. For most simple ICE or accessory wiring, a modest iron will be perfectly adequate. But for heating up thick pieces of wire (such as a battery cable) you need some real oomph from your iron, and you'll require around 150W of it (electrical) or around 4oz of gas iron.

Gas

Gas irons are often favoured by the professional; they produce masses of heat quickly and are totally portable. Clearly, they need some care in their use and, more importantly, some thought as to where they are placed while not in use. They can be bought as part of a kit, which usually includes a variety of 'bits' and other accessories which facilitate its use other than as a soldering iron, for example, a small blowtorch. This is usually worthwhile, as gas irons are generally more expensive and multi-use helps spread the cost. Gas refill canisters are available from electrical specialists, tobacconists (some gas cigarette lighters use them) and even chemists, where some hair-styling devices use the same type of refill.

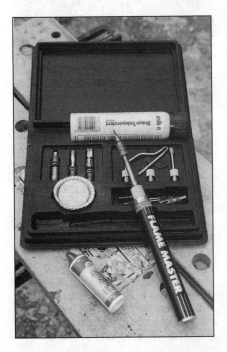

This is a typical gas iron with an accessory kit beneath it. The fluxed solder is shown in a handy tube and the canister at the top would more usually see service in a hair-curler.

General electrical tools

Electrician's tape is not all the same. If you're working on your classic, you'll want the job done right, and good tape like this from 3M will stick well for years without going brittle and peeling off. It's not cheap, but then you get nothing for nothing. If you're actually looming the wiring, then use proper harness tape (available from Auto Sparks) which is self-bonding whilst not actually being self-adhesive.

Crimpers

You can't afford to be without a good set of crimpers which will provide cutting, crimping and stripping capabilities in a single tool.

On the right is the most basic sort of crimper, which allows you to cut wiring, strip the plastic protective sheath and to crimp the three sizes of solderless terminals. However, they can be described as 'manual' in that you have to know (or more likely, guess) the size of the wiring to be stripped and there is no restriction on the amount of pressure applied to crimp a join. On the left is the semi-automatic type, which works out for itself exactly how thick the wire is.

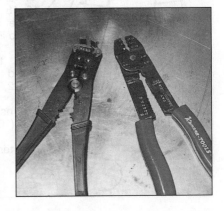

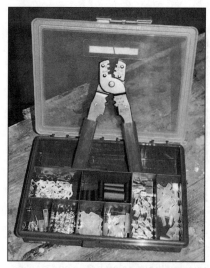

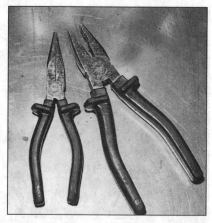

A good way to start your electrical toolkit is to buy a collection of connectors complete with insulators and a quality crimper. This is the Vehicle Wiring Products N9M kit designed for use with British vehicles (there's a separate one for Japanese cars which use smaller connectors). The pliable plastic box keeps things neat and tidy and makes it easy to see when to re-order a particular type of connector.

For absolute ease of making good, solid crimped joins, you need a ratchet crimper. The VWP DV5 model works in the same way as a 'manual' device, but it does both crimps at once and the ratchet mechanism ensures that you always crimp exactly the right amount – not too little so the connector falls off, or too much so that you all but cut it in half!

You'll need pliers to hold, cut and twist. Make sure the pliers you choose have plenty of thick insulation to guard against electric shock. Note the difference between standard pliers on the right, and the long-nosed (often called 'electrician's') pliers on the left. Use the former for heavy work, and the latter for more delicate work and where access is difficult – it's horses for courses.

This diagram shows the versatility of the MP71 crimping tool shown as part of the previous kit. It can handle most types of connector likely to be found on your classic. As ever, it's important to use it correctly to get the best results.

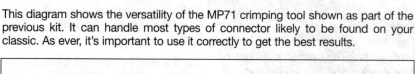

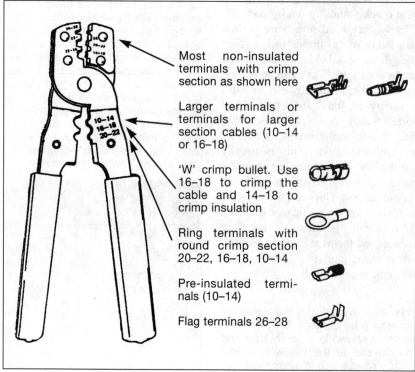

Most non-insulated terminals with crimp section as shown here

Larger terminals or terminals for larger section cables (10–14 or 16–18)

'W' crimp bullet. Use 16–18 to crimp the cable and 14–18 to crimp insulation

Ring terminals with round crimp section 20–22, 16–18, 10–14

Pre-insulated terminals (10–14)

Flag terminals 26–28

Any auto electrician will know the usefulness of a sharp knife. It can be used for stripping off sheathing where a crimping tool can't reach, cutting electrician's tape and plastic cable ties, removing awkward-to-get-at rubber grommets, cutting pieces of carpet where a wire needs to pass through – the list goes on. A craft knife is a good idea, preferably one with a retractable blade, as it is very easy to find it with your knee when you're embroiled in the intricacies of in-car wiring!

Alternatively, the sort of blade found on the current crop of super multi-tools (from makers such as Leatherman and Gerber) are extremely sharp and useful, giving the correct degree of care. Remember that a knife with a blunt blade is a very dangerous item; if you have one, then either have it sharpened, or throw it in the bin!

Anyone working with cars will know the feeling of needing a third hand – the classic electrician can have it! This clever device comprises multi-jointed 'arms' with crocodile clips on the end and is ideal for holding, say, two wires to be joined while you use your hands to do the soldering.

Slave battery

On the face of it, a battery isn't a tool, but it can easily be just that. Many of us replace a battery when it is clearly past its best, but not actually totally defunct. Rather than take it to the local tip (the only safe way to get rid of a battery), I put mine beside the bench and connected a Battery Sava to it. This meant that it always had some charge in it, though giving it a regular trickle charge with a battery charger would have a similar effect, albeit less convenient. It was often called on (particularly during the winter months) to jump start a car which had had its lights left on all night – it's far easier than messing around with two cars. Equally, when testing products (for example, the horn), it's often far simpler to do it on a bench rather than have to fit them to the car – especially if there is a fault and you have to remove them again! There's no doubt, a portable source of 6V or 12V power is a real boon.

Cleaning

When you're working on many of your classic's electrical components, particularly those living under the bonnet, you'll often be dealing with an oily, greasy mass – the starter motor and dynamo/alternator are two that spring instantly to mind. There's little point in trying to work on them in this condition; so cleaning them is the first priority. Use a standard degreasant (Gunk, Jizer, etc.) but not flammable liquids and certainly never petrol. To do the job properly, you'll need something watertight (or degreasant-tight) to stand them in so that they can have a good soaking and you can work the liquid in well with a stiff brush (the type usually supplied with alloy wheel cleaners is ideal).

It's always handy to have a few ready-made bridging leads and, of course, it gives a little practice in using some of the tools you've bought. For manually 'bridging' a component (either to cut it out of a circuit or to bypass a switch or relay) make up wires with a selection of male/female terminals attached. Up to a ½ metre of wire should be enough for most applications. In general, a 14/0.30 wire, as used for radio/cassette installation, will be sufficient (for heavier applications, thicker wire will be required and it may be worth considering getting an expert opinion before going this far). This is yet another advantage of running a classic car rather than a 'modern'. For example, many of us have had an overheating engine caused by the failure of the electric fan thermostatic switch. On more than one occasion, I have had cause to be glad that my tool kit of many things contained a simple spade-to-spade bridging lead which enabled me to simply jump the plug to the fan and turn it permanently on.

Where you're bridging a component carrying power, make up a lead with an in-line fuse holder in its centre. You can change the fuse rating (up or down) to suit the job in hand. In some cases, you can use two or more of the leads in order to get the correct terminals at each end.

The terminals can be crimped or soldered as required.

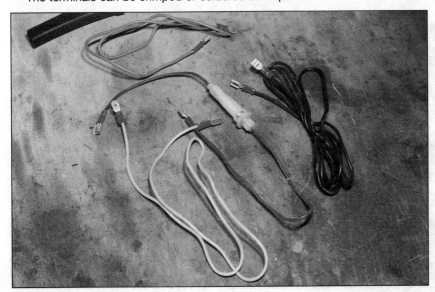

As already mentioned, in the classic world it is generally going to be American cars that will be fitted with catalytic exhausts. The Lambda sensor is mounted in the exhaust close to the exhaust, and when it fails, it can cause lots of problems. Gunson's Lambda sensor probe is able to reveal whether it is working properly – vital if you're going to save a highly-expensive 'cat'.

If you do a lot of DIY, you will soon reap the benefits of a purpose-made parts washer like this one from Clarke. This oily mess is a starter motor, and it requires some serious cleaning before stripdown begins.

The washer contains a submersible pump and a reservoir for the degreasant. The starter is placed on a tray (with a perforated grid to let the excess cleaner back into the reservoir) and the fresh cleaner is pumped up through the flexible nozzle to be directed where required. After five minutes in the washer and a little effort with a stiff brush . . .

. . . the starter looks like new, and working on it is a realistic proposition. Note the use of the air gun with the compressor, which dramatically reduces the drying time and gets the cleaning liquid out of all those nooks and crannies.

Chapter 3
Basic principles and techniques

Your classic's wiring is a means to an end, a way of getting power from the battery to electrical devices all over the car. In the case of the dynamo/alternator, the wiring is a way of topping up the battery in order to feed those devices. They may be as simple as a light bulb or as complex as automatic air conditioning, but they all work on the same system.

Wiring goes around in circuits, which means, by definition, there must always be a start and a finish – if the circuit is broken or incomplete, then the device in question will not work. Imagine a lap of Silverstone 'circuit' where someone had been along with a JCB and dug up the tarmac past Becketts; that's effectively what you get with a damaged wire, poor earth or broken fuse.

You don't need to know the detailed workings of electricity to City & Guilds standard, just a basic grounding (no pun intended!) is all that is required to give confidence to work on your classic. Learning the true ins and outs, charting the course of charged particles as they rocket around conductors is for those taking examinations at the University of Clever Things – us classic car owners tend to have a resistance to too much technical talk, preferring to know simply what's watt and how to make light work of making the lights work.

The almost universal standard analogy used to simplify the principles of car electrics is water; it's something we all understand and, more important, it's something we can see. And there lies the major problem with electricity – it's hard to understand something you can't see.

Volts and current

Imagine a tank containing water with a pipe attached to it – rather like the cold water tank in your loft. Water flows out of the tank down the pipe, and the flow of electricity down a wire is called the current, and current is measured in amperes (or amps). By definition, water will flow out of the pipe as long as there is some pressure caused by the tank water level being above the level of the pipe. In electrical terms, the force 'pushing' the current along the wire is called voltage. The more voltage available, the more current will flow down a particular wire.

Current thinking

There are two types of current that affect the classic car owner – alternating current and direct current, abbreviated to AC and DC. Cars work on a DC system, because although AC has many advantages it can't be stored in a battery. The only AC item you'll find on your classic is likely to be an alternator, and that has to have its current rectified (by a rectifier, strangely enough) to DC.

Water flows from high to low – it just can't go the other way. In your classic there is a similar irrefutable law, which is that DC electricity must flow the same way all the time, from the battery around the system and back again thus:

● POSITIVE EARTH SYSTEM
From negative to positive.

● NEGATIVE EARTH SYSTEM
From positive to negative.

Electricity always flows *towards* the earth terminal, regardless of the polarity.

Resistance

If, for whatever reason, our water pipe becomes constricted – let's say that cricket bat you've kept in the attic for 25 years drops on it – then two things happen; the amount of water coming out of the pipe is *reduced*, but the amount of pressure at the point where the restriction occurs *increases*. There is a *resistance* to the natural flow of water. In wiring, too, there can be a resistance to carrying the current along it. Usually, the resistance is very low indeed, although it increases as wiring gets older. Switches, too, have a resistance, as do the electrical applications themselves, by and large, to a greater extent than wiring. Resistance is measured in ohms; a tribute to the man who had a law named after him, German physicist Georg Simon Ohm.

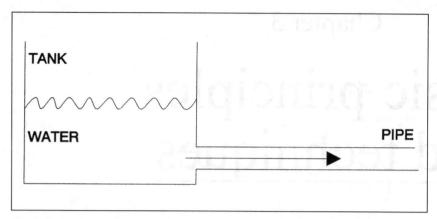

The standard water/electricty analogy works well. Water flowing from this tank and down the pipe represents current (amps) and the pressure governed by the volume of water in the tank and the bore of the pipe represents voltage.

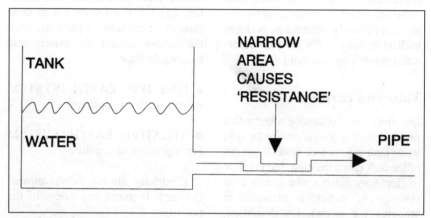

When the exit pipe is squeezed, less water can get through, i.e. it resists the flow of the water. Similarly, a smaller wire has more 'resistance' to passing electrical current than a larger wire.

The important point here is to use the right size of wire (or pipe) for the job in hand; where there is a large current trying to get down a small wire, the resistance creates heat in the wire. On some occasions, the heat can fire materials around the wire or even get hot enough to melt its insulation and cause short circuits. If in doubt, opt for larger to be on the safe side.

So there you have it, but remember that the water analogy is just that, a resemblance alone in certain characteristics, because water and electricity most definitely do not match!

Ohm's law

Georg Simon Ohm (1787–1854) discovered the following:

Current = voltage divided by the resistance of the wire or appliance in question. To make life a little more complex (but not much), the electrical denotations of those items are V for voltage (volts), I for current (amps) and R for resistance (ohms). So our original equation goes like this: I = V/R, and like all such equations it can be turned around in various ways in order to discover one value when you know the other two. So it could also be written: R = V/I (resistance = voltage divided by current) or V = I x R (voltage = current multiplied by resistance).

Just as more water can flow down an unrestricted pipe, then more current can flow down wiring and through applications which have a low resistance.

Save your meter

A multimeter is a worthwhile investment but you need to use it properly. The basic rule is simple: to test for everything, you need to have a connected circuit with the component in question operating (or trying to) EXCEPT when measuring resistance (ohms). For *resistance* measurements the ignition should be switched **off** and the item you're testing should not be trying to operate – if in doubt, remove the battery earth lead. If you've a really advanced classic with one of those dreaded ECUs under the dash, then even more care is required and you would be well advised to consult an expert – it is possible to ruin an ECU simply by putting the meter probes to the wrong terminals.

Watts the story

Electrical power is measured in watts, and every electrical item with a job to do uses it, the exceptions being the battery – which is simply a storehouse – and the alternator/dynamo – which creates it. Once more, there are basic formulae that enable you to work out current, watts and voltage. Using the abbreviations mentioned earlier, together with 'W' being the abbreviation for watts, we get the following:

I = W/V (current = watts divided by voltage)
or
V = W/I (voltage = watts divided by current)
or
W = V x I (watts = voltage multiplied by current)

Probably the most useful equation is the first one, which is ideal for working out the current requirements (and from there, the wire size) of accessories to be added, for example, fog lamps. Remember also that other components, such as switches and connectors, also have current ratings, so make sure that everything in a particular circuit is rated correctly. Always opt for a larger current rating rather than a smaller one. (See Appendix 3 for typical power consumption figures.)

In brief

● Current is measured in amperes, abbreviated to amps or 'A' (as in 8A).
● The force pushing current along the wiring is voltage, abbreviated to volts or 'V' (as in 12V).
● Resistance is measured in ohms.
● Power is measured in watts, abbreviated 'W'.

Wiring

The electrical components in your classic are joined to each other and/or relevant parts of the electrical system by lengths of wire. Each wire comprises a number of thin copper strands housed in an insulating sheath. Multiple strands are used to reduce the risk of the cable breaking as it is twisted and bent during installation.

However, it must always be remembered that most classics are upwards of 25 years old and during that time could well have fallen victim to our friend the 'bodger' owner. As such, it is quite possible for incorrect sizes and colours of wiring to have been substituted at some time in the past, something that usually denotes that the wire used was the first piece out of the owners' 'box of bits'. The basic rule is simple – unless you have seen it and checked it yourself, believe nothing to be as it should be!

Colours

So that you can have some chance of following which wire is which, the sheaths are colour-coded and, although there has never been a world-wide universal agreement on these codes, in the UK most classic cars are British and most electrical items came courtesy of Mr Lucas. Consequently, the table given here will apply to a vast number of UK classics. This is the basic Lucas colour-coding chart which applied to most classics from roughly 1950. The plain colours are obvious, but some are denoted by two colours. In these cases, the first colour given is the colour of the sheath and the second colour is the stripe or, to be more precise, the 'tracer' colour. Thus,

'black/green' is a black wire with a green tracer, but 'green/black' is a green wire with a black tracer. In the interests of cutting costs, most electrical diagrams are printed in black and white and so the colours are denoted by abbreviations (some colours are confusingly abbreviated to be a letter other than their own – for example, 'U' for blue). A brown/white combination would be given as N/W.

The most commonly used colours and abbreviations are as follows:

B	Black
G	Green
K	Pink
N	Brown
O	Orange
P	Purple
R	Red
S	Slate
U	Blue
W	White
Y	Yellow
LG	Light green

This table shows typical classic usage and colours. It isn't definitive, but it's a good start, especially for British classics.

From	To	Colour
Battery/solenoid	Ammeter	Brown
Battery/solenoid	Control box	Brown
Battery/solenoid	Switches (not via control box)	Brown
Battery/solenoid	Alternator	Brown
Ammeter	Control box	Brown/white
Ammeter	Switches	Brown/white
Control box	Switches	Brown/blue
Dynamo (D terminal)	Control box	Brown/yellow
Dynamo (F terminal)	Control box	Brown/green
Ignition switch	SW terminal on coil	White
Ignition switch	Fuse (ignition fed)	White
Ignition switch	Petrol pump	White
Ignition switch	Ignition warning light	White
Ignition switch	Oil light	White
Ignition switch	Accessory fuse	White/blue
Ignition switch	Starter solenoid	White/red
Ignition switch	Wiper motor	Green
Ignition switch	Indicator	Green
Ignition switch	Stop/tail light switch	Green (sometimes white)
Ignition switch	Heater motor	Green

From	To	Colour
Ignition switch	Reversing light switch	Green
Ignition switch	Instruments in console	Green
Light switch	Side & tail lights	Red
Light switch	Side & tail light fuse	Red
Light switch	Panel light switch	Red
Panel light switch	Panel lights	Red/white
Side & tail light fuse	Nearside side & tail lights	Red/black (sometimes Red/brown)
Side & tail light fuse	Offside side and tail lights	Red/orange (sometimes Red/brown)
Side & tail light fuse	Side & tail lights on both sides	Red/green (sometimes Red/blue)
Light switch	Dip switch	Blue
Dip switch	Dipped beam	Blue/red
Light switch	Main beam	Blue/white
Wiper switch	Motor (field wound)	Black/green
Wiper switch	Motor (permanent magnet)	Blue/green (sometimes red/green or brown/green)
Stop light switch	Stop lights	Green/purple (sometimes green/yelow)
Reversing light switch	Reversing lights	Green/brown
Indicator unit	Indicator switch	Light green/brown
Indicator unit	Indicator warning light	Light green/purple
Indicator switch	Nearside indicators	Green/red
Indicator switch	Offside indicators	Green/white
Petrol gauge	Sender in petrol tank	Green/black
Temperature gauge	Temperature sender	Green/blue
Oil warning light	Oil warning sender	White/brown
Ignition warning light	D Terminal on dynamo or 'ind' on an Alternator	Brown/yellow
Coil	Distributor	White/black
Fuse	Horn	Brown (or purple if fused)
Fuse	Interior light	Brown (or purple if fused)
Fuse	Clock	Brown (or purple if fused)
Horn-push	Horn	Purple/black (some times brown/black)
Horn relay	Horn	Purple/yellow
Interior light	Door switch	Purple/white
Earth	Various	Black

It's important to stick to the original colours when you're adding features or repairing your electrics. If you're unfortunate to have inherited a vehicle owned by J. R. Bodger, you'll know only too well the confusion that can be caused by someone who has simply tacked in a piece of the wrong coloured wire just because it was to hand. Empathise, too, with the unfortunate buyer of a Moto Guzzi motorcycle who's owner told him it had been rewired after a fire; the previous owner had done the work himself and, to save money, had invested in just one roll of cable – and wired the whole machine with the same thickness and same colour wire!

You're never alone with a strand . . .

As well as the colour, wire is also denoted by its size. Within the sheath, wire isn't just a thick piece of copper, rather a collection of thin copper strands. The wire size is given as a number of strands and their diameter

Imperial sizes		
Size strands	Diameter *(inches)*	Current rating *(amps)*
23	0.0076	5.75
9	0.012	5.75
14	0.010	6.00
36	0.0076	8.75
14	0.012	8.75
28	0.012	17.5
35	0.012	21.75
44	0.012	27.5
65	0.012	35
97	0.012	50
120	0.012	60
60	0.018	70

Metric sizes		
Size strands	Diameter *(mm)*	Current rating *(amps)*
16	0.20	4.25
9	0.30	5.5
14	0.25	6.0
14	0.30	8.5
21	0.30	12.75
28	0.30	17
35	0.30	21.0
44	0.30	25.5
65	0.30	31.0
84	0.30	48.0
97	0.30	55.5
80	0.40	70.0

(i.e., how thick they are). The table here shows the main wire designations you're likely to come across – as with most things today, there are imperial and metric figures; make sure you don't mix and match!

Heat

As you explore your car's electrical system, you'll note that some wiring is thicker than others. There's a reason for this and, when repairing, you should NEVER use thinner wire; if the correct size wire is not available, then either leave the job until it is or err on the side of caution and use a thicker wire.

In general, a thicker cable will dissipate heat better than a thinner one for any given current load, which in turn means that high current loads require thicker cable. If you use a thinner wire for a given application, it will overheat, to a lesser or greater extent. Obviously, the main point to make here is that hot cables in a car can ultimately only lead to one thing –

fire. Just about everything inside your car is flammable, and in particular you're sitting on a tankful of petrol.

It should be noted that if wiring is bunched together (as it often is) the heat from one cable will affect another, thus reducing each cable's efficiency and creating a potentially dangerous 'hot-spot'.

Current capacity calculation

All wire has a current capacity which, if exceeded, will lead to overheating of the wire and the possibility of a fire. When you are wiring in a new product, it is usual that the current requirement is given by the manufacturers. However, if you are unsure, use this simple formula to work it out: Amps = Watts/Volts. As a simple example, let's say you're fitting a pair of fog lamps, and reading the side of the box tells you that each takes 35 watts. Using our calculation, we can see that amps = 70 (i.e. 2 x 35W lamps) divided by 12 (in a 12V

electrical system). Basic maths tells us that 70/12 = 5.8 amps. So, check the wiring table and select the correct size of wire – in this case 14/0.010 is the closest, rated at 6A.

Togetherness

In general, it's neater and safer to run wires together in bunches called looms (or small bunches called sublooms). The obvious exception is that when wiring in audio products, speaker leads must be kept away from any wiring carrying power. The manufacturers did a good job when they built your car, but the original loom will be old and worn by now, and if it's had some 'enthusiastic' owners, may be the worse for wear. Professionals use proper looming tape, which looks like electrician's tape but isn't; it's not sticky but designed to stick to itself – you have to use it to understand! There are alternatives, as shown here and, of course, when you're adding wiring, either create your own loom or try to include them in an existing loom.

VEHICLE WIRING

Vehicle wiring comes in many diameters and colours, each with its place in the electrical pecking order, and it's important that you keep to it. The basic premise is simple – more current equals thicker wire. If in doubt, then check beforehand. When push comes to shove, choose the thicker wire, rather than run the risk of overheating – or even fire.

3 This, however, is not as impressive and bodes ill – the vehicle manufacturers didn't fit lumps of black electrician's tape part way down lengths of wire. This kind of bodge is always the work of a previous owner; expect to find wires twisted together and called a join (it's not!), damaged sheaths 'repaired' or wires joined together, again, usually by twisting the strands together. What's worse here is that the tape is old and has started to become brittle and crack, so it's being less protective every day.

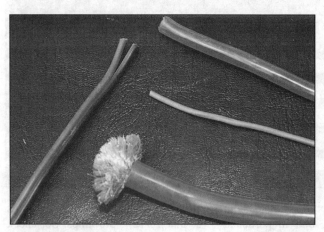

1 Some extremes of wire thickness. On the left is an example of standard thin twin-core speaker cable. At the top is thick cable of the sort typically used to power up power amplifiers, and beneath it is much thinner cable for running 12V to a set of foglamps, etc. The really thick cable at the bottom of the photo would be used for very heavy current loads, such as supplying a separate fuse box.

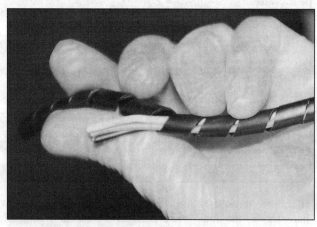

4 To loom your wiring, use electrician's tape around the wires at a slight angle. It's cumbersome and tricky to carry out in the way the professionals do. Much easier is spiral binding, which comes in 6mm and 12mm diameter from VWP. It wraps around the wires in question and can be cut to length. Better still, it's easy to remove if you are taking out the wiring at a later date, or have problems, or even if you want to add another wire or two.

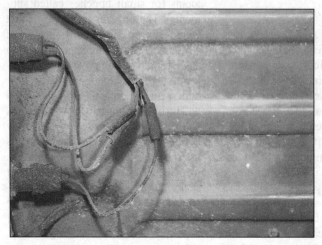

2 Old, but still functional, this original loom serves the stop, tail and indicator lamps.

5 One of the great innovations of recent years is heat shrink sleeving. It looks like pieces of small bicycle inner tubes, but with a harder feel to it. It can be used in small sections for insulation, or over whole sections to form a mini-loom.

Grommets

All the correct wiring, connectors and pretty soldering can come to nothing if you then pass the wiring through an unprotected hole in the bodywork. Typical examples are where wiring is passing from the cabin to the engine bay through the bulkhead, or where wiring is leaving the 'A' pillar to the door (for items such as electric windows). Even the sturdiest loom will move at some point as the car is driven, and over time the protective sheath around the wire will chafe to the point where the copper strands can make contact with the car body. As the body is the earth of the electrical system, you will then get a short circuit. If you're very lucky, there will be a few sparks, a blown fuse and an inoperative electrical function. What is more likely to happen is that the sparks create fire and . . . well, you can guess the rest.

(Owners of fibreglass cars are not immune – even though the wiring can't earth with the body, there are plenty of other metal parts around . . . and fibreglass lights up far quicker than most would imagine.)

Even if you're using an existing grommet, the fact that it's getting on a bit makes it worth having a close look. If it is cracking and generally showing its age, then replace it now, rather than later, at which point you could also be sorting out the charred remains of your loom.

Whenever you pass a wire through a hole, in steel, plastic, fibreglass or even card trim, it is vital that it should also pass through a grommet. As you can see from this VWP boxed selection, sizes and types are many and various, so there's no excuse. Where you have holes that need blanking, you can use a blanking grommet – just like a standard grommet but without the hole. The most common use is where someone has previously drilled a hole for an aerial in the wrong place. They are available in sizes ranging from ¼in to 1in.

It's important to get the right size grommet for the hole, these tables show how to choose, courtesy of Auto Sparks.

These grommets are all suitable for use in metal bodywork of standard thickness. The last one listed (marked *) allows for a ¼in thickness panel and is ideal for use in fibreglass, where grommets are just as essential as in steel panels.

Wiring diagrams

For the amateur car electrician, it is a wonderful thing to come across a totally schematic diagram, i.e. one where the various components are drawn to look like what they are. It would be wonderful to find that all wiring diagrams were drawn in this way, but they're not. Moreover, diagrams tend to use a 'mix 'n' match' selection of symbols, schematics and drawings so that swapping and changing between different manufacturers' diagrams is harder work than it should be. Trying to memorise every single symbol is pointless and unnecessary, as almost all diagrams include a key, which helps enormously.

Interpreting

By definition, a wiring diagram is a complex piece of work; so the main requirement in interpreting the diagram for your classic car is patience. Following a specific cable along the length of the vehicle and across the page can send you cross-eyed, and it's easy to pick-up on a different cable part way through. It's a good idea to have pen and paper to hand and make your own diagram of the specific items you're checking. But, at the end of the day, it's only the electrical version of a road map, with the towns and cities being electrical components and the roads being the wires.

PVC type		Rubber (Lucas)	
Hole size	**Bore size**	**Hole size**	**Bore size**
¼in	⁵⁄₃₂in	½in	⅛in
⁵⁄₁₆in	⁷⁄₃₂in	¾in	⅛in
⅜in	⁵⁄₁₆in	1in	⁷⁄₃₂in
⁷⁄₁₆in	⁵⁄₁₆in	1¼in	⁵⁄₃₂in
½in	⁵⁄₁₆in	1⅜in	½in
⅝in	⁷⁄₁₆in	1½in	½in
¹¹⁄₁₆in	½in	1¾in	½in
¾in	½in	*1³⁄₁₆in	⁹⁄₃₂in
1in	¾in		
1¼in	1in		

1 Alternator or dynamo
2 Control box
3 Batteries – 2 x 6 volt
4 Starter solenoid
5 Starter motor
6 Lighting switch
7 Headlamp dip switch
8 RH headlamp
9 LH headlamp
10 High beam warning lamp
11 RH parking lamp
12 LH parking lamp
13 Panel lamp switch or rheostat switch
14 Panel lamps
15 Number plate lamp
16 RH stop and tail lamp
17 LH stop and tail lamp
18 Stoplamp switch
19 Fuse unit
20 Interior courtesy lamp/map light (early cars)
21 Door switch (RH)
22 Door switch (LH)
23 Horns
24 Horn push
25 Flasher unit
26 Direction indicator switch or
26 Direction indicator/headlamp flasher or 26
     Combined direction indicator/headlamp
     flasher/headlamp high-low beam/horn push switch or
26 Combined direction indicator/headlamp flasher
     headlamp high-low beam switch
27 Direction indicator warning lamps
28 Front flasher lamp (RH)
29 Front flasher lamp (LH)
30 Rear flasher lamp (RH)
31 Rear flasher lamp (LH)
32 Heater motor switch
33 Heater motor
34 Fuel gauge
35 Fuel gauge tank unit
36 Windscreen wiper switch
37 Windscreen wiper motor
38 Ignition/starter switch
39 Ignition coil
40 Distributor
41 Fuel pump
42 Oil pressure gauge
44 Ignition warning lamp
45 Speedometer
46 Coolant temperature sender
46 Coolant temperature gauge
47 Coolant temperature sender
49 Reverse lamp switch
50 Reverse lamp
53 Fog and driving lamp switch
54 Driving lamp
55 Fog lamp

57 Cigar lighter
59 Map light switch (early cars)
60 Radio
64 Instrument voltage stabiliser
65 Luggage compartment lamp switch
66 Luggage compartment lamp
67 Line fuse
68 Overdrive relay unit
71 Overdrive solenoid
72 Overdrive manual control switch
73 Overdrive gear switch
74 Overdrive throttle switch
76 Automatic gearbox gear selector lamp
77 Windscreen washer pump
82 Switch
95 Tachometer
101 Courtesy or map light switch
102 Courtesy or map light
115 Heated rear window switch (GT only)
116 Heated rear window
118 Combined windshield washer and wiper switch
131 Combined reverse lamp and automatic
     transmission safety switch
147 Oil pressure sender
150 Heated rear window warning lamp
152 Hazard warning lamp
153 Hazard warning switch
154 Hazard warning flasher unit
159 Brake pressure warning lamp and
     lamp rest push
160 Brake pressure failure switch
168 Ignition key warning buzzer
169 Ignition key buzzer warning door switch
170 Front side marker lamp (RH)
171 Front side marker lamp (LH)
172 Rear side marker lamp (LH)
174 Starter solenoid relay
198 Driver's seat belt buckle switch
199 Passenger seat belt buckle switch
200 Passenger seat switch
201 Gearbox switch seat belt warning
202 Warning light 'fasten belts'
203 Line diode

Cable colour code

N	Brown
U	Blue
R	Red
P	Purple
G	Green
LG	Light Green
O	Orange
W	White
Y	Yellow
B	Black

Though this diagram looks like the proverbial spider with ink-covered legs has been at work, it's actually not as bad as it seems. It represents the wiring for a pre '67 MGB and shows instantly that it has a positive earth. Check out item 3 which shows the positive terminal going to the bodywork and note that there are two batteries (both 6V) wired in parallel to provide the 12V required.

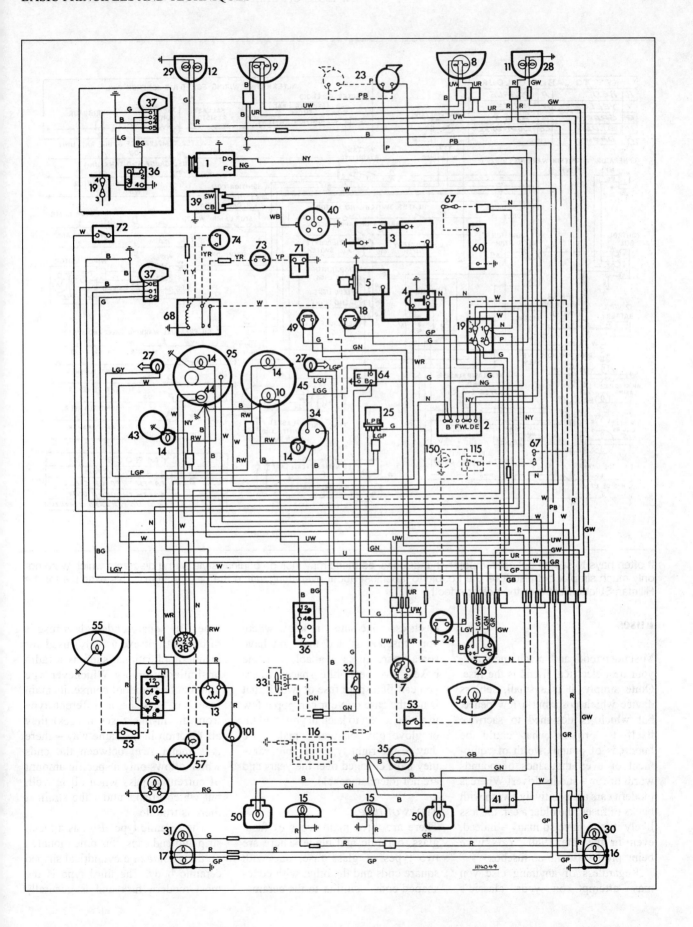

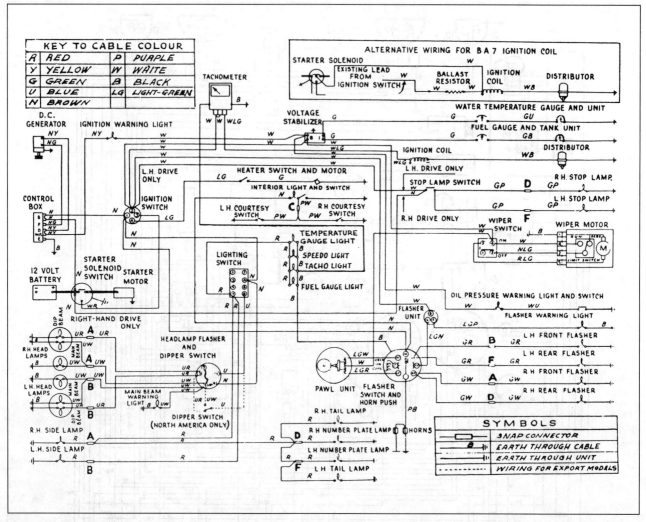

It often pays to search out contemporary handbooks, as these may include original-style wiring diagrams which were not only much simpler but also took the trouble to label just about everything within the diagram itself. This example for the Hillman Stiletto illustrates the point perfectly.

Fuses

Misunderstood and much maligned, your best electrical friend is the fuse. Quite simply, it is a small, selfless device which costs but a few pence, but which is designed to sacrifice itself to protect what could be hundreds of pounds worth of equipment or even thousands of pounds worth of car – and its driver! Whereas modern cars are positively awash with banks of fuses, the older a car, the less likely it is to have so many – indeed, even in the late 1960s, cars were being produced with no fusebox.

Regardless of anything else you may attempt on your classic's electrics, make sure you know where your fusebox is and that you have some spare fuses available – some boxes have neat little spaces where you can fit a spare fuse or two. If that is not the case on your car, pop a few in a plastic bag to keep in your tool kit or glove box. Naturally, make sure they're the right type for your car – they have changed over the years and are not interchangeable.

Types of fuse

There are three main types of fuse: glass, ceramic and blade. There are two types of glass fuse, one with square ends and the other with cone-shaped ends – similar to the ceramic type. The square-ended glass fuse is often (but not exclusively) used for in-line applications, such as a radio or similar accessory. Whichever type your car has (and, of course, its main fuse box may be a different type from the in-line fuses it uses) they all function in the same way – there is a metal strip between the ends which allows only a specific amount of current to pass when all is well, but which breaks under the strain if there is trouble.

The ceramic type also has a metal strip and end caps, this time mounted on the *outside* of a cylindrical shaped ceramic body. The third type is the most modern fuse and is generally referred to as a blade fuse. The thin fuse wire is in its plastic body.

In general, it is easy to see if a fuse has blown just by looking at it. However, sometimes it's a tricky call, so use your multimeter on 'resistance' setting and attach a lead to each end (or terminal) of the fuse. If you get a reading, the fuse is sound; if not, it's dead and heading for the bin.

Changing a fuse is a simple operation. All three types are a push fit into some sort of spring clip. The difficult part may be knowing which one has blown. Normally the circuits protected by each fuse will be listed in the handbook and in some cases marked on the fusebox. It's a useful exercise not only to know where the box is sited, but what fuses are in it and what circuits they protect.

Ratings

Each fuse has an amperage rating, and it is vital that you do not change it. Many owners, faced with a fuse which blows on a regular basis, 'solve' the problem by fitting a fuse of a larger value. This solves nothing, it just puts off a small problem until it becomes a big one. Fuses don't blow because they feel like it, there has to be a reason; this could be a simple matter of a broken wire touching the chassis and causing a short circuit, or it could be more complex involving the protected component's delicate electrical innards. Whatever, sort the problem properly, not by uprating the fuse.

Which fuse?

Your handbook or relevant Haynes workshop manual will tell you which fuse protects which circuit, but if your classic is catered for by neither, then a simple process of elimination will soon give the answer – remove each fuse one at a time and note what now doesn't work. You can guess at roughly what's what by the rating of the fuse – high amperage applications require high amperage fuses.

Puffing and blowing

A fuse will usually protect more than one circuit. If you have a constantly blowing fuse, then you can isolate the problem area by a process of elimination. Check what components are served by the fuse in question and turn them all off (a fuse will only blow when power is being requested by the item). Then turn on one of the components. If the fuse doesn't blow, turn it off and turn on the next component. When you turn something on and the fuse blows, you've found the culprit.

Clean

Sometimes there's a lack of power to a component and the fuse is suspect yet seems to be intact. This apparent contradiction in terms can often be explained by good old-fashioned dirty contacts. Remove the fuse and rough up the ends with fine sandpaper (or, of course, substitute a new fuse). Use a small sliver of sandpaper to clean up the terminals on the fuseholder which (unless it's the blade type) will be spring-loaded.

Smoking is bad for you

It's a legendary classic tip from the '50s and '60s that you can use a piece of silver paper from inside a cigarette packet (more likely chocolate wrapping today) as a makeshift fuse. This is not recommended. OK, when it's 2am, raining and blowing a gale and your car is stranded by a blown fuse on the remotest part of Dartmoor ten minutes after your mobile phone battery beeped its last, then this is the exception. The rule, though, is to replace a fuse with a fuse. By being prepared and carrying some spare fuses you won't have to break the rule. Many fuse boxes actually have compartments where spare fuses can be carried and where they are, by definition, exactly where you want them when another one blows.

Fuse values

The amperage ratings shown here are all continuous unless denoted otherwise.

Colour	Rating (amps)
Glass fuses (cone end)	
Blue	3 max
Yellow	4.5 max
Nut brown	8 max
Red on Green	10 max
White	5 max
Glass type (flat end)	
Red on Blue	2
Red	5
Blue on Green	8
Black on Blue	10
Light brown	15
Blue on Yellow	20
Pink	25
White 5 Yellow	50
Ceramic	
Yellow	5
White	8
Red	16
Blue	25
Flat blade	
Purple	3
Pink	4
Orange	5
Brown	7.5
Red	10
Blue	15
Yellow	20
White	25
Green	30

Other types of 'fuse'

Some electrical products are almost certain to get to an overload situation on a regular basis. Using a standard type fuse would be annoying for the driver, so the manufacturers often fit a 'thermostatic interrupter'. As the name suggests, this device is ruled by heat; if the circuit gets overloaded, the heat created bends the metal contact inside the interrupter in such a way as to break the contact. Once it has cooled, the circuit is restored. These are ideal for such applications as electric windows, where sticking or rusting guides could cause trouble or, of course, a child could get his hand stuck.

A different sort of 'fuse' (in that it serves the same purpose) is the fusible link. This is fitted into the main battery wire and is designed to protect every circuit in the vehicle except for the starter. For it to melt, the overload would have to be tremendous and is unlikely to occur except in extreme circumstances, such as an accident – when you would be very glad of it indeed! With a car upside down and a ruptured fuel tank splashing petrol everywhere, various loose wires spitting and sparking would not be a good thing.

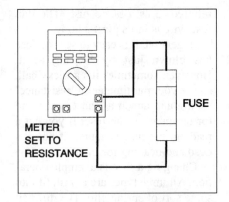

Your all-powerful meter can be used to check a fuse which appears to be good but doesn't pass any current. Remove the fuse, set your meter to 'resistance' and touch a probe to either end of the fuse.

Terminals

Wires have to be linked to one another, and this requires that terminals of differing types be fitted at the relevant points. When a car leaves the factory, the wiring, like everything else, is (or should be) perfect. However, it's usually not too long before an enthusiastic owner wants to add something here and move something elsewhere, and the opportunity for a bodge or two presents itself. As the car gets older, worth less (as opposed to *worthless*) and in the hands of ever poorer owners, then the corner-cutting increases apace. Expect, therefore, to find a large number of distinctly unsavoury connections in the depths of your under-dash or engine bay. Bits of wire twisted together do **not** constitute a proper connection; moreover, they lend themselves to all sorts of nastiness ranging from intermittent operation to outright fire.

It's important to make a check when buying a classic that you are not purchasing a monument to the bodgers' art – but if you find you have already bought such a car, you need to de-bodge it straightaway. And, of course, if you are adding accessories or replacing sections of wiring, etc., you should use only the right sort of connectors fitted in the correct manner.

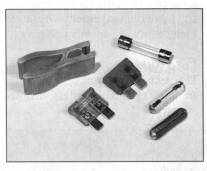

A collection of fuses you're likely to meet. From left to right is a fuse remover (eases wear and tear on patience and fingernails), two later-style 'blade' fuses, a glass fuse (used mainly for in-line fusing) and two ceramic fuses, common on classics.

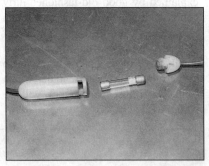

Many components are fitted with an in-line fuse, usually of the glass type. The two halves of the holder twist apart and the fuse falls out. As always, replace like for like – don't fit a larger amperage fuse. Corrosion on the inner terminals is common.

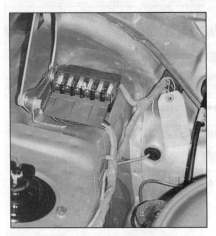

It was very much *de rigeur* to fit the fuse box under the bonnet on classic cars. Sited here they're subject to extremes of heat, cold and moisture – keep a weather eye on yours for signs of corrosion, and spray regularly with WD40.

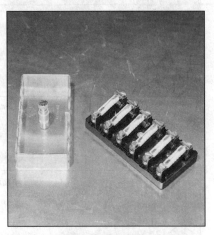

Like most classic electrics, you can get hold of classic style fuses and even complete fuse boxes from the specialists. These are older-style ceramic fuses with colour-coded ratings.
(Courtesy Vehicle Wiring Products)

Popular types of terminal

Lucar

Popularly known as a spade terminal, this is available in male and female versions. The female is often used on the end of wires leading to a fusebox, where suitably sized male terminals form part of the box itself. They are generally used in this fashion, rather than to join two separate pieces of wire – this is more usually the province of the butt connector (see later).

Bullet

The bullet terminal is available in male and female versions and is used where there is a need to join a wire which will probably need to be disconnected at some point.

A common accessory usage is to join speaker cables where, by thoughtful fitting of the male and female terminals, it is easy to maintain the correct polarity of the system.

Ring

Ring terminals are most often used for earth connections where they can easily be fitted under an existing fastener (bolt or screw) or where a fastener can be fitted for that purpose. Applications such as amplifiers also often require the use of ring terminals for the power, earth and remote switching connections.

Fork

Like the ring terminal, the fork is often used for earth connections or for accessory applications such as some amplifier connections. It is usually used where removing a fastener to place a ring terminal in place is not possible or is very difficult. As such, the fastener can simply be loosened and the fork terminal slid into place.

Butt

A connector used to join two pieces of wire.

Buying new terminals

All the above examples can be purchased as either solder or crimp versions. Most aftermarket accessory stores sell bubble-packs of modern-style Lucar and bullet connectors, but they're usually only in packs of four or six and are far from cheap. If you only want a few, they'll do the trick, but if you're a thinking-ahead person and/or you need soldered and/or older types of terminal, it's much cheaper to buy in bulk from one of the mail order electrical specialists such as Auto Sparks or Vehicle Wiring Products. Keep different types of terminal together to save aggravation – you could follow the (caffeine-addicted) author's habit of using old coffee jars as a cheap and convenient method of storage.

Self-stripping connectors

Unless you're really stuck, it's best not to use the self-stripping type of connector – certainly, they would not have been used as original equipment on your classic. Any you might find lurking in your loom must have been fitted by a previous owner, one who probably didn't know (or care) too much about electrics. They're usually used as a quick way to add electrical accessories and almost universally to wire in towing brackets.

In essence they are a good idea – a simple plastic cover hides a sharp metal 'blade' which is forced down on to the original wire in the car and the end of the wire to be spliced in. But, they can often also strip the plastic cable sheath off and bite into the copper strands within. This obviously makes the cable thinner at that point (less wire, of course, means more resistance) and it makes for less cable for the connector to hold on to. Conversely, if it doesn't bite deep enough, then there could be no electrical contact at all – or worse, intermittent contact. Moreover, if they are used in the engine bay, they are very open to attack by oil and water and the extremes of heat and cold.

Crimped connections

The most common classic electrical tasks involve connecting bits of wire to various types of electrical connectors. Despite what you might have been led to believe by a previous owner, twisting two bits of wire together and covering the resultant mess up with electrician's tape is categorically NOT an electrical join! At best, it's a shoddy piece of work which will look unprofessional (because it is) and could well lead to electrical trouble. At worst, it could short circuit and lead to a vehicle fire.

The simplest way is to use a crimped join, although most professional electricians will prefer to solder just about all electrical connections.

Soldering

For many, soldering is a black art to rival astral projection, but it needn't be with the right gear and a little patience. The most important aspect is to practise beforehand on an old piece of scrap wiring and a terminal or two from your collection.

SAFETY NOTE: By definition, working inside a classic car with an iron, heated to over 700°, is a recipe for disaster – just about everything inside the car is flammable, and what about that fuel tank! Most of us have rags and dusters to hand, and it takes only the smallest spark for them to catch fire.

- **Always have a fire extinguisher to hand.**
- **Stop frequently to make sure that a fire hasn't started out of your immediate eyesight.**
- **Use a piece of scrap steel or similar to protect flammable bits of trim or upholstery.**
- **Never hold a wire or terminal with your fingers – heat travels quickly as you'll soon find out!**

Having chosen your iron (see Chapter 2) ensure that the solder you have is specifically for electrical joins. Wherever possible, remove the electrical components from the car and work on the bench – it's easier and safer. Always make sure you have a damp sponge within reach of the iron, so you can tap off excess solder without damaging the iron.

Continued on page 35

MAKING THE RIGHT CONNECTION

Making the right connection is not just a question of technique, you'll also need the right type of terminal. There are dozens of different types and, though many have passed out of favour over the years, specialists such as Auto Sparks and VWP can supply just about any style of classic connector required. This way you can complete a good job and keep your classic looking right, too.

3 Classic bullet connectors come in various sizes to suit different wire thicknesses. This type is available in four sizes (wire size 9, 14, 28 and 44 strands of 0.30 wire) and can be soldered or crimped, but there are similar-looking terminals (available in 28 and 44/0.30 sizes) that are soldered only. *(Courtesy Auto Sparks)*

1 A selection of commonly-used aftermarket terminals. Left to right: ring, butt, female bullet, fork, male bullet, female and male Lucar. Note the distinctly dubious self-stripping connector (the white item to the right). Empty coffee and condiment jars make perfect containers! For starters, try a complete set including crimping tool and a selection of connectors, as seen in Chapter 2.

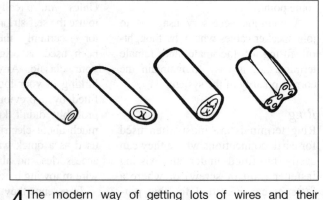

4 The modern way of getting lots of wires and their respective terminals to join at the same point is to use thin-wall wire and a multi-plug. Back when wiring was thicker and electronics less complex, multi-bullet connectors were as complex as it got. Connecting sleeves of one, two, three, five or even ten-way are available. *(Courtesy Auto Sparks)*

2 Close-up, the most popular connectors, the Lucar (spade) and bullet, seen here in female and male formats respectively (there are male/female counterparts for each). All connectors must be insulated regardless of whether the insulation is part of the connector itself or a separate entity.

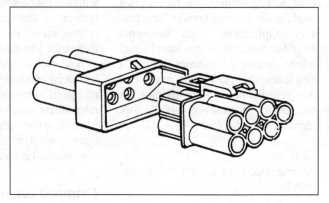

5 However, if you have a more recent classic, then the odds are you'll find at least one of this type of multi-pin connector tucked away somewhere. This is the 3mm pin and socket type and comes in one, two, three, four, five, seven and nine-way assemblies. *(Courtesy Auto Sparks)*

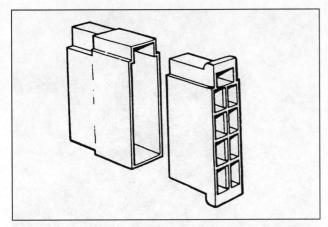

6 This ¼in spade and tab type also comes in a variety of styles and sizes, notably two, three, four, six, eight, nine and eleven-way assemblies and an eleven-way unit specifically designed for panel mounting. *(Courtesy Auto Sparks)*

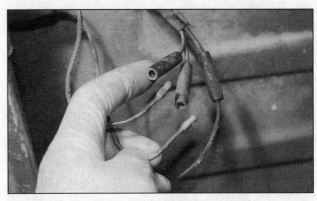

8 A typical sub-loom to the rear lamps, as simple as it can get – three wires, three male/bullet connectors, three lamps. Corrosion is a common problem as the terminals corrode within the plastic sheaths. It pays to undo this type of connection occasionally and brush off any corrosion and treat it to a dose of WD40.

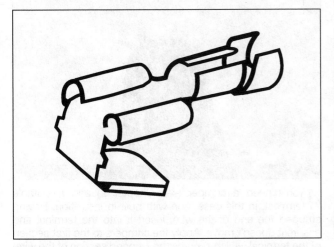

7 The way to get two wires on to one connection (say, at the fusebox) is not to cram them both into one terminal, but rather use a neat piggy back terminal like this. *(Courtesy Vehicle Wiring Products)*

9 Connecting the battery earth terminal to the body means that you're never far from somewhere to run a separate earth lead for a given component. Here, a ring terminal has been crimped to a wire and fitted under a bolt in the bodywork – after the area has been thoroughly cleaned using a wire brush. The finished connection has been covered in copper grease to keep it sound.

Once you've made the join, resist at all costs the temptation to blow on it to help it cool – it doesn't need it and, moreover, this could lead to a dry join, where the wire is loose inside what appears to be a solid join. The intermittent faults this could cause could send you grey overnight.

When soldering bullet terminals, it pays to 'doctor' the format somewhat; push the bared wire up into the bullet itself and through the hole in the end. Bend it over and hold the terminal itself in a vice (or third hand) to prevent the wire slipping out as the heat from the iron melts the plastic sheath. Solder the

wire to the end of the terminal and, when cool, snip off the excess and crimp the sheathed part as usual for a good physical join.

IMPORTANT NOTE: In general, soldered joins are about the best you can get, but in classic cars particularly, a mixture of old age and more vibration than on modern vehicles, can cause the join to break. If the join comes loose but doesn't actually disconnect altogether (or if it breaks inside and makes a dry join) this can lead to hair-tearing

intermittent problems. So, it pays never to believe what your eyes tell you – a join that *looks* sound might just be the cause of your problems. Test by wiggling it gently.

Clean, clean
You would not consider trying to weld dirty, greasy or rusty metal, and the same principles of cleanliness apply to soldering. Where applicable, use emery paper to remove any surface

Continued on page 39

MAKING A CRIMPED CONNECTION

Problems with electrical connections often have their origins in the apparent simplicity of the job of stripping a wire and fitting a terminal. Many owners just don't take enough time to do the job properly, with the result that they end up with poor joins leading to sporadic electrical contact and infuriating intermittent faults.

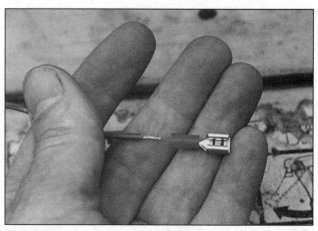

3 Here, the wire has been readied prior to making a crimped join.

1 To fix any terminal to a piece of wire, you'll need to strip away the last 6mm (around ¼in) of the protective plastic sheath. Most owners use a combined cutter/stripper/crimper, of which the best type is one which automatically judges the thickness of the sheath and . . .

2 . . . cuts through that but not the actual wire. Having cut off enough of the plastic, twist the copper strands together to prevent fraying – unless you're going to solder the wire, in which case the strands should be left so that they can be spread later. If you're going to make a 'Y' shaped join where one wire joins an existing run of cable, cut off more of the sheath to allow for the bared end to be wound around the join area prior to soldering.

4 You'll need a crimper (see Chapter 2) and a suitable terminal, in this case, one with built-in insulation. Having stripped the end of the wire, insert it into the terminal and ensure it doesn't move. Apply the crimpers to the first section of the terminal (which secures the stripped section of the wire) and press hard. Then make a second crimp at the lower part of the terminal. If you've room to make a third crimp, then do that, too, as a belt and braces measure against the terminal pulling loose from the wire. And that's it – ultimately, it's not as desirable as soldering, or as professional, but if you can't solder, then it's the next best thing.

5 On the finished join, you can clearly see the twin crimp marks. The principle remains the same for non-insulated crimp joins.

SOLDERING A CONNECTION

When soldering any join, make sure that you have secured both wire and terminal as much as possible – when working on a bench it's simplest to use the vice or a 'third hand' type tool. It pays to have some pliers on hand. If you're using a new iron, 'tin' in before you start on the workpiece by melting some solder on the end and then tapping it off on your sponge. Also, it pays to 'tin' the bared end of the wire to aid a good solid join.

3 When soldering a connector on to the end of a wire (the most common type of soldered join) strip the wire and crimp the sheathed part into the end of the terminal, as described earlier. This is because soldering makes purely electrical joins, not physical joins. Without this, any tugging and pulling at the wire could result in the join coming adrift. Here comes the essential part of soldering: apply the heat TO THE WORKPIECE – do not melt the solder on to a cold workpiece! The object is to heat the terminal from one side until it's hot enough to draw the solder into it when applied from the other. Not doing this is the reason for most failed soldered joins.

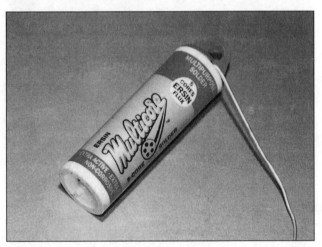

1 Using a ready-fluxed, multi-core solder like this one is simple and ideal for in-car electrical work.

4 Remember that the object is to end up with a nice smooth coating of solder, not a huge, unsightly lump of the stuff. Note that the insulator is there waiting for the join to cool. We have all made the mistake of fitting the terminal and then realising that the insulator had not been slotted down the wire beforehand!

It's advisable to keep the blades of spade and other similar terminals pointing upward to prevent the solder running into the ends and making connection impossible.

2 Here you can see a gas iron being used to heat up the wire before the solder is applied. Don't forget that the join will stay hot for a few minutes, so resist the temptation to touch it straightaway.

5 Complete the insulation and tidying process by sliding on some heat shrink tubing. In many cases, it will be necessary to put the heat-shrink in place **before** the terminal is connected – think it through beforehand!

JOINING WIRES TOGETHER

Adding one wire to another along its length can cause problems, but only if you try to cut corners. One way is to cut the original wire and use a two-socket bullet connector; fit suitably-sized male bullets at either end of the (now cut) original wire and also to the end of the new wire. An alternative, favoured by many professionals, is to splice into the original wire with a soldered join, as shown here.

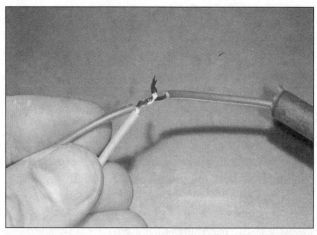

3 Twist the new wire around the old – the amateur would finish at this stage by adding a little electrician's tape. But not you!

1 Apply heat steadily to the tubing – you can see here how it has shrunk considerably from its original diameter and forms a neat and water-tight covering. It's a good idea to buy a couple of one-metre lengths of different diameters – VWP can supply from 3.2mm to 25.4mm original diameter. Use a hair dryer, gas soldering iron or, with some care, a heat gun on the tubing.

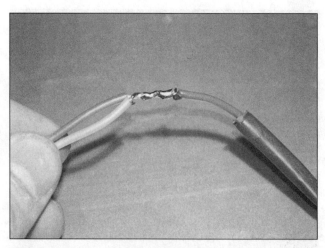

4 Add heat from your soldering iron and a little solder. It should run into the strands enough to colour them, but you don't want great blobs of the stuff.

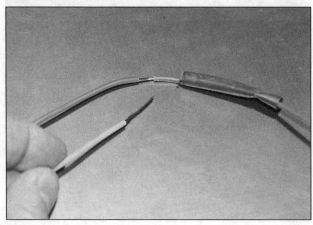

2 To join a wire by soldering, cut the insulation away from the original wire and bare about 12mm of the end of the new wire. Note that a piece of heat shrink insulation has already been put in place.

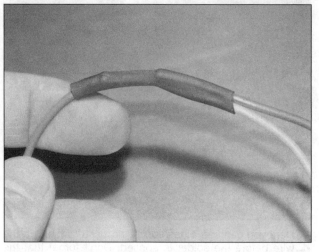

5 Then ease the heat shrink over the join and apply a little heat. Neat, professional and electrically sound.

oxidisation or rust from metal surfaces. Make sure that there is no oil or grease contamination by wiping the areas with methylated spirits (naturally, do this well away from the hot iron!).

Flux facts

When soldering, you will need to use a flux, although most modern solders include a flux in the reel of solder itself. This is because when the metal is heated it oxidises, preventing the solder from sticking to it. It's advisable to touch the solder on to the workpiece before it will actually melt, in order to ensure that there is some flux in place before the soldering proper starts.

Soldering hints and tips

● Always use specific electrician's solder for in-car electrical work.
● 'Tin' a new iron before starting work.
● Never blow on a join to help it cool, or you could get a 'dry' join.
● Soldering makes an electrical join, not a physical one – always crimp the sheathed cable.

Relays

Basic description

A relay is nothing more than a heavy duty switch placed in-between a conventional switch (any type) and the component that is being switched – headlamps, fuel pump, electric horns, etc.). On the surface, this looks like adding some more complication just for the sake of it, but, in fact, it saves complication and makes life much easier – certainly for the car-maker, anyway.

The reason is down to the amount of current that the device takes; for example, high-powered driving lamps. As we've already seen, the typical wire size throughout most of the car is capable of handling around 6A. But on a heavy application, 15A–20A could be required, and if smaller wiring was used, it would soon overheat and maybe even catch fire.

The same principle applies to the on/off switch. This, too, is current

rated, and has to be physically much larger to handle bigger current loads. Both of these present problems for the car manufacturers, who don't want to fill the car with swathes of heavy and clumsy wiring or scatter the dash with a dozen different switch sizes. The answer then is to fit a matching set of lower-rated switches and use standard-sized (thinner) wire, but instead of connecting them directly to the components, they are linked to a relay. A relay is an electronic switch which can take a low current input (typically 175mA) but operate something which requires a hefty current, up to 25A or 30A.

Inside every relay is a coil, which is wrapped around an iron core. When the switch current goes through the coil, the core is magnetised and a small steel plate is attracted to it – this movement of the plate, between two (or more) contacts (see next section) is the on/off action required to operate the device.

A simple relay will normally have four terminals, two for the winding and two for the contacts carrying the heavy current. Often these are shown as C1 and C2. When a (small) current is passed through the winding (terminals W1 and W2) the central core becomes magnetised and attracts the clapper plate, so closing the two contacts and providing a circuit between C1 and C2 for the heavy current. Some form of spring is used to open the contacts when the winding current is interrupted.

Four- and five-pin relays

There is a standard type of four-pin relay which is commonly used for many simple applications. The pins are usually marked in the plastic relay casing and numbered as shown in the picture below, that is 85, 86, 30 and 87. Pins 30 and 87 are the two that switch the electrical device on and off; in the 'resting' state the pins are held open by a spring and the device is off. To some extent, they look like contact breaker points. When the switch is turned on, a current flows across terminals 85 and 86, and as the coil is energised the other two contacts are forced together and the

device is switched on.

But for its extra pin (which is usually held closed to pin 30) a standard five-pin relay is very similar to the four-pin version. When current is applied to terminals 85 and 86, as previously, the switch is opened and connection made between pins 30 and 87.

These two types of relays are the most common, but for specific applications, where these could not be used, manufacturers had to use different relay combinations, though all work on the same principle.

Three-pin relays

Some relays only have three pins because the earth connection is made by the casing directly to the earth on the vehicle, or by a separate connection to the case.

Relay numbering

There is no universal standard for relay pin numbering, and although most conform to the accepted norm there are exceptions to prove the rule. The most common four-pin numbering systems are shown in this table:

	PIN 1	PIN 2	PIN 3	PIN 4
Type 1	C1	C2	W1	W2
Type 2	87	30	85	86
Type 3	88A	88	85	86
Type 4	H	B	P (or S)	Not marked

Simple relay tests

1. The simplest test for any relay involves using nothing more complex than your ears! Get close to the relay whilst it's *in situ* and get someone to operate the electrical device it controls (fuel pump, etc.) – if it is required, switch on the ignition. Listen to the relay and you should here a sharp metallic click as it operates. If you don't, then either the relay is not receiving power or it is faulty.

2. Do NOT try to perform this test with power to the relay. Remove the relay and check that there is NO continuity between the power terminals (typically 30 and 87). Clip the leads

To check your relay, refer to your car's electric circuit diagram so you know which wires go to which terminals. Some relays make life easy by having a simple diagram on the casing. When removing a relay, be careful not to damage the pins as you wiggle it out of its holder.

Most relays have removable tops which clip-fit on to the bases. The only benefit of being able to look inside is to check that there is nothing obviously physically wrong – wires adrift, etc., and that the points are OK. The electronic testing can be carried out from the terminals without removing the top.

Relays can be purchased from electrical component suppliers, rated to suit your application. This one is suitable for high-wattage auxiliary lamps and for added protection (of which you can't have too much) it has its own fuse built-in.
(Courtesy Hella Limited)

On this five-pin relay, pins are again marked as to which is which together with a simple diagram. Being of German origin, the pins are numbered slightly differently from most – just as well they did include a diagram!

on to the terminals with the meter set to 'resistance' (ohms) – if the reading shows continuity, the relay must be discarded and replaced.
3. Use a fused bridging lead, connecting one terminal to a positive feed from the car and the other to one of the output terminals on the relay. Put another bridging lead to the other output relay terminal and touch it to a good earthing point. As the contact is made, you should hear a sharp clicking sound as the contacts in the relay operate. If you don't, try swapping over the leads on the relay, as some relays need a specific polarity. If there's no sound and you're sure that the power and earth connections are good, then the relay is dead and must be replaced – although if you want belt and braces confirmation, go to the next check.
4. With the bridging leads as previously, set your meter on 'DC/Volts' and put the red and black leads

across the power circuit terminals. The meter should show battery voltage (i.e. approx. 11V–13V). If not, the switching is simply not working properly and the relay is dead.

Three-pin relay tests
The tests for these relays follow the same pattern as already described, with the difference being that the earth connection is not a pin on the relay, rather it is via the case of the relay or a separate wire.

The fault-testing procedure is the same as described for four-pin relays, using the casing as an earth where required.

Solenoids

A solenoid of the type usually found on starter motors, works on the same principle, in that a small wire from the ignition switch triggers the unit which can cope with the massive currents – often upwards of 250A – to the starter motor. The main difference is that the internal windings move a plunger or rod.

Chapter 4
The battery

Introduction

A great many classic car problems can be traced to the battery, largely because the (relative) lack of use allows it to go almost or completely flat between infrequent drives. One problem is that the electrical effort required to turn the engine over can often be so much that there isn't enough left to provide enough to generate a decent spark at the plugs. Thus, whilst you may think that the ability to make the starter motor operate means that the battery can't be at fault and that the non-starting troubles must lie elsewhere in the ignition system, you may well be wrong. As such, lesson one is simple – ALWAYS make sure your battery is fully charged (and holding the charge) before you charge off on a wild goose chase, looking for the fault that never was.

Modern batteries are efficient beyond the wildest dreams of motorists of the 1950s, and doubtless they would have given an eye tooth or two to fit one to their cars at that time. In retrospect, however, the classic motorist of today is likely to think as much of original appearance as of outright efficiency, especially as the classic car tends to be a second, third or even fourth car. As such, a good business has grown up to supply batteries that are not only electrically efficient, but also that look the part under the bonnet (or seat, etc.). To this end, there are still a number of specialist battery manufacturers (see Appendix 1) who can build – or rebuild – a battery that looks just as it did when new. Moreover, they can make it work like a modern unit, giving the best of both worlds.

What is a battery?

Although battery technology has improved greatly over the years, several inherent problems remain, notably that of weight and safety. However you throw the dice, it is still a plastic (more specifically polypropylene) box filled with sulphuric acid, bolted into a bumping, vibrating, high-speed vehicle.

A battery is made up of individual 2V cells. Each cell is made up of a number of lead plates which are suspended in an electrolyte solution of diluted sulphuric acid. The cells are connected in series whereby three are required for a 6V battery and six for a 12V battery. As the battery discharges (i.e. as it is drained of its energy by electrical products on the car) the electrolyte solution chemically reacts with the surface of the lead plates to form lead sulphate. It is this chemical reaction that creates the electrical current. The lead sulphate collects on the plates, and as this happens a concentration of sulphuric acid in the electrolyte solution is reduced. When the battery is being charged, the opposite takes place, in that the sulphate on the plates is converted back to sulphuric acid.

If the battery is not used (charged or discharged) for long periods of time, lead sulphate is formed which can change to a hard crystalline state which prevents the correct chemical reaction occurring. Recharging can sometimes redress the balance, but more often, a battery allowed to stay in this state for too long becomes permanently damaged to the point where it will never accept a full charge again.

Why fit a battery?

The main reason road cars need a battery is to supply the massive current required for the starter motor to turn the engine over. In addition, it can also power electrical items (such as side lights or a radio) whilst the engine is switched off. When the engine is running, a relatively small amount of current is taken from the battery for the ignition system and, where required, lights, wipers, etc., but to counter this, it is being charged by the dynamo or alternator (see Chapters 6 and 7).

Battery designations

Until the late 1990s, all batteries were designated in terms of amp/hours, i.e. amperes per hour (AH). A reasonably powerful battery would be, say, 45AH, with a diesel or larger-engined model requiring perhaps a 65AH battery. The description of the first example means that it would provide a total of 45 amps for a full hour or 4.5 amps for ten hours or . . . well, you can get the picture from this. Nowadays, thanks to yet more Euro harmonisation, battery specification is nowhere near as simple and is usually denoted in terms of *Cold Cranking* and *Reserve Capacity*, explained as follows:

Cold Cranking (CC) is the current discharge the battery can maintain from fully charged at –18°C before the voltage in each cell drops to 1.4V.

Reserve Capacity is the time (in minutes) taken for the voltage in each cell to drop to 1.75V from fully charged whilst the battery is being discharged at a rate of 25 amps. So now you know! The larger the two figures are, the more capable the battery is.

Of course, these figures are only true of a brand new, fully charged battery. As with everything else on your classic, the battery wears out and becomes less efficient over time.

Battery care

The battery has always been an easy item to ignore, even before the 'maintenance-free' era. Make it a point to check-up on your battery on a regular basis. Not only can it save you some grief (when the car won't start or it fails on the road) but it can also save your bank balance. If you don't use your classic on a regular basis, then keeping it charged up is one of the most important maintenance tasks (see later in this chapter).

Physical checks

Make sure that the battery is physically sound, that it is strapped in securely (an MoT failure point) and that there are no signs of cracks in the battery casing. Always look around the battery tray, as spilled battery acid corrodes metal very quickly. If you do find signs of this, disconnect and remove the battery and thoroughly rinse the area with a neutralising agent, such as a mixture of hot water and ammonia, or washing soda. Let the affected areas soak for a while and then wipe off, making sure the area is totally dry – using a hair dryer or heat gun will get into all the awkward areas. Brush on anti-rust agent and/or primer and, when dry, apply a top coat of paint,

ideally a thick product like Hammerite. While the battery is out, it's worth charging it up on the bench (it's so much easier!) and checking all around it for hidden cracks. Make sure you wipe over the battery with your neutralising solution and dry it thoroughly before replacing (don't use the hair dryer, of course). Check the electrolyte level is correct (see below) and that the earth connection is sound to the chassis/body and/or engine.

Check that the positive and negative connections on the battery are tight (but don't get too excited with that spanner – over-tightening can do more harm than good). If there's any 'fur' around the terminals, remove the leads, clean them and the battery posts using a wire brush, and replace the leads. (Some recommend using boiling water as well, although this has to be used with no small amount of care for obvious safety reasons.)

Coat both terminals and posts with either a purpose-made spray-on protectant, or Vaseline to prevent another attack of the 'green furries'.

Electrolyte

The battery electrolyte level should be kept topped up (using only **distilled** water) to the point specified on the side of the battery (just above the level of the plates when viewed from the top). In normal use you'd expect to be doing this around every 1,000 miles, but as classics aren't usually used 'normally', it's a question of regular checking to establish how often your particular car needs topping up. It's myth that topping up with neat acid or even anti-freeze will prevent a battery freezing up in cold weather – it won't, so don't do it! Keeping a battery up to the mark with electrolyte and correctly charged will keep it ice-free in all but the most extreme of conditions. Always wipe the top of the battery **before** starting to top-up, to prevent debris dropping into it.

If any electrolyte is spilled, wipe it up immediately and wash off skin where applicable – it is highly corrosive. If you need to remove your battery, wear rubber gloves and goggles, and always keep it upright.

If you find that the electrolyte in all the cells needs topping up with increasing and irritating regularity, then it is possible that it is being overcharged and the battery is heating up too much. In this case, make a thorough check of the charging system. It is also possible that the battery is physically too close to a source of heat, the engine or exhaust. Here, fitting the battery elsewhere probably won't be feasible (although desirable), but fitting heat-shield material either around the battery or the exhaust, should improve things.

If just one cell constantly needs topping up, it suggests a crack in the battery casing. Examine thoroughly and wear strong gloves. There are many proprietary products for mending casings, although great care must be taken with regard to the electrolyte. Remember that a leak will have attacked the metal in the battery tray and it will need attention, as mentioned earlier.

Possible problems

Sulphated plates

As already discussed, not using any battery for a period of time leads to sulphation of the plates. In extreme cases this can make it hard for the battery to accept charge, even from a mains charger. Typical signs of this problem can be seen when the cells affected by the sulphation (maybe all of them) get particularly hot during charge and a general low output. In extreme cases, the battery is fit only for scrap. If you're lucky, trickle charging the battery will put some life back in.

Open circuit

The cell plates are welded to a cell bridge which links them all together and if this is broken, or if a cell connector is loose, it will lead to an open circuit situation. In this case, the battery will give no voltage reading and appear to be totally dead, even after charging. An open circuit fault is

Continued on page 44

THE BATTERY

The battery is the heart of your car's electrical system and, like the human heart, it can suffer many kinds of ailments which result in everything else coming to a dead stop. A little TLC in the form of a simple maintenance schedule will keep it ticking over nicely.

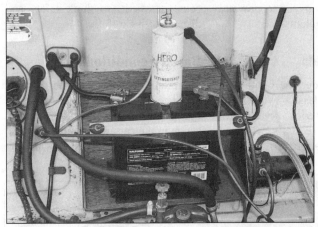

1 A well-restored '61 Morris Minor with a classic battery – or not, as the Halfords logo shows! Thankfully, there is an increasing trend for even mainstream suppliers to produce modern powerful batteries in classic black. (The extinguisher doesn't live there all the time – only while it's on display.)

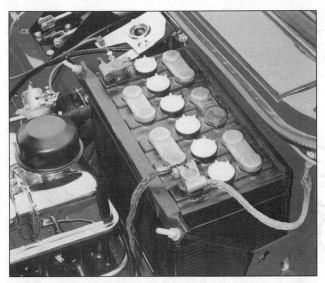

2 That's one serious lump of power, there! This 1962 TR4 has a real heavyweight power plant which looks as if it's straight from the factory. There are a number of specialist companies who can create (or re-create) batteries just as they used to be. (See Appendix 1.)

3 Access to the electrolyte is gained by removing the caps; this is a later style three-in-one cap (two off) whereas some batteries are screw type. Take care not to damage the (relatively) soft plastic, or to splash acid on your hands. Check that the electrolyte level is over the plates (by looking down into the battery), or on some batteries there is an easy-to-read level indicator on the side.

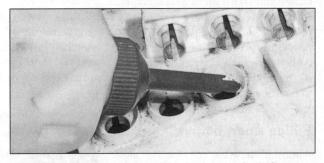

4 Where necessary, top-up the battery – don't forget to only ever use *distilled* water, not the stuff straight from the tap. A purpose-made filler like this has a special nozzle which stops water coming out before you're in position and so keeps the top of the battery dry.

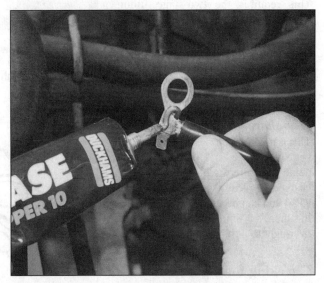

5 It's important to make sure that the contacts are clean and fur-free, otherwise you'll get general poor electrical performance. It pays to remove the leads from the terminals occasionally, wire brush the battery terminals and connectors and apply copper grease, Vaseline or similar.

often one of the trickiest to diagnose because the physical link to the cell bridge can touch occasionally and result in an intermittent fault.

Short circuit

It is possible for the negative and positive plates to short circuit against each other if conducting material gets stuck between them. Equally, the separators may be faulty. Whichever, in this case the result will be a constant discharge of the battery and, realistically, the best option is a new battery.

Post traumatic stress

The battery posts on a well-used classic can take a bit of a hammering, especially if the battery is regularly removed for charging, and it is possible for them to work loose. Although the cell tops can be replaced, it's often cheaper (and more reliable) to opt for a replacement battery.

Filling a new battery

Almost all new batteries are supplied 'dry-charged' and these require a different filling method from uncharged batteries.

Uncharged

This requires the two-stage filling method, where each cell is filled halfway up the battery and then left for anything from 6-12 hours before the filling process is completed. It should then be trickle-charged until it reaches full charge.

Dry-charged

This is much simpler – just fill each cell with electrolyte, and that's it. At this point, the battery will be almost fully charged (typically between 85% and 95%) and can be used straightaway or, if there's time, trickle charged overnight to bring it up to full charge.

Checking for a good earth

As ever, using the car's chassis/bodywork as a giant earth terminal has its drawbacks, notably that of corrosion. Where an earth lead is bolted to more

rust than metal, it follows that the connection is going to be less than good. This good earthing has to start at the very beginning, at the point where the earth lead from the battery is attached to the car itself and (usually) also to the engine. These points are almost universally ignored and are the source of many weird and wonderful faults. It pays to remove them on a regular basis, clean up the terminals and the mounting points with a wire brush and replace using Vaseline or copper grease to prevent corrosion-based problems.

Battery terminals

A quick glance under the bonnet of any selection of classics will show you that, just as batteries vary considerably, there are equally various different types of battery terminals.

This is the screw-down type, available, as most are, from the specialists or even from high-street shops such as Halfords.

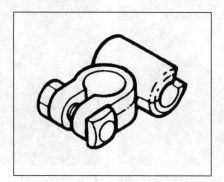

This is a soldered version of the same type of connector. These two will fit all sizes of battery cables and earthing braids. (Courtesy Auto Sparks)

Battery disposal

No battery lasts for ever, but some care needs to be taken when getting rid of one that is dead. It should be taken to the local council tip or your nearest dismantlers (the latest name for scrap yards!) where once upon a time you'd a get a few bob for your trouble. Whatever, even a duff battery contains some very unpleasant things for both the environment and any people (especially children) who come across it, so think safety and dispose of it carefully.

Battery condition

There are plenty of ways to discover the state of your battery; keeping an eye on the ammeter and/or voltage gauge in the car are the most obvious. A simple, general test is to switch on

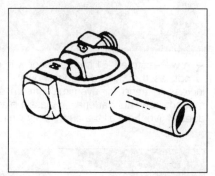

This solder type of connector is a universal, with two wire sizes being available; either 37/0.90 or 61/0.90. Conversely . . . (Courtesy Auto Sparks)

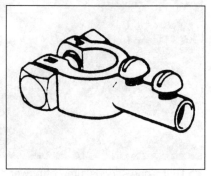

. . . the screw-type version of the same connector is suitable for all sizes of wire. Smear the cable with copper grease before fitting. (Courtesy Auto Sparks)

the headlamps without the engine running. They should shine bright and clear for some time before showing any signs of weakening. A battery which has no charge (or which shows an apparent 12V but which is actually on its last legs) will light them for just a few seconds before they dim. But this is only a general indication, and there are other aspects which could influence the result, such as poor earth contacts, faulty wiring, etc. So, it's wise to run some more definitive tests to find out if your battery is on its way out.

If you have a hydrometer (still available from most car-spares shops), relate the readings to the ambient temperature as shown in this table:

Each cell should be more or less the same reading. If there is a difference between cells of more than 0.040, then it points to a problem with that cell and a probable battery failure.

NOTE: Never take a hydrometer reading immediately after topping up the battery with distilled water – if you have just topped up, it should be charged for at least 30 minutes before taking a reading. To ensure that the acid and water have mixed properly, fully charge the battery at the normal re-charge rate.

Battery condition	Hydrometer reading *Climatic temperature usually below 25°C (77°F)*	Hydrometer reading *Climatic temperature usually above 25°C (77°F)*
Full charge	1.27–1.29	1.21–1.23
3/4 charge	1.23–1.25	1.17–1.19
1/2 charge	1.19–1.21	1.13–1.15
1/4 charge	1.15–1.17	1.09–1.11
Flat	1.10–1.12	1.05–1.07

Testing the battery and using a multimeter

Having invested in a multimeter, let's make it work for a living. Apply the red and black leads of the meter to the positive and negative terminals of the battery without the engine running (i.e. without an electrical load or charge) and look for a voltage reading of 12V+. With the engine running (not in a confined space), the voltage should rise to around 13.5V. With electrical loads (headlamps, electric fan, etc.) the voltage should still read 13V+, as the dynamo/alternator recognises that the battery needs topping up. Where adding electrical loads causes the battery voltage to be seriously depleted, it indicates that the charging system is not operating correctly. Details can be found in the relevant chapters, but simple checks you can make start with the state of the drivebelt – it should be physically sound (not frayed or shiny, so it slips around the pulley) and it shouldn't be too slack; typically, there should be around 10/12mm of play in

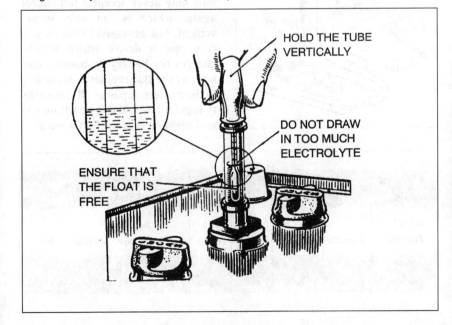

Diagram of hydrometer in use. *(Courtesy Lucas Automotive)*

HOLD THE TUBE VERTICALLY

DO NOT DRAW IN TOO MUCH ELECTROLYTE

ENSURE THAT THE FLOAT IS FREE

A more modern version of the hydrometer is the Hella Optilux Hydro-volt. It's smaller, easier to use and simpler to take a reading, but the results are interpreted the same way.

the belt in-between the pulleys. Turn the cooling fan by hand (cold engine) and check the belt to see if it turns the pulley. If not, tighten the belt as specified in your handbook and check again.

Most multimeters have the facility to check the charging rate of an alternator/dynamo. It's important to run such tests with no load and then a heavy load (heater fan, heated rear window, headlamps, etc.) and see if there is any great difference. Certainly, an alternator should easily be able to compensate for the extra load, although a slowing down of tickover speed is to be expected. If either alternator or dynamo register as not charging properly on your meter, then you've probably found your problem. But don't forget that it could be double trouble – a faulty charging unit *and* a duff battery as well!

Where the battery and charging system appear to be OK, then the battery may be on its last legs, but there may be excess current leakage – that is, something is draining too much current out of the battery whilst the car is standing. Clearly, with most cars there will be some drain at this time, even if it's only a clock or a radio (taking a little current to keep its pre-set memories alive). All things being equal, the battery should shrug off this kind of drain for weeks before feeling any ill effects. The most common culprits are interior lights or the glovebox light staying on (in each case check the pin switches for operation), or leaving on an electrical item, such as a radio, when leaving the car. See later for checking details.

Excess current leakage

Battery consistently flat overnight? There's no need, as this table supplied by Gunson Limited shows:

This assumes that the battery is in absolutely top order, but even so, the small amount of current required for, say, running a clock or radio memory, should make virtually no difference to the state of battery charge. Even at a massive 10A discharge, a heavy duty battery should still stand up to be counted for six hours.

Connect your meter as illustrated and relate your readings to the table. Expect less than 0.05A as being typical. Even with quite a few items requiring more current (such as an immobiliser) it shouldn't go much above that. If you're getting quite noticeable sparks as you disconnect the battery lead, it indicates that something is taking too much current. To find the culprit(s), check the obvious first. Is the interior light staying on with the doors shut? This could be the fault of a sticking or damaged door pillar pin switch. If you've a glovebox light, confirm that it goes off with the glove box closed. If you're not sure, remove the bulb and run the test again.

This diagram shows how to use your meter to test the amount of current drain on the battery. It depicts Gunson's Testune meter, which makes life easy by dividing the scales into red and green areas – green for good and red for bad. The wiring connections are the same for a digital meter; select current (amps) and, on a negative earth system, remove the red (positive) lead from the battery and connect it to the black lead from the meter. Then connect the red meter lead to the positive battery terminal. *(Courtesy Gunson Limited)*

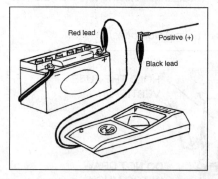

If nothing obvious shows itself, then you'll have to remove fuses one at a time and run the check again. When you note a large drop in the current being taken, the appliance is connected via that particular fuse. There may be more than one component per fuse, so a further process of elimination (disconnecting where appropriate) and re-testing should nail the culprit.

Charging

Batteries like to be charged at a steady rate over a period of time, so a 'trickle' charger is your best option. A boost charge (of the type delivered by heavy-duty chargers normally only used by garages) should be regarded only as an emergency measure. Unless you have a fully automatic charger, you'll have to remove the filler caps to allow gases to escape (rest the caps sideways in the holes to prevent detritus getting in) and keep an eye on it so that it doesn't overcharge.

SAFETY NOTE: When charging the battery in the car, always remove both negative and positive leads to prevent possible damage to the vehicle's electrical system. The time when a battery is most under threat is during the cold winter months. A battery allowed to discharge too far for too long may never accept a full charge again, which is not only inconvenient, but expensive! One answer is to use a device which trickle-charges the battery 24 hours a day, such as the Battery Sava. According to the makers, it passes all Euro safety regulations and can be left on day and night for a mere 4p per week.

Current drain	0.01A	0.02A	0.05A	0.10A	0.20A	0.50A	1.00A	10A
40AH battery	6 months	3 months	5 weeks	17 days	8 days	3 days	40 hours	4 hours
60AH battery	9 months	4.5 months	7 weeks	25 days	12 days	5 days	60 hours	6 hours

CHARGING A BATTERY

When charging a battery, it is vital to fit the charger leads (red to positive and black to negative) to the battery BEFORE you plug in and switch on the charger. This is to avoid sparks and the possibility of an explosion of the battery gases. Also, the charger should be switched off AND unplugged before removing the leads.

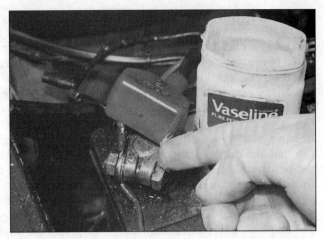

3 . . . smear on copious amounts of Vaseline. It pays to repeat the cleaning and protecting routine at the earth cable-to-chassis point.

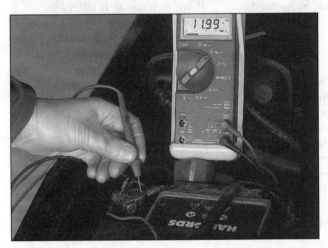

1 Testing battery voltage using a multimeter is simple. Take care not to breathe in fumes from the engine and watch out for the drive belts and fan, etc.

4 The author has used this Gunson Automatic charger for almost ten years with perfect results. The benefits are that there is no need to remove the filler caps and that, being automatic, it can be left on charge for as long as required, perfectly safely.

2 Keeping your battery terminals clean can save endless hassle on cold winter mornings and dark rainy nights. Clean them with a wire brush and use a purpose-made spray-on battery protectant or . . .

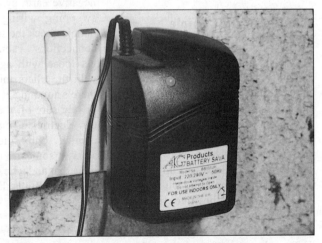

5 The Battery Sava is a simple device which supplies a small trickle charge to a battery to prevent it discharging completely during long idle periods.

Gas and explosions

Even basic chemistry tells us that when hydrogen and oxygen get together, the resulting mixture is potentially explosive. Unfortunately, during the battery charging process, this is exactly what is created – the negative plate gives off the hydrogen, and the oxygen emanates from the positive plate. It follows, therefore, that great care is required when you're in the vicinity of a charging (or even a recently charged) battery, avoiding such things as naked flames or sparks, say, from a grinder or cold chisel. Another possible source of sparks is if you connect or remove the clips from the battery terminals whilst the charger is still switched on at the mains – DON'T do it! It is extremely dangerous.

Charging tips

● Unless otherwise advised, loosen the filler caps to allow excess gasses to escape.
● Charge the battery in a well-ventilated area.
● Fit and remove the charger connections with the mains plug disconnected.
● Top up the battery with distilled water before charging.
● Prefer a trickle charge to a massive boost – it's kinder to the battery.

Changing the vehicle polarity

As we've seen, batteries have two terminals, positive and negative. Almost all cars since the early '60s were produced with an alternator and a **negative** earth electrical system, i.e. the negative terminal of the battery is connected to the vehicle body, engine and/or chassis. However, up to then, many cars were produced with a good-old dynamo and a **positive** earth electrical system, notably of British manufacture, such as the original (3.8 litre) E-Type Jaguars. If you're running a positive earth car, you will soon find that life is more difficult than it should

be, especially if you want to add an accessory or two, because most electrical products are produced with the negative earth market in mind. In addition, it makes upgrading from a dynamo to an alternator much easier; although positive earth alternators are around (the Lucas 10AC and 11AC models, for example), they're far from common – and thus expensive – and one of the great benefits of running with the negative earth herd is that your motoring life gets cheaper as well as easier. Unless you're desperate to keep your car original (in which case, skip this bit), you can make the swap from one to the other without tears. In essence, changing this way is swapping the polarity, this being the direction the electricity flows around your wiring loom.

Order

Though it may sound like a complex task, polarity swapping is quite easy. However, there are lots of things to check and individual sub-tasks to complete, so it's vital to have a grand plan. Read this section carefully and make yourself a check list, and work through it in order. It pays to do a 'dry run' first, checking out what you'll need (there's nothing worse than having to break off a job to fetch terminals, etc.) and that you understand which items need wiring amendments and which can't be used at all in a negative earth system. Where you're swapping wiring over, check and double check the security of your new connections – some spade terminals get loose with age, so a gentle nip with the pliers might be in order. If there's anything at all you're not completely sure of, then ask – your local car electrician, classic expert or, of course, club members – there's always someone who's been there, done that and who will happily let you learn the pitfalls the easy way.

Battery

Clearly, the battery leads have to be swapped over – before you do, see the 'washing and wiping' section for a quick check you might need to make.

Sometimes the terminals have to be swapped and in many cases, the leads just aren't long enough to reach the opposite terminal. It will usually work to physically remove the battery and turn it around – it will make the terminals slightly further away, but much less than previously. It's the time to check out the condition of your battery terminals – if they look old and careworn, they probably are, so blow a tenner or so, and get a new pair from one of the specialists. Having worked out how they're physically going to fit, do NOT reconnect the leads – leave them off until everything has been changed and checked.

What else does it affect?

Lots of items really don't care which way round they get their volts, just as long as they arrive. These include light bulbs and switches. Electric motors won't usually be affected except that they could spin in the opposite direction. The simplest way to deal with this is to swap over the power and earth cables on the motor itself.

Some products contain electronic components designed to handle just one polarity, and it's here that the DIY stops. These include such things as clocks, radios and some gauges, for example. Some period radios have a polarity switch built into them – just flick it the other way, turn on, tune in and . . . well, you know the way it is.

If your 'wireless' hasn't got a switch, you'll have to have it converted, or fit a different model. If you've a really old valve set, it usually does not matter about polarity, but you'd be wise to check with an expert first (a) because of the relative value of such old and working components, and (b) because valve sets can generate enormous voltages, and getting it wrong has the makings of real trouble. Clocks also can't be changed over at home and neither can electronic tachometers. (Bowden cable driven rev counters aren't affected, of course). Again, some were designed with polarity switching on the back, but otherwise you're faced with either a professional internal swap over (where possible) or a new unit. If you have an ammeter, the positive and negative terminals on the back will need to be swapped (otherwise 'charge' would read into the minus and visa versa). Look out for stickers or labels using wording which includes the word 'diode(s)' – this is an electronic one-way valve and won't go well with you swapping the polarity. If you have the luxury of an electric fan in the heater, run the fan once the battery leads have been reconnected, and see what happens. If it blows in hot air as normal, then it's not polarity sensitive. However, if it sucks instead of blows, it is, and will need the leads swapped over.

Most ignition coils will work with either polarity, but there's no easy way to tell. Swap the thin leads on the coil marked SW (+) and CB (–) and see if the car runs. However, how old is the coil already *in situ*? If it's any age, now may be the time to invest in a new one.

Washing and wiping

There are two basic types of washer and wiper motors. If the washer motor has two terminals, simply swap them over. If it has three, use your multimeter to find out which one is the earth and then swap over the other two. Field motor wiper motors can handle a polarity change with no ill effects, but the permanent magnet type will run backwards, causing unnecessary strain on the whole mechanism and bearings, etc. Before you do the swap-over, run the wiper motor to ascertain the direction of rotation. Having swapped the polarity, run the motor again; if it's the same, no problem. If it has changed, the wiring will need to be swapped over.

Fuel-ish things

You don't need to be told that any-

thing involving petrol and electricity needs to be treated with enormous respect, and that's what we need when considering an electric fuel pump (those with mechanical pumps can feel smug and skip this section). You need to establish what type of fuel pump you have – some early pumps don't mind which way round the volts go, but later models are polarity sensitive. The latter should be marked in some way and you should be able to see this. If you are not 100 per cent sure that your pump is suitable, then check first – your club or local specialist should be able to tell you.

Charging

Finally, it remains to remind the regulator and dynamo that something is

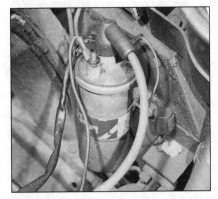

The coil may or may not need changing – but it's probably time for a new one anyway.

different since they were last connected to the battery. First of all, ensure the battery is still disconnected then remove the wire from the regulator terminal marked 'D'. Use your electrician's tape to cover the connector and tape it up out of harm's way. Then remove the wire from the terminal marked 'F' and reconnect the battery, being aware that if you've made any glaring errors you may need to disconnect it pretty quickly! Expect the usual tiny spark as you replace the earth lead, which indicates that a small current is being drawn for items such as a clock, radio memory or interior light. The sort of flash that makes you jump back pretty smartly implies all is not well; remove the earth lead a bit sharpish and do some checking before going on to the next section.

Assuming no mistakes thus far, hold the 'F' wire and simply 'stroke' it on terminal 'B' on the regulator (the input from the battery) half a dozen times. (on earlier, two-bobbin regulators, the terminal was marked 'A' – see Chapter 6). Allow a few seconds between each contact and expect to get a small spark as you do it (make sure there's no leaking fuel, etc. nearby). Replace both wires to the regulator – don't mix them up now! Then it's the moment of truth; turn the ignition key and check that the panel warning lights illuminate as they should and that there are no obvious signs of trouble – cracking of blown

The RB340 is typical of Lucas regulators of the '60s, with terminal positions clearly marked on the case.

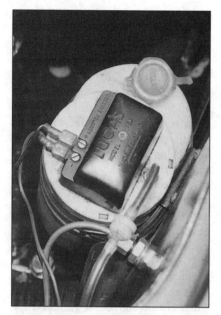

A typical two-terminal washer motor – simply swap the two around. On a three wire unit, find the earth then swap the other two over.

As you can see, you will find it's a similar situation with the wiper motor.

fuses, wreaths of smoke from beneath the dashboard. It's wise to stick at this stage for 30 seconds or so and have a helper looking under the bonnet for engine-bay trouble. If all is well, start her up. If you've an ammeter, you're looking for a '+' charge. If not, use your multimeter on the battery to run the same test. Let the engine run for a while (not in a confined space, of course) while you make a thorough visual inspection around the car. When you're happy, switch on the various electric appliances one at a time to make sure they work properly.

Chapter 5

The ignition system

A car's ignition circuit is a source of mystery to many drivers, but for classic owners it's a relatively simple affair. Certainly, anyone who thinks it's complicated should take a peek under the bonnet of a modern, electronically-managed car! The basic classic car petrol ignition system (diesel cars don't need this, of course) is shown in the first diagram, and until the advent of the ECU most cars worked on this basis. The job of the system is twofold; first, it has to create a spark in each combustion chamber at exactly the right time. Second, it has to boost a mere 12V input to many thousands of volts at the spark plug tip in the cylinder head.

SAFETY NOTE: Any car's ignition circuit will, at some point, have many thousands of volts running through it – and it's vital that you take care that they don't also run through you! Remember, also, that whilst a sharp shock may not do any great injury in itself, it could provoke an involuntary spasm causing, say, your hand to pull back quickly from a plug lead into a rotating cooling fan.

The typical classic ignition system uses six basic components:

1 The battery – clearly, there's no voltage of any sort without this. (A battery which is on its last legs will cause all manner of problems. Just because it starts the car and is charging, doesn't necessarily mean it's OK – always ensure the battery is in good condition when trying to sort out ignition problems.)
2 The coil, which has the unenviable task of boosting the battery voltage of around 12V to 10,000V and more.
3 The contact breaker assembly, found in the distributor, which has to make and break the spark thousands of times per minute.
4 The distributor, which has the job of sending the boosted voltage to the right plug at the right time.
5 The spark plugs – one (or in some exotic cases, two) per cylinder, which has to take the boosted voltage and produce a fat spark of between 20,000V and 40,000V at up to 3,000 times a minute.

This simplified diagram shows a typical contact breaker ignition system set-up. The ballast resistor (see later) is not fitted to all systems. The thick black cables from the coil to the distributor cap and from there to the plugs, are HT – high-tension – and carry many thousands of volts. The others are either earth wires or leads carrying just battery voltage (or less).

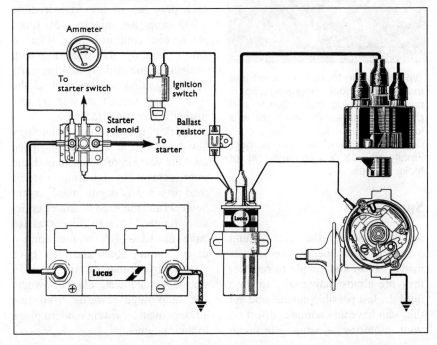

A classic car with classic ignition problems – the Mini is legendary for the 'water on the electrics' syndrome. With the coil, distributor cap and plug directly behind the grille, whereupon they can be showered with water, there's no wonder! Protected plug leads and protective rubber caps over both coil and distributor help no end on any car, as will a regular spray with WD40 or similar. This will help dispel moisture, especially in the form of overnight condensation which causes so much havoc on early morning starts with a reluctant battery.

Because of increasingly stringent emission regulations, it has been necessary for the major plug manufacturers to increase the firing voltage of the plug and the electrode gap. For example, in the early 1970s a typical voltage across the gap would be around 15,000V – nowadays it is nearer 40,000V. In addition, modern plugs are capable of working extremely well over periods of 20,000 miles – unimaginable in 1965.

Other areas of improvement include the development of copper-cored electrodes and subtle design changes to get heat away from the critical tip area as quickly as possible. This way the plug can be kept as close as possible to its optimum working temperature and thus be more efficient for longer.

Heat

The terms hot and cold are often used with regard to spark plugs. The tip of the plug typically has a temperature of between 450°C (842°F) and 850°C (1,562°F), so you can see that 'cold' is a relative term! Below this lower figure, the plug won't be running hot enough to burn off the carbon which then accumulates and so will tend to soot up; the result being rough running, poor idling and bad starting. At the other extreme, if the plug runs too hot, the plug tip will glow bright red and fire the petrol-and-air mixture in the cylinder head too early – i.e. before the spark. This is the pre-ignition syndrome and can be extremely dangerous for your engine and your wallet. Over the years, this has led to problems for plug manufacturers because some engines (high performance ones) run hotter than others, so that plugs had to be supplied in different heat ranges. The advent of copper-cored plugs helped their situation enormously, because of copper's ability to dissipate heat so well. As such, it has reduced the number of plugs required in a given heat range.

Typical ignition tools. On the left is a multi-function tool comprising a spark plug brush, plug gap adjuster and plug gap gauges. On the right is a long file suitable for plug electrodes or, more usually, the points gap. Finally, there's a complete set of feeler gauges.

Spark plugs

Spark plugs are the true unsung heroes of every petrol engine ever made. Cheap and simple to replace, they are almost universally ignored until the last possible minute, and yet they can have an enormous effect on your motoring – worn plugs can cause poor starting, uneven idling, rough running and low mpg figures. The last link in the ignition chain, they provide the spark which ignites the fuel-and-air mixture in the combustion chamber.

In an engine turning at 6,000rpm, each plug has to fire an incredible 3,000 times per minute – 50 times per second! And, of course, it has to fire at exactly the right moment, something due initially to other parts of the ignition system, but if the spark plug doesn't answer its call instantly, then trouble awaits.

Spark plug design and technology has developed at a frightening pace over the years in response to both the improvement in ignition systems (and particularly engine management devices) and the need to reduce emission levels. Though few classics have an ECU (electronic control unit) to worry about and most have either high emission limits or a simple smoke test, classic owners can reap huge rewards from this advancement by fitting modern plugs to their engines.

Spark plug removal

Always use the correct tool for the job, in this case either a pukka spark

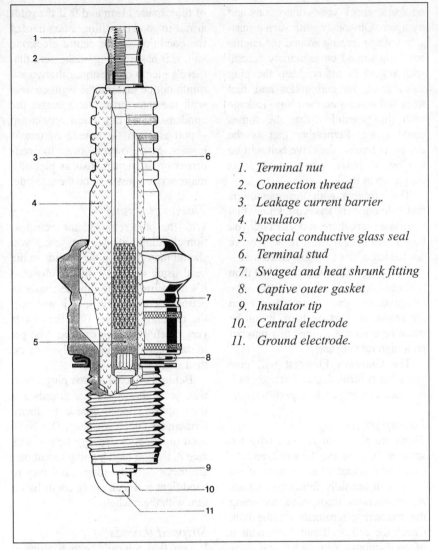

1. Terminal nut
2. Connection thread
3. Leakage current barrier
4. Insulator
5. Special conductive glass seal
6. Terminal stud
7. Swaged and heat shrunk fitting
8. Captive outer gasket
9. Insulator tip
10. Central electrode
11. Ground electrode.

The spark plug isn't as simple as it seems, as you can see here! *(Courtesy Robert Bosch GmBH)*

This 1961 Morris Minor is still using metal plug caps, but most manufacturers were turning to the safer and more efficient plastic type. Note: lots of other electrics here; the coil bolted to the dynamo for ease (the small cylinder at the lower mounting is an anti-interference capacitor), the horn at front left and, just behind it, the windscreen washer pump.

plug spanner or a long-reach socket, both of which should have rubber inserts to grip the top of the plug. This protects the ceramic insulator and also holds the plug so you can't drop it down into the engine's innards or on to the floor. Better still, it makes replacing the plugs much easier. A plug spanner will usually have a universal joint in it, which is useful for getting to awkward plugs hidden at the back of the engine and obstructed by wires and pipes. Most socket sets include UJ (universal joint) adaptors, so use that instead. Whichever you choose, make sure it's exactly the right size for the plug in question.

Clear away all the debris from around the spark plug before you start to remove it. Muck and oil seem to make a bee-line for the area around the top of the plug, and if it gets down into the bore when the plug is removed, it could lead to some mechanical mayhem. If you've a compressor, connect up your air gun and give it a blast (protect your eyes, of course). If you haven't, a long (dry) alloy wheel-cleaning brush will get right to the top of the plug.

If you're using a socket, you'll probably also need a medium extension to make removal easy. Many DIY owners believe that they're tight-

ening for England when fitting plugs, so be prepared for a tough tussle. Remember, also, that when applying lots of torque to remove a plug, when it does eventually give, it's likely to do so suddenly – so consider where your hand will end up, the better to save the skin on your knuckles. If you're unsure of the previous owners' attitude to maintenance, err on the side of discretion. If there is any reluctance at all to unscrew easily, wind the plug out one turn and back a half. This way, if the plug has been there since the Napoleonic wars, it will have the effect of breaking down the carbon deposits that will have accumulated on the threads. In extreme cases, this could wreck the thread as the plug comes out. Equally, if the plug has been cross-threaded on the way in, then taking your time on removal could give you advance warning. If you suspect this is the case, it's best to wind the plug back in while you ponder your next course of action. (See later in this chapter.)

Checking the plug

See your handbook or Haynes manual for details about recommended plug life, bearing in mind that plug technology has progressed apace, and modern plugs are far more capable than their counterparts of 30 years ago. Typically, around 10,000 miles is suggested as a plug-change limit, with a check-up and clean at 5,000 miles. Balancing that, many modern plugs are said to be good for 20,000 miles, but as classics tend to do many fewer miles than modern cars, and use their plugs in a different way from most cars, it does no harm to check-up at the very least annually. Given that a set of plugs is likely to be one of the cheapest maintenance items on your list, halving the suggested mileage will do no harm at all. Equally, some engines are harder on plugs than others and are more prone to plug problems if they're not totally up to scratch.

When checking a plug, look first at the centre electrode; if it's seriously worn down, then bin the plug. If it's in good condition, then it's a question of checking the gap between the two electrodes and adjusting where necessary. DON'T use the centre electrode as a lever when adjusting the gap!

Check the colour of the plug, which should be a mid-grey colour. If it's light grey, nearly white, then the fuel mixture is too lean. At the other extreme, if it is black and/or showing oily deposits, the mixture is much too rich and the plug is unable to burn off the excess of fuel.

Checking the spark

Your engine won't start if there's no spark at the plug, but equally, it won't run at its best if the spark getting there isn't powerful enough. The simplest method of spark checking is to remove the plug, fit the HT lead and rest the metal body of the plug on the cylinder block to earth it. Remove the positive connection from the coil to prevent the engine from firing. Hold the plug lead with insulated pliers and have someone turn the engine over (if you've a good old push-button type solenoid, you can do it yourself, of course) and watch for a nice fat spark across the gap. If there's

no spark, check your connections and try again. Obviously, with such a massive voltage leaping around the engine bay, you should be extremely careful with regard to safety; keep the plug away from the carburettor and fuel lines and make sure there's no leakage with the possibility that the fumes could ignite. Remember that as the engine is turning the drive belt will be turning, so make sure you can't get caught up in it.

The problem with this method is that, although it lets you know that there is a spark there, it doesn't tell you how much of a spark it is. And we're not talking a bit of a sharp crack here – a spark plug with a gap of 25–30 thou will need upwards of 3,000 volts to be effective. And that's at tickover; when the engine is working hard, it can be twice or even three times that number on a high revving car!

The Gunson's Flashtest will give you a better idea of spark strength, as it includes a sliding scale of performance.

Low spark to plug

There are plenty of reasons why the spark at the plug may be weak, and the first check is that all other parts of the HT circuit are fully functional. Check all connections throughout, including the spade/ring terminals on the coil. Check the coil itself and the condition of the distributor cap – a hairline crack can cause many problems. While the cap is off, ensure the contacts in the top

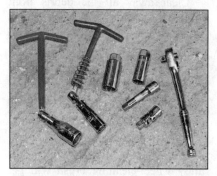

Using the right tool for the job. On the left are two different sizes of 'T' handle style plug wrenches, and on the right are two sizes of long-reach socket and ratchet. All have rubber inserts to hold the plug, once removed.

of the cap are clean and that the rotor arm is in good condition. Look hard at the condition of the centre electrode and, if it has a spring, make sure that there's plenty of tension, otherwise it might not be making the right contact with the rotor arm. Don't forget the condenser. This tiny – and very cheap – part is often the source of untold hassles. Many owners swap the condenser on an annual basis as part of a major service, just to be on the safe side.

Thread cleaning

With the plug removed for examination/cleaning/replacement, etc., you should then clean up the threads in the head using a specific thread chaser – it's not a bad idea to dip the chaser in petrol before doing this, as it will help the cleaning process. Turn the chaser very carefully, taking care that you get it started true. Wind steadily forward then slightly back.

Before replacing a used plug, use a wire brush to clean up its threads and then apply copper grease to them. Remember that spark plugs DO NOT need to be eye-wateringly tight – let's face it, they're hardly going to fall out, are they? Turn the plugs until they're hand tight and then apply about half a turn with the ratchet.

Stripped threads

If you find yourself with a stripped spark plug thread, it isn't the end of the world, although it could be mightily inconvenient and, in some exotic cases, similarly expensive. If you've sussed that a plug has been cross-threaded when it was fitted, then don't remove it all the way, rather wind it back in. This gives you a usable car to take to a professional, or to drive to the local spares shop for a thread repair kit.

Many machine shops offer a thread replacement service, and if you're not totally confident when dealing with cylinder heads, this is probably the best option. Remember that special care is required when dealing with aluminium cylinder heads because that soft metal is particularly unforgiving of cack-handedness. As a rule, it's a while-you-wait job, if you book your car in.

Don't remove the plug until you've cleaned away any oily debris so it can't drop into the cylinder head and cause damage. You can use a small brush or, if you have a compressor, blast away the dirt in efficient fashion. Remember to wear eye protection for this job.

Having removed the plug lead, check it for security on the cap itself – they often come loose with years of pulling and tugging. Apply the spanner, making sure it is a good square fit before starting to turn. This kind of spanner has a universal joint to make getting into an awkward spot (like this!) much easier. Though it may not seem it, the spark plug is quite delicate, particularly the ceramic insulation around the top half. Pukka plug spanners have rubber inserts so there's less likelihood of dropping it.

Companies such as Mr Fast'ner offer a range of DIY thread repair kits which are available through distributors or by mail order. Remember, though, that it may be necessary to remove the cylinder head on some engines, which will add considerably to the time and hassle.

HT cables

The HT leads from the coil to the distributor and from there to the spark plugs, are historically and almost universally ignored. However, they can be a source of trouble, as they break-down steadily over the years, something which leads to poor starting, poor fuel economy and a general loss of performance. This can be particularly noticeable in the wet, when the spark will take the path of least resistance, which in many cases, can be via the moisture in the engine bay and not to the spark plug.

In really bad cases, running the engine in a slightly darkened garage will reveal a 'fork lightning' type of effect all around the engine bay. However, this is extreme and usually it is less obvious.

Faulty HT leads cannot be repaired, and must be replaced. Most classics were originally fitted with copper-cored leads, which were good for transmitting the spark, but not so good at suppressing the inherent interference.

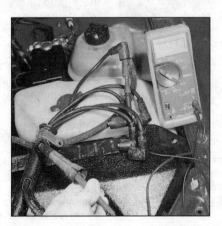

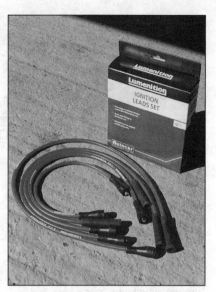

Unless originality is a key point, it is often worth changing to the more modern silicone type such as the Lumenition leads seen in the section dealing with conversion to performance electronic ignition. This gives superior insulation characteristics and improved reliability even in extreme conditions of temperature and humidity. The 8mm diameter ignition lead cable is specifically manufactured to high specifications. The leads have braided glass fibre reinforcement. In technical terms, they will remain flexible over a wide range of temperatures down to -50°C, resist oil, petrol and brake fluid but won't crack. Because of the pure silicone construction, they are capable of firing up to 60,000 volts and have improved resistance to damp and water. Like conventional leads, they are available in matched sets (made to the correct length for the vehicle) or individually (though buying leads separately isn't advised, as this can lead to an imbalance).

You can do a simple check with your multimeter (set to 'resistance'/ohms) by taking a reading from the earth wire at the distributor cap end of the lead and at the plug end. Your manual should tell you an exact figure (although if the leads are any age, you can't expect to get a perfect reading) but around 10–15 KOhms is about right for most cars. If it's noticeably more than that, then you've found a potential trouble-maker. Make sure that the leads are reasonably similar in their readings. Like springs and dampers, it's wise to replace HT leads in a set.

CLEANING A SPARK PLUG

When cleaning a spark plug, don't restrict yourself merely to the electrodes. Use a wire brush to get carbon deposits from the end of the plug and get those threads clean at the same time.

3 To check for a spark, remove the plug, fit the cap to it and hold it (using a pair of well-insulated pliers) against the engine block. Remove the positive LT lead from the coil (to prevent the engine starting) and have an assistant turn the engine over. You should see a fat spark jumping across the plug elec-

trodes. If you don't, or if the spark is weak, then there's something amiss – possibly the plug, but possibly elsewhere in the system resulting in less voltage getting to the plug.

1 It pays dividends to clean out the plug threads when you perform a major service and when you've just bought a new (i.e. different) classic. There are various sizes to suit all threads. Run it carefully down the threads, remembering always how easy it is to strip a thread in aluminium. They can be turned

using a spanner or socket, but hand-turning gives more 'feel' and reassurance. Even small amounts of gunge and bits of baked-on carbon could be enough to baulk the plug whilst tightening and strip the thread altogether.

4 A much more scientific method of checking the spark (rather than the plug) is to use a Gunson's Flashtest. By fitting the Flashtest to the

plug cap and earthing the device to the engine block, the spark jumps across the two terminals here. By adjusting one 'leg', the strength of the spark can be read-off the scale beneath.

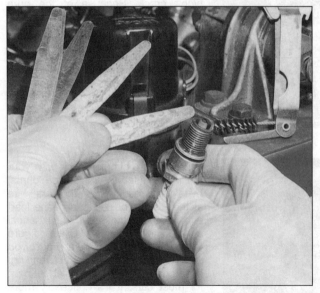

2 Use quality feeler gauges to check the gap. You need to be able to fit the required gauge (check your Haynes manual) in between the gap with just a hint of friction – not sloppy, but not tight. Use a special plug gapping tool to adjust the GROUND electrode only.

5 Cleaned and gapped, it pays to apply a little copper grease to the threads before replacing the plug. Not too much, mind, and you don't want it smeared all over the electrodes. Hand-tighten the plug until it's almost home. Use the plug

spanner/socket to tighten, but not too much – it's not a wheel nut and it's hardly likely to come loose!

The coil

A standard coil comprises two electrical windings – a primary and a secondary – wound around an iron core resting on an insulated base. The whole assembly is housed in a cylindrical aluminium case which is filled with insulating oil to prevent internal flashovers and also to provide some measure of heat dissipation. It's job is to turn a 12V input into an output of many thousands of volts.

The primary winding comprises around 200 turns of heavy gauge wire with each layer insulated from the next by paper. It is wound around the exterior of the secondary winding in order to dissipate the heat more easily. It is connected between the two by the LT (low tension) terminals on the top of the coil. The secondary winding is typically 20–30,000 turns of fine enamelled wire insulated as previously.

One end of the secondary winding is connected to the primary and the other is connected to the central core laminations (which in turn are connected to the coil chimney high tension terminal).

The large terminal at the centre of the coil is for the HT (high tension) lead which takes the now-boosted voltage from the coil to the distributor. There are two smaller terminals, each on either side of this, which can be Lucar (spade) or screw-on type. One of these is the 12V input and is marked '+' and/or SW (switch)/15. The other is the earth wire, which goes to the distributor, and which is marked '–' and/or CB (contact breaker)/1. The two thinner wires are relatively harmless, but great care must be taken with the thicker lead

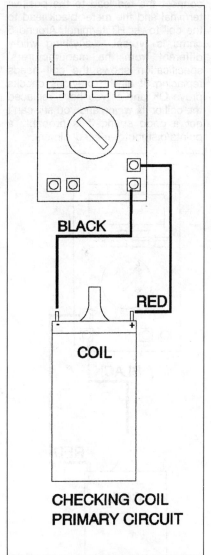

CHECKING COIL PRIMARY CIRCUIT

To check the coil primary circuit, first switch the ignition off and remove all leads from the coil, including the HT lead to the distributor. Set your meter to 'resistance' (ohms) and connect the red lead to the positive (+ve) coil terminal and the black lead to the negative (–ve) terminal. The reading should be around 2 ohms. A high reading indicates a faulty primary circuit and that a new coil is required.

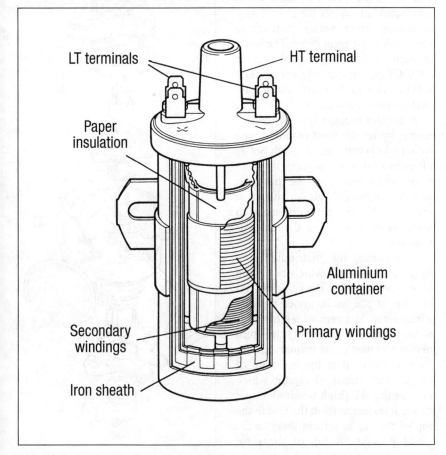

A cross-section of a typical coil, showing its component parts. Thankfully, the appearance of the coil has changed little over the years, so buying a new one, and having it look right under the bonnet, is easy. The choice is mainly between a standard coil and a high-output version. If you're going for the latter, take specialist advice beforehand to be sure you're matching all components in the system and, of course, that you'll actually get some benefit from the extra expense. The coil is not a user-serviceable item; it works, or it doesn't. If it is faulty, then it must be replaced. *(Courtesy Lucas Automotive)*

because of the massive voltages produced with the engine running.

The coil is often ignored when it comes to diagnosing electrical faults, largely because they tend to

To check the coil secondary circuit, remove the coil leads as previously, leave the meter set to 'resistance' and connect the red lead to the positive terminal and the meter black lead to the coil tower HT terminal. Around 5 ohms is typical – anything wildly different from the manufacturers' specification shows the coil needs replacing. If all the previous checks prove OK and/or you have replaced the coil or its wiring and you still can't get a good spark, it is probably a points/distributor-related ailment.

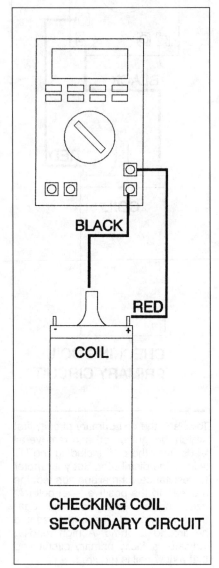

CHECKING COIL SECONDARY CIRCUIT

last for so long. Consequently, the coil in your classic could well be original, despite the fact that many other body and mechanical parts may have been replaced. There are ways to check a coil with your meter, although a sure sign that it is on the way out is to remove the central HT lead (engine/ignition off) and see if it is wet. If so, it means that the insulating oil is leaking and the coil should be replaced.

The distributor and contact breakers

Description
(Thanks are due to Holden Vintage & Classic for their invaluable help with this section.)

The basic job of a distributor is to provide enough voltage at the sparking plugs to ignite the mixture of petrol and air which has been fed into the cylinder in question. The distributor must make the sparking plug in question 'spark' at exactly the right time – something which varies from car to car – and in the right order. The exact amount before top dead centre (BTDC) depends on the vehicle and will be given in the handbook or relevant Haynes manual.

A contact breaker type of distributor is by far the most common type found on classic cars. Though not as efficient as its more modern all-electronic counterpart, it has the great benefit (for the DIY classic owner, at least) of being relatively easy to understand, work on and replace if required.

In essence, the distributor is a long rotating shaft which is geared to the movement of the camshaft. At the top of the shaft, under the distributor cap, is a cam which operates a movable contact which in turn makes and breaks the primary circuit from the coil. It is the breaking of the LT (low tension) circuit which creates the HT (high tension) surge; this is transferred from the coil to the top of the cap and from there to the metal contact on top of the rotor

arm. As the name suggests, this rotates, touching each of the contacts for the individual plug leads in rotation. This surge continues to the plug, whence the spark is created.

This exploded diagram reveals the complexity of the device. The most common distributors are those made by Bosch and Lucas and can usually be identified by their red and black caps respectively. There are different makes and types, but all operate on the same basic principles.
(Courtesy Lucas Automotive)

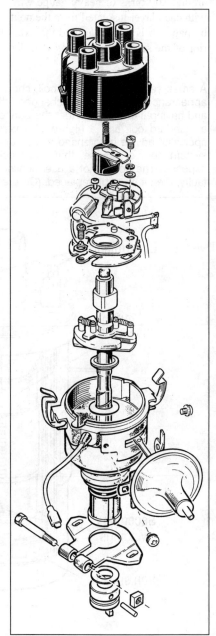

Contact breaker points

The contact breaker mechanism itself comprises two contact points (usually made of tungsten) one of which is fixed to the base plate, the other being attached to a heel which rests against the cam on the distributor shaft. As the cam spins around, the points open and close, alternately making and breaking the contact. The cam turns at half engine speed on a four-stroke engine. Each lobe of the cam can be seen as being the point where a piston is reaching the very top of its compression stroke and so needs some impetus to send it on its way to complete the next cycle – the impetus being the spark and resultant explosion.

The gap between the fixed and movable points can be adjusted in accordance with the car makers' specifications – if it is too large or small, then the performance of the car will suffer. On distributors which don't have a vacuum advance/retard unit, the movable plate is actually fixed. On a four-cylinder engine, one complete four-stroke cycle sees the contacts open and close four times. Keeping the points gap as the manu-

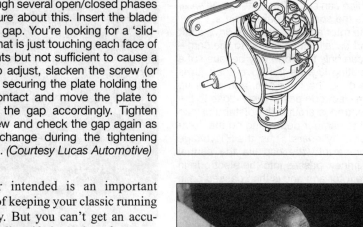

Use a set of feeler gauges to select the correct thickness, this is typically 0.0014in–0.0016in (0.35mm–0.40mm). Check your handbook or Haynes workshop manual to be sure. Turn the engine over (ignition off) until the points are wide open – you'll probably need to go through several open/closed phases to be sure about this. Insert the blade into the gap. You're looking for a 'sliding' fit that is just touching each face of the points but not sufficient to cause a drag. To adjust, slacken the screw (or screws) securing the plate holding the fixed contact and move the plate to change the gap accordingly. Tighten the screw and check the gap again as it can change during the tightening process. *(Courtesy Lucas Automotive)*

facturer intended is an important aspect of keeping your classic running properly. But you can't get an accurate reading if the points faces are damaged. What usually happens is that the massive voltages cause pitting on one point's face and a corresponding pip on the other. When this is minor, you can solve it by using a small file in-between the points (ignition off!). If it's too bad, the points should be replaced.

This shows a typical contact breaker arrangement. *(Courtesy Lucas Automotive)*

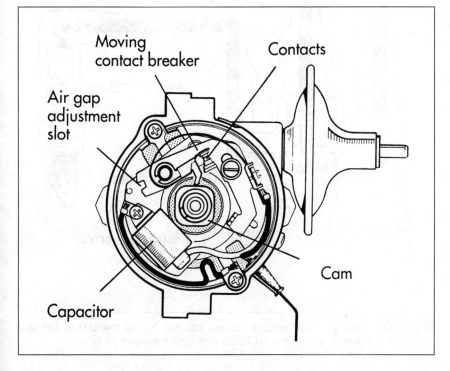

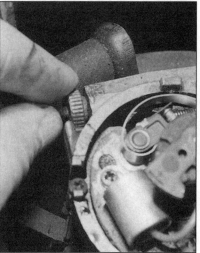

Many classic distributors have a knurled knob on the side of the distributor which enables very fine adjustment of the points without the need to keep slackening the base plate screw.

Distributor cap

Naturally enough, this cap fits on top of the distributor, protecting its innards and acting as a method of getting the high voltage from the coil to the right plug at the right time. There are electrodes around the outside of the cap corresponding to the number of cylinders, and a central electrode in which is fitted the HT lead from the coil. A carbon brush, under light spring pressure, ensures contact between the central electrode and the rotor arm.

Some caps are screwed into place, but most are like this one and are secured by strong spring clips. Gentle pressure from a flat-bladed screwdriver usually does the trick, but be careful not to damage the cap itself. Check the condition of the electrodes, which can suffer from pitting and wear like the contact breaker points.

The rotor arm sits atop the drive shaft and usually push-fits on to the cam – it can only fit in one way because of a locating lug. As the drive shaft turns so does the rotor arm, and at its tip the electrode passes very close to the electrodes around the distributor cap – the number depending on the number of cylinders. Thus, the HT voltage comes into the cap via the central chimney, passes into the electrode in the rotor arm and is then passed on in sequence to the HT leads and, ultimately, the spark plugs.

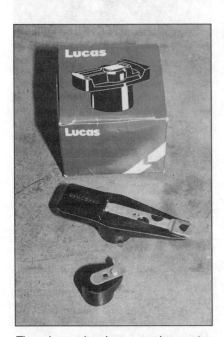

Though coming in many sizes, rotor arms are all essentially the same. Keep the rotor arm clean, as the constant high voltage sparking can damage the surfaces. Remove any grease by using methylated spirit, and use wire wool or similar to clean-up the contact areas at the centre electrode and on the outer contact (don't use a harsh abrasive or you'll wear away too much of the soft brass surface). Like the capacitor, the rotor arm is a cheap and easy-to-replace part, and it pays to renew it regularly – you'll get better starting, running, performance and mpg. *(Courtesy Holden Vintage & Classic)*

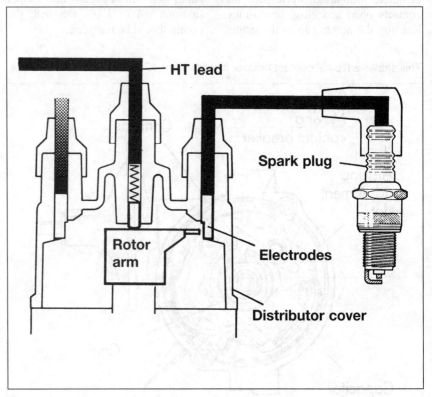

This shows how the high voltage comes into the top of the distributor and passes via the rotor arm to the HT leads and then the spark plugs. *(Courtesy Lucas Automotive)*

Distributor Maintenance

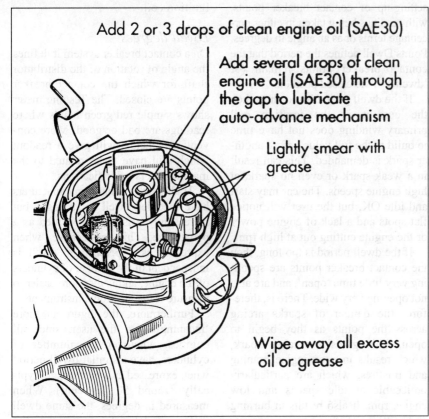

Add 2 or 3 drops of clean engine oil (SAE30)

Add several drops of clean engine oil (SAE30) through the gap to lubricate auto-advance mechanism

Lightly smear with grease

Wipe away all excess oil or grease

Keeping your distributor and its contents in good order can save you a lot of hassle (when your car won't stop and you're in a hurry), irritation (when it takes ages to start) and cash (an out-of-adjustment distributor and/or points, etc., will cost pounds in poor performance and excessive fuel consumption). When it comes to checking up and making adjustments, it's hardly rocket-science. Make a regular check that the various leads are all sound and not working loose. Look for signs of physical damage and keep the distributor free from oil mist and damp. Check the contact breaker points gap at the specified intervals, make sure that the faces of the points are not pitted and/or burned, and keep the 'heel' of the points assembly lubricated with a smidgen (don't overdo it!) of light grease to keep it free-running on the distributor cam. Use a few drops of SAE30 oil to lubricate the mechanical moving parts as shown in this diagram. *(Courtesy Lucas Automotive)*

Capacitor

Contact breaker systems feature a capacitor (sometimes referred to as a condenser). This is fitted either alongside the points under the cap or on the outside of the distributor body. It is wired across the points between the insulated LT connection point in the distributor and earth. It is important that the making and breaking of the spark should happen quickly and efficiently, and the capacitor aids this process. In doing so, it also reduces pitting of the points faces.

A typical capacitor from a Ford four-cylinder engine. The device earths itself via its securing screw. Easy to remove and refit and low in cost, the capacitor can cause all manner of problems when it starts to fail. Don't mess about, just fit a new one – some owners fit a new one at every major service, just in case.

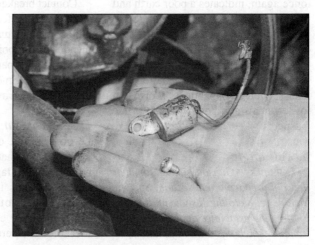

Classic car owners are well-advised always to carry a spare capacitor – they're cheap and easy to fit. More important, capacitor problems can cause a host of weird and not-so-wonderful symptoms that can appear to be everything from incorrect timing to carburation. When problem solving, many owners start by replacing the capacitor as a matter of course.

Ballast resistor

We've already seen that battery condition is vital to the correct starting and operating of your classic. It's possible that the current required of a battery to turn over the engine – especially on a cold day – can leave too little to create a decent spark; with the coil getting perhaps 9V or lower, rather than its full 12V. With less voltage in, there's less voltage out. Hence, the engine turns but doesn't fire, especially if the rest of the ignition system is below par – dirty plugs, pitted points, damp HT leads, etc. To help overcome this problem, some car manufacturers produced a coil which could operate at just 7/8 volts, and put in a little electrical widget called a ballast resistor to cut down the 12V from the battery to that level – but only while the engine is actually running. When the starter is operated, the resistor is automatically by-passed meaning that the reduction from normal battery voltage has little or no effect on the spark.

Checking the distributor earth

Check 1

It's very important that the distributor should be earthed correctly, and checking this is simple. Select 'resistance' (ohms) on your meter then connect the black lead to the battery earth terminal and the red lead to the metal distributor body. The reading should be low – typically around 0.15 ohms. If it is considerably higher (say, 12–15 ohms), the earth is bad, which could lead to a misfire or reluctance to start, etc. If you're unsure of your results, cross-check by using one of your bridging leads to connect the distributor body directly to the battery earth terminal. If this gives you a meter reading wildly different from your first reading, there's an earth problem to be solved.

Some distributors have a braided connection actually inside the distributor itself which links the baseplate to the distributor body. Make sure the connections have not vibrated loose (or off!) and, when running the meter tests, put the red lead to the baseplate to take a reading.

Check 2

The second check is to select 'DC/Volts' on the meter and connect the black lead to the positive battery terminal (on a negative earth system) and the red lead to the distributor body. With the engine ticking over there should be only nominal voltage – typically around 0.5V. Any more, once again, indicates a poor earth and the higher the figure, the worse the problem.

If you have earth problems, check all the earth points in the system, starting with the battery-to-chassis/body connections. Corrosion of terminals and bodywork are prime suspects.

Dwell angle

(My thanks to Gunson Limited for their help in preparing this section. Specific details relate to the Testune multimeter, though the principles apply to any multimeter which has a dwell function.)

The dwell function is used for the setting-up of contact breaker points, with readings being taken in either percentage terms or as an angle in degrees. Points Dwell defines the period that the contact breaker points remain (or 'dwell') in the closed position.

If the dwell period is too short then the current in the ignition coil primary winding does not have time to build to the full value before another spark is demanded. This can result in a weak spark or even no spark, at high engine speeds. The car may start and idle OK, but the user will notice flat spots and a lack of engine power or the engine cutting out at high rpm.

If the dwell period is too long, then the contact breaker points are spending very little time 'open', and are also not opening very wide. There is, therefore, the danger of sparks arcing across the points as they begin to open. This gives a weaker spark, which results in poor engine running and misfires, which are particularly noticeable at idle speeds and low engine rpm. It also results in burning and pitting of the contact breaker points, which further adds to the problem of engine misfires. The car may be difficult to start, and may clearly be running 'rough' at idle and low rpm.

It should be remembered that:
● Increasing the points gap reduces the dwell
● Reducing the points gap increases the dwell

Contact breaker points can be set up statically, using feeler gauges, although motor manufacturers usually recommend that the points are set up using dwell data, particularly using a dynamic dwell meter such as Testune, as this is a much more accurate method.

Dwell per cent

Dwell per cent defines the percentage of time that the test meter is receiving a voltage signal. In particular, for points ignition it measures the percentage of time that the points are closed. For electronic ignition it measures the percentage of time that

the current is flowing through the ignition coil.

Dwell degrees

On a contact breaker system it defines the angle of rotation of the distributor shaft for which the contact breaker points are closed. The Testune meter shows simple red/green bands where readings are bad or good. More conventional meters will give a readout which will have to be related to the manufacturers' specifications.

Traditionally, motor manufacturers have specified dwell as an angle, but increasingly it is being specified as a percentage. This is because, when expressed as a percentage, dwell is independent of the number of cylinders of the engine, and is therefore easier to measure using electronic instruments.

Furthermore, the figure is more 'meaningful' to the user, since all engines, whatever the number of cylinders, have a similar dwell period when expressed as a percentage (typically around 50 per cent). When measured in degrees, the same dwell differs widely depending on the number of cylinders (e.g. 50 per cent dwell is 22.5° for an eight-cylinder engine, and 180° for a single cylinder engine).

The table opposite shows percentage across the top line, with degree conversions for various cam lobe configurations.

When it doesn't add up

If you get your dwell angle correct but find the points gap ridiculously small, it's possible that you have distributor problems such as the cam of the distributor being worn, or wear in the bearings of the distributor shaft. If you have difficulty in setting points dwell to precisely the manufacturer's recommendation, remember that the points method is a mechanical system, operating near the limits of its performance, yet subject to the vagaries of mechanical wear and tear (electronic ignition was introduced to solve these problems). Absolute perfection (unless all related components are new) is rarely achieved on a classic.

Comparison of dwell percentage and angles

All engines	40%	45%	50%	55%	60%
4 cam lobes	36	40.5	45	49.5	54
6 cam lobes	24	27	30	33	36
8 cam lobes	18	20.25	22.5	24.75	27
1 cam lobe	144	162	180	198	216
2 cam lobes	72	81	90	99	108
3 cam lobes	48	54	60	66	72

Note: the number of cam lobes refers to the contact breaker points cam under the distributor cap.

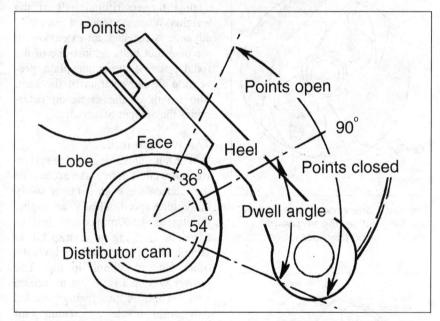

This diagram shows a typical four-lobe cam which has, by definition, four periods of 90° (thus making up the 'circle' of 360°). If the quoted dwell is 54°, then the points are open for 36° of each dwell period. By using the table this can be seen to equate to a dwell of 60 per cent. *(Courtesy Gunson Limited)*

Auto advance and timing

As we've seen, the spark at the plug gap is used to trigger an explosion (or more precisely, a 'burning') of the petrol-and-air mixture in the cylinder head. The plugs fire slightly before the piston has got to the very end of its stroke (at TDC – top dead centre) to allow time for the mixture to burn completely for the downward 'power' stroke. The higher the engine revs, the greater the angle before TDC the spark plug has to fire.

As well as the engine speed, other factors affect the timing, notably the degree of suction in the inlet manifold and whether the use of unleaded petrol requires the ignition timing to be retarded.

Incorrect timing will result in poor performance or economy, or both. Though many classics aren't required to pass MoT emission tests, it's ecologically friendly (and cheaper!) to produce as low a figure as possible, and having the timing spot-on is one

way to achieve it. Moreover, a timing advance that is too high can result in audible 'pinking' (a tinkling noise from the engine) which could lead to engine damage. Timing advance that is too low may cause engine overheating with high fuel consumption and low performance.

Advancing the cause

Distributor life isn't quite as simple as that, though, because the ignition system is not only required to develop the HT spark, it also has to deliver it to the correct spark plug and at the correct instant. In addition the spark timing must be varied in accordance with engine speed in order for the engine to maintain optimum performance. For some years this was not possible, and units such as the DJ4A (used on the MG TA among others) had no internal means of advance; the shaft was a single piece item with a drive gear fixed to the bottom end. The top of the shaft was machined into the form of a four-lobed cam which operated a simple set of contacts. In the mid-1930s, this model distributor was replaced by a more sophisticated unit; the DK4A. It was quite a step forward, as it incorporated an automatic advance mechanism, in the form of weights and springs – the same system still being used today on some cars! This now meant that the distributor could be built to each engine's requirements. As the engine revs increased, the weights in the distributor were forced outward, each one held back by differently tensioned springs. The first (primary) spring controlled the low revs advance, and as the revs rose the secondary spring came into action. By varying the tension of these springs, the distributor could be tailored to fit individual engines with surprising accuracy. This is the advance curve and it simply has to be right for an engine to function properly.

Automatic centrifugal advance

Normally, a spark should occur just before the piston reaches top dead centre on the compression stroke, but as the engine speed increases, the HT spark must be timed to occur a little earlier (before top dead centre) in the cycle. The reason for this is that, however quickly the petrol-and-air mixture burns when ignited by the HT spark, a finite amount of time is involved and this has to be taken into account. So, advancing the spark timing automatically ensures that maximum power is applied to the piston just as it passes TDC and begins to come down on its power stroke. This is achieved by using a centrifugal type of advance mechanism attached to the distributor shaft.

The distributor cam is rotated around the shaft, within limits, by the action of two weights which are forced outwards by centrifugal action. Most distributors use two steel weights, each of the same weight, size and shape. The weights are coupled to the cam which is able to move around the top of the shaft. Springs connected between the anchor posts of the action plate and the cam foot retain the cam in its static timing position.

As the engine speed increases, the distributor shaft speed increases and the weights are thrown outwards by centrifugal action against the tension of the springs. Movement of the weights rotates the cam slightly in advance of the shaft in the direction of shaft rotation. In effect, what has happened is that the point at which the spark occurs has been moved in advance of its static firing point.

The rate of advance is controlled by the tension of the springs reacting against the centrifugal pull of the weights. When the required amount of advance is reached, an extension on the cam foot butts against one of the fixed posts of the action plate, preventing further rotation of the cam. The length of the extension determines the amount of advance.

The vacuum unit

Whilst this automatic advance system worked well, it didn't take account of the load on the engine, rather solely the engine speed. Clearly, an engine turning at 4,500rpm could just as easily be slogging up a steep hill at 10mph in first gear as going down the other side at 70mph in top. The answer was, and is, to use a vacuum unit. This is a spring loaded diaphragm inside a vacuum unit which is responsive to the changes of depression in the inlet manifold. One side of the diaphragm is connected to the inlet manifold by a small bore pipe. The other side is linked by an actuator arm to the plate on which the contact breaker is mounted.

As the diaphragm flexes (i.e. as the accelerator is depressed), the contact set mounting plate rotates around the cam against the direction of rotation for spark advancement. When the depression in the inlet manifold decreases, the diaphragm is returned to its static position by a spring incorporated in the vacuum unit.

The vacuum unit, therefore, depends for its operation on the

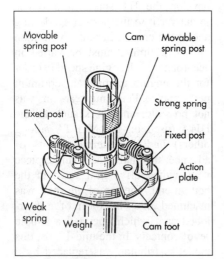

This diagram shows a typical centrifugal advance set-up. *(Courtesy Lucas Automotive)*

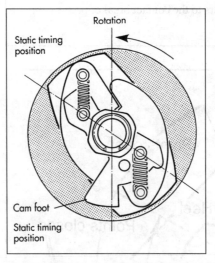

The static timing position would look like this, but as the engine gathered speed . . . *(Courtesy Lucas Automotive)*

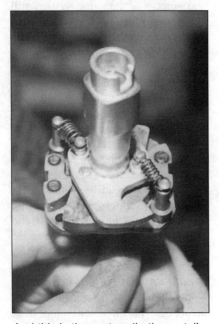

And this is the system 'in the metal'.

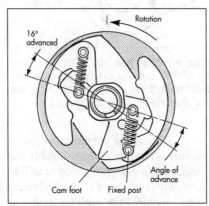

. . . centrifugal force would force a timing advance. Note how the springs have extended – the tension of the springs can be set to give particular advance characteristics by the manufacturer. Moreover, worn springs can accidentally give a wrong advance figure – less than is required at speed. *(Courtesy Lucas Automotive)*

amount of depression created in the inlet manifold. The amount of vacuum advance required is determined by the timing manufacturer. A code number, stamped on the case of the unit, indicates its operational characteristics. The code number, for example 3-24-12, is interpreted as follows:

(a) Vacuum (inches of mercury) at which the unit begins to function.
(b) Vacuum (inches of mercury) at which maximum advance (or retard) occurs.
(c) Maximum advance (or retard) in degrees. (Retard vacuum unit usually has 'R' at the end of the code.)

Alternatively, vacuum codes are now given in metric values where the amount of advance/retard is measured against mm of mercury.

Vacuum advance

The vacuum unit provides additional advance at high engine speeds when there is only a small load on the engine. The throttle is then only partially open and the restricted air flow creates a vacuum (or depression) in the inlet manifold. The vacuum tapping is taken from very close to, but slightly upstream of, the throttle butterfly. When the throttle is closed, at idle or on over-run, there is no vacuum at the tapping, and so no advance is given. It is only when the throttle butterfly is opened slightly that the tapping is uncovered and the vacuum is applied. This is known as edge control because it is only when the 'edge' of the throttle butterfly uncovers the tapping that vacuum advance occurs. However, when the throttle is fully opened, the depression is reduced and the vacuum unit ceases to operate.

Under conditions of low load and high engine speeds, the amount of residual gases (burned gases from the previous firing stroke) remaining in the cylinder increases. This has the effect of diluting or weakening the mixture on the next firing stroke. As a weaker mixture takes longer to burn, the spark must be timed to occur earlier in the engine cycle.

Always make sure that the vacuum advance connections are sound both at the distributor and at the carburettor. At both ends, it's a simple push-fit and it can become loose. Check the tube itself for signs of perishing or cracking with age.

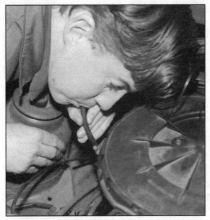

The advance mechanism inside the distributor can be checked quite easily. With the engine off, remove the vacuum pipe from the distributor and ensure that the connection to the distributor is sound. Clean up the end of the pipe and suck on it hard. There should be some resistance and as you stop sucking, you should hear the base plate (spring-loaded of course) click back to its original position. If it doesn't, then either the mechanism is damaged or has seized solid or, more likely, the diaphragm inside the vacuum unit has failed.

Checking and setting the ignition timing

The timing can be set statically, although it is generally agreed that dynamic timing (using a light and with the engine running) is more accurate and gives better results.

Before starting to check/adjust timing, it is important that the rest of the ignition system is operating as it should (cleaned/replaced points with correct gap, cleaned rotor arm, etc.) and that the engine is at full operating temperature (i.e. not running on full choke). You'll need your handbook or Haynes workshop manual for such details as timing advance figures, engine idle speed, whether the vacuum pipe should be connected/disconnected, etc. Check also the location of the timing marks – usually on the fan belt pulley or engine flywheel – and what these marks mean (a single mark will usually mean TDC – often denoted as '0' or 'V') and if there are other markings what angles they represent. In order to see them easily, even with static timing, it's a good idea to highlight the mark you're using with liquid paper (Snopake, etc.) or a dab of quick-drying white paint. Timing is usually carried out on No. 1 cylinder, but there are variations, so check first.

Static ignition timing

By definition, this is carried out with the engine not running. Connect your meter (set to 'DC/Volts') or test lamp between the ignition coil 'CB' or '-' terminal, and earth. Remove the distributor cap and ensure the ignition is switched off.

Find the location of the timing marks on the vehicle, then rotate the engine until the marks are correctly aligned with No. 1 piston on its compression stroke. Then check that the rotor arm is pointing to the correct HT contact for the timing cylinder. If the timing is correct, the contact points should be just at the point of opening with the cam rotating in the correct direction of rotation. Check this by using your meter/lamp. Switch on the ignition and, as the points open, the lamp will light or the voltmeter will register battery voltage.

If the timing is incorrect, slacken the distributor pinch bolt (adjustment bolts) and rotate the distributor body to the point at which the contacts are about to open, with the timing marks correctly aligned.

Dynamic timing

SAFETY NOTE: Using a timing light involves at least some time spent with the engine running. Take the following safety precautions to ensure you're not injured:

● **Ensure that the car is parked on level ground with the handbrake on.**
● **Do not wear loose clothing that could be caught in moving engine parts.**
● **Route timing light cables away from hot/moving parts.**
● **Take care not to touch HT leads.**
● **Don't place tools where they could be dislodged or vibrate into the engine bay.**
● **Make all electrical connections with the ignition 'off'.**
● **Keep children and animals away from the area you're working in.**
● **Don't work in a confined space – carbon monoxide can kill in minutes.**

Finally, remember that the point of using a stroboscopic timing light is to make the moving pulley appear stationary – it isn't, so don't absent-mindedly stick your fingers in to adjust something!

The inductive lead clips on to the HT lead for No 1 cylinder. It receives a pulse every time that spark plug gets its voltage, and thus the light 'fires' exactly at the right time, every time.

Having wired up the light as described, start the engine and run it at the speed recommended, disconnecting the vacuum pipe where appropriate (check your handbook). When the light is pointed at the pulley, the white mark will show up and appear to be stationary, and it should align with the mark on the engine block. If it does, the timing is correct. If it doesn't, adjust the timing by rotating the distributor body as described earlier. This particular light can be set to zero degrees for conventional timing at idle speed or at a higher figure to check increased advance at higher engine speeds.

Timing lights with a Xenon beam, such as the Gunson heavy duty version, give the brightest light. Like most strobe lights, it will only work off negative earth and requires a 12V supply. Cars with positive earth systems and/or only 6V, can circumvent this problem by using a suitable slave battery.

Checking the centrifugal advance mechanism with a timing light

As we have seen, this mechanism should advance the timing with engine speed. To check, remove the vacuum pipe, start the engine and point the gun at the timing marks. As a helper increases the engine speed, the marks should remain aligned initially, but gradually begin to 'move' in the opposite direction to the pulley/flywheel rotation. The 'move-ment' will stop eventually – advance typically begins between 500rpm and 1,500rpm and ends at between 4,500rpm and 5,500rpm.

Excessive advance during this test generally indicates broken advance springs. Too little advance points to sticking or wear at the pivot point of the rotating weights.

Distributor rebuild

No matter how well you tend your distributor's needs, it's going to wear out eventually, notably the cam and the associated bearing. Also, of course, the HT spark cannot make a true path to the plugs if the rotor arm and distributor cap are not in top order. This is when you'll need the services of a good rebuilder – unless you're capable of doing it yourself. Holden Vintage & Classic rebuild and supply probably more classic distributors than anyone else in the UK, so their experience has been more than useful for this section.

All units receive a new cap, rotor, contact points, condenser, new bearings/bushes, oil seals and drive dog (where necessary). The new weights and springs are set up to the original advance curve and the new vacuum diaphragm is set up to the original specification. Vacuum units are usually not interchangeable between different distributors. Holden's actually cut the original unit apart with a special tool, insert a new diaphragm and spring into a new housing and refit to the distributor body. They say that it is very rare for an elderly vacuum advance to work perfectly, so they are renewed as a matter of course.

Also working on the same plate is the centrifugal advance mechanism. The two coil springs can be 'tuned' to let the advance occur faster or slower, as required (the advance curve). There is a 'stop' to give the distributor its maximum advance. Holden's restorers always fit new springs and ensure that the 'stop' is the right length for the model of car in question – which is why you will have to tell year, engine size and state of tune.

And the same is true of a worn distributor drive slot at the bottom end of the unit. Holden's will put in a new spindle when wear is found; it will be up to you to replace the distributor drive shaft in the block. Luckily, distributor drive shafts usually screw or pull up and out of the block once the distributor is out, depending on type, but consult your manual. Wear with the geared type of distributor drive is extremely rare.

Holden Vintage & Classic could easily be called the distributor capital of the universe, with shelves stacked high with all manner of distributor, old and new, complete and in kit-form.

With the distributor removed from the car, they take off the cap and rotor arm and try moving the spindle from side to side. (If you try this in the car, the drive gears at the lower end of the unit could mask play in the spindle bushes.) A waving spindle equals variable points gap, equals variable spark timing, equals lowering efficiency.

Having stripped the old unit down, Holden's send various bits, including the cam pillar, away for plating. The shaft itself is checked for true running and reground 5 thou undersize. Old bushes are pressed out of the cleaned body, the Holden engineers using a special machine to remove them.

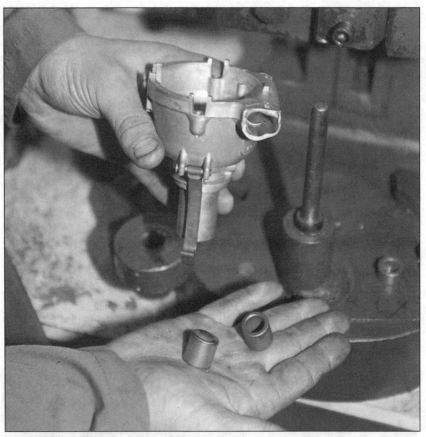

This is the newly-reground spindle and base plate, together with brand-new advance weights.

The same machine is used to insert new sintered bushes – these are made from particles of metal and carbon compressed to form a perfect self-lubrication material. By fitting them this way (rather than tapping them in) helps prevent the relatively delicate bushes from deforming or collapsing. Weights wear out and are always renewed while pivot posts, which almost never wear, are checked and only replaced if necessary.

It is inevitable that some compression of the new bushes will take place, and so they have to be carefully reamed to size.

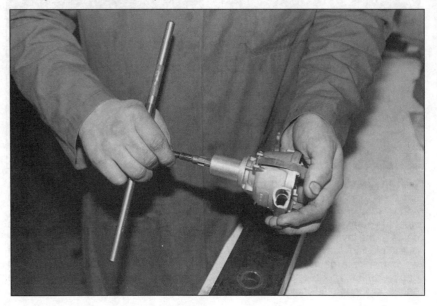

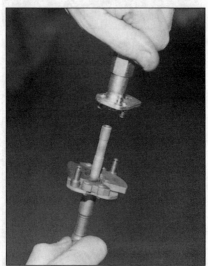

The related rotor shaft pushes on to the spindle, and pegs in the base locate the weights. As the weights swing out at speed, they advance the rotor shaft. The rotor shaft is held normally back at first base by a pair of springs which pull on posts mounted on the base plate. One of the posts is also the stop for the advance limiter, built into the front of the rotor shaft. This can be added to by welding a bit on, in order to limit the advance. Conversely, grinding a bit off, increases the advance. The correct amount is stamped in it.

The final step is to bench-test the complete distributor to ensure the advance characteristics are exactly as required. The Holden's testing machine is as much a classic as the cars it works for. The newly rebuilt distributor will ensure that the engine's vital sparks are fed in at precisely the right time. The bushes keep the spark exactly at the position you put it in; the correctly positioned 'stop' ensures the optimum maximum amount of advance, while the new springs control its rate. At the same time, the new weights and vacuum device ensure that the advance or retard is graduated correctly in accordance with the amount of acceleration and speed. A distributor's innards are a brilliantly evolved piece of precision engineering.

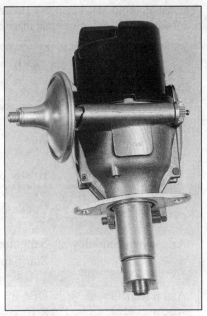

The much misunderstood MGA has half the cylinders. All three distributors are physically very different but serve the same basic purpose.
(Courtesy Holden Vintage & Classic)

Distributor distribution

All distributors are the same – or not, as can be seen in this selection from the Holden Vintage & Classic shelves. This is a Triumph-only unit, suitable, with various designations, for such cars as the TR2/3/4/4a, Spitfire, Herald, Dolomite, etc. Note the rev counter take-off.
(Courtesy Holden Vintage & Classic)

A distributor with three times as many plug lead sockets! This is for the 12-cylinder Jaguar range. *(Courtesy Holden Vintage & Classic)*

This table, reproduced courtesy Holden Vintage & Classic, shows typical classic distributor fitments. Where a number is prefixed by 'A', it signifies that these are particularly popular models, such that they are literally off-the-shelf at Holden's.

Manufacturer	Model	Year	Distributor type	Distributor number
AC	16HP	1948-56	DX6A	40143
	Ace	1955	DX6A	40143
		late 1955-60	DX6A	40462
	Bristol engine	1956-63	DXH6A	40551
Allard	J/J2/J2X	1949-55	D4A8	40068
	Cadillac engine	1951-55	DULFH8A	40523
	TD21	1958-60	DM6	40641
Armstrong Siddeley	Sapphire 234	1956-57	DM2P4	40542
	Star Sapphire	1959-60	DMBZ6A	40650
Alvis	14HP	1946-50	DKY4A	40071
Aston Martin	DB6	1966	25D6	41083
Austin	8HP		DK4A	400206
	10HP/12HP		DK4A	405601
	A30	1952-56	DM2P4	40299
	A35	1957-62	DM2P4	40561
	A40	1959-62	DM2P4	40675
	Sheerline	1949-54	DVX6A	40147
	1300GT	1970-74	25D4	41238
	3 litre	1968-71	25D6	41201
Austin Healey	100	1954-56	DM2P4	40495
	100M	1956	DM2P4	40520
	100 six	1958-59	DM6	40662
	3000	1959-63	DM6	40662
	3000	late 1963-64	25D6	40920
	MKIII late	1964-65	25D6	40966
	Sprite LC	1958-61	DM2P4	40561
	Sprite HC	1958-61	DM2P4	40656
	Sprite/Midget	late 1961-62	DM2P4	40752
		1963-66	25D4	A40919
		1967	23D4	40819
		1968-69	25D4	A41198
		late 1969-71	25D4	A41270
		1975-on	45D4	A41449
Bentley	S2/S3/Continental/ T series	1962-68	20D8	40898
Bristol	400/401	1949-50	DX6A	40109
	401	1951-52	DX6A	40235
	401/403/404/405	1953-55	DX6A	40345
	405	1956-58	DX6A	40489
	406	1958-61	DX6A	40592/40629
Citroën	15HP	1946-49	DKH4A	40100
		late 1949-52	DKYH4A	40219/40236

Manufacturer	Model	Year	Distributor type	Distributor number
Citroën *(continued)*	15HP	late 1952-55	DM2P4	40332
	23HP	1946-55	DK6A	40173
Daimler	SP250 (Dart)	1960-64	20D8	40676
	2.5 litre V8 saloon	1963-69		
	2.5 litre Consort	1950-53	DZ6A	40175
	4.2 Auto	1969-71	22D6	41065
	4.2 models	1969-71	22D6	41060
Ford	Anglia/Cortina HC	1962-66	25D4	40857
	Cortina/ Capri/			
	Corsair GT	1963-66	25D4	40927
	Lotus Cortina	1964-66	23D4	40953
	X-Flow			
	competition spec (twin carbs)		HVCXF1	N/A
Frazer Nash	Mille Miglia/Targa			
	Florio/Sebring		DX6A	40346
Healey	16HP/Sportsmobile/			
	Silverstone/			
	Tickford Abbot	1948-54	DKY4A	40081
Hillman	Minx side-valve	1946-54	DKYH4A	40050
	Minx ohv	1955-56	DM2P4	40428
	Minx ohv HC	1957-58	DM2P4	40530
	Minx Series IIIA/			
	Husky Series II	1959-61	DM2P4	40681
	Imp	1963-65	25D4	40905
	Imp	1966-71	25D4	41122
Humber	12HP	1935-37	DKY4A	404347
	Imperial/Pullman/			
	Snipe & Super	1946-53	DK4A	410700/40135
	Hawk	1961-62	DKY4A	40723
		late 1962-63	DKY4A	40800
Jaguar	XK120 7.0:1	1949-53	DVXH6A	40198
	7.0:1	late 1953-54	DVX6A	40249
	8.0:1	1949-54	DVX6A	40199
	XK140 7.0:1	1955-57	DVX6A	40435
	8.0:1	1955-57	DVX6A	40436
	8.0:1	1955-57	DVX6A	40199
	8.0:1 Spec Equip	1955-57	DVX6A	40293
	9.0:1 Spec Equip	1955-57	DVX6A	40445
	XK150 7.0:1		DVX6A	40578
	8.0:1		DVX6A	40576
	9.0:1	1958-61	DMBZ6A	40616
	XK150 3.8 litre	1958-61	DMB6A	40640
		1958-61	DMBZ6A	40665
	XK150S 3.4	1960-61	DMBZ6A	40670

Manufacturer	Model	Year	Distributor type	Distributor number
Jaguar *(continued)*	XK150S 3.4	1960-61	DMBZ6A	40616
	3.8	1960-61	DMBZ6A	40617
	XKSS (USA only)	1960-61	DMBZ6A	40473
	E-Type	1961-63	DMBZ6A	40617
		late 1963-64	22D6	40887
		1965-71	22D6	41060
		1971-72	36DE12	41321
		late 1972-74	36DE12	41387
	MKII 2.4 7.0:1	1960-63	DMBZ6A	40557
	8.0:1	1960-63	DMBZ6A	40528
	7.0:1	late 1963-67	22D6	40883
	MKII 3.4 7.0:1	1960-63	DMBZ6A	40578
	8.0:1	1960-63	DMBZ6A	40576
	9.0:1	1960-63	DMBZ6A	40617
	MKII 3.8 8.0:1	1960-63	DMBZ6A	40640
	9.0:1	1960-63	DMBZ6A	40665
	MKII 240	1968-69	25D6	41208
	3.4 /3.8 models		22D6	40885
	7.0:1/8.0:1	1963-on		41063
	XJ6 2.8 (M & A)	1969-71	22D6	41335
		1972-74	25D6	41366
	XJ6 3.4 (M & A)	1975-81	45D6	41620
		1982-83	45D6	41861
		1983-on	45D6	41914
	XJ6 4.2 (M & A)	1969-71	22D6	41060
		1972-75	22D6	41367
		1975-79	45D6	41915
		1980-83	45DM6	41797
		1983-on	45DM6	41913
	XJ12 5.3 (M & A)	1981-89	36DM12	42647
	XJS 3.6 (M & A)	1983-86	45DM6	41921
	XJS HE 5.3 (M & A)	1981-89	36DM12	42647
Land Rover	2.25	1969-76	25D4	40944
		1977-85	45D4	41630
		1980-82	Ducellier	6501
MG	TC, TD	1946-52	DYK4A	40162
	TD	1953	D2A4	40368
	TF	1953-55	D2A4	40367
	MGA	1956-61	DM2P4	40510
	MGA (1600 MKII)	1962	DM2P4	40761
	MGA twin cam	1960	23D4	40718
	MGB	1963-68	25D4	A40897
		late 1968-69	25D4	A41155
		late 1969-74	25D4	A41288

Manufacturer	Model	Year	Distributor type	Distributor number
MG *(contiued)*	MGB	1975-on	45D4	A41610
	MGB V8	1975-76	35D8	41394
	MGC	1968-69	25D6	41201
	Midget	1961-62	DM2P4	40752
		1963-66	25D4	40919
		1967	23D4	40819
		1968-69	25D4	41198
		late 1969-74	25D4	41270
		1975-on	45D4	41449
	Magnette	1954-56	DM2P4	40414
				40509
		1957	DM2P4	40510
		1958-59	DM2P4	40587
	MKIII	1959-61	DM2P4	40644
		1962-67	25D4	40823
		late 1967-68	25D4	41154
	MG1100	1963-67	25D4	40853
		1968	25D4	41028
	MG1300	1968-70	25D4	41214
				41238
	MGB comp special	—	43D4	41844
Mini	Cooper 'S'	1965-69	23D4	40819
		1970-71	23D4	41033
	Cooper 'S' comp	—	43D4	41843
	850	1969-74	25D4	A41026
		1974-on	45D4	A41570
	1000 & Clubman	1969-74	25D4	A41254
		1974-81	45D4	A41418
		1981-on	59D4	A41765
	1275 GT	1970-74	25D4	A41257
		1974-on	45D4	A41419
Morgan	Plus 4 (TR2/3 Eng)	1955-59	DM2P4	40480
		1960-63	DM2P4	40698
		late 1963-66	25D4	A40795
	Plus 8 comp spec	—	HVC81	N/A
Morris	Minor 1000 HC	1963-66	25D4	A40849
		1966-68	25D4	A41148
		1969 on	45D4	A41513
	Minor LC	1966-68	25D4	A41025
		1969 on	45D4	A41422
Triumph	TR2, TR3	1954-59	DM2P4	40480
	TR3A, TR4, TR4A	1962-67	25D4	A40795
	TR5/TR6	1968-72	22D6	41219
	TR6	1973	22D6	41501

Manufacturer	Model	Year	Distributor type	Distributor number
Triumph	TR6	late 1973-75	22D6	41542
	TR7	1975-on	Delco	
	TR8 (carb)	1978-82	35DE8	41682
	TR8 (injection)	1980-82	35DE8	41794
	Spitfire	1963-75	Delco	
	(alternative)	1964	25D4	40902
		1976 on	5D4	A41449
	GT6	1967-75	Delco	
	(alternative)	1969-74	22D6	41168
	Herald 1200	1963-on	25D4	A40791
	Herald 13/60	1968-on	25D4	A41127
	1300	1969-on	25D4	A41127
	1300TC	1969-on	25D4	A41213
	1500	1971-on	25D4	A41381
	Dolomite 1300/1500/1500HL		45D4	A41449
	Dolomite 1850	1972-81	Delco	
	Dolomite	1974-75	44D4	41589
	Dolomite Sprint	1976-81	44D4	41655
	Toledo 1.5	1974 on	45D4	A41449
	Stag single points	1970-72	35D8	41336
	Stag twin points	1973-77	35D8	41525

Uprating to electronic ignition

Whilst the contact breaker points system is a good idea, the physical making and breaking of the spark starts to wear the points faces as soon as they are fitted. By definition, although they may be set-up perfectly, it isn't long before their performance starts to degrade, which leads to poor starting, acceleration, top speed and worsening fuel consumption. These features will be barely noticeable at the beginning of the wear pattern, but as the miles rack up, then they will become more evident. By the time that the scheduled service interval comes along, the need for new points will be obvious; if they're not replaced on time, poor starting will become a common feature of the engine's performance (or lack of it).

To some extent, all these problems can be offset by regular checking and cleaning of the points faces, but the other and permanent method is to replace the points with electronic ignition. Lumenition have kits to suit most classic cars and can provide a standard optical electronic ignition system, a high performance set-up or a points-less system based on magnetism. One vital aspect to bear in mind is that if originality is important, the original points/condenser can easily be replaced. So, if your car is used regularly but is also entered for concours competitions, you could run day-to-day on electronic ignition and swap when necessary.

Once fitted, it will never require any further maintenance for optimum timing. Until recently this kind of uprate was suitable only for NEGA-TIVE earth cars, but Lumenition's technical advances mean that it can be fitted to positive earth cars. However, there are a number of specification precautions that have to be taken, details of which Lumenition are pleased to supply on purchase of a specific system.

Optronic system

This is for straightforward points replacement using the existing coil, offering excellent all round performance, and is ideal for all road and classic cars. Instead of having a mechanical contact set, Lumenition Systems use three basic components; an Optical Switch (mounted in the distributor), a Power Module and a distributor fitting kit (most makes of distributor are covered, e.g. Lucas, Bosch, Ford, Ducellier, MotorCraft, Mallory, Marchal, A.C. Delco, Magneti Marelli, etc.).

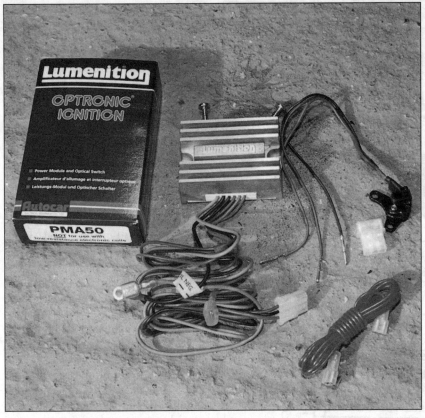

This is the basic Optronic kit, showing power module, wiring and distributor optical switch. If you're more interested in performance than originality, it is suitable for a wide range of classic cars and to tailor this to your specific vehicle, it has to be used in conjunction with . . .

. . . a distributor fitting kit specific to the vehicle. The number of blades on the chopper relates to the number of engine cylinders.

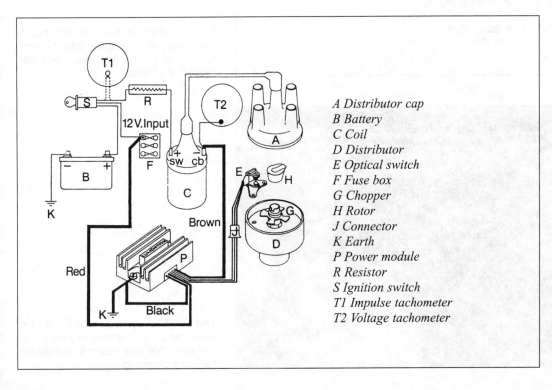

A Distributor cap
B Battery
C Coil
D Distributor
E Optical switch
F Fuse box
G Chopper
H Rotor
J Connector
K Earth
P Power module
R Resistor
S Ignition switch
T1 Impulse tachometer
T2 Voltage tachometer

Installation is surprisingly easy, as this simple diagram shows.
(Courtesy Autocar Electrical Limited)

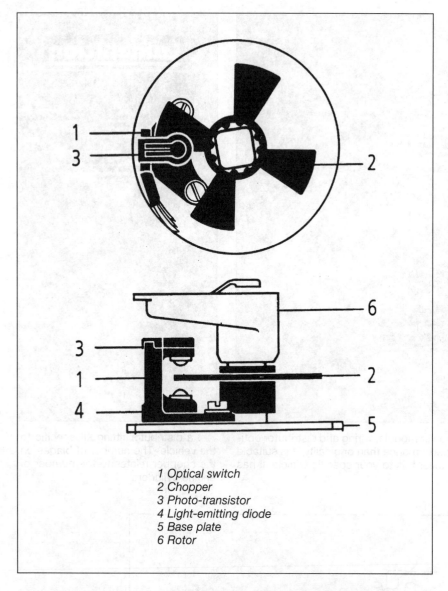

1 Optical switch
2 Chopper
3 Photo-transistor
4 Light-emitting diode
5 Base plate
6 Rotor

Operation

An infra-red light beam is detected by a silicon photo-transistor. This beam is interrupted by a revolving chopper fixed to the distributor cam and has one blade for each cylinder. It is unaffected by light, dirt and dampness. The optical switch is fixed to the same plate as the points were, so that speed and vacuum advance remain unchanged. The power module (amplifier) receives the electronic pulses from the optical switch and, using an internal high-power Darlington transistor, charges the coil. The exact positioning of the chopper determines spark timing, and dwell time is determined either by the width of the chopper or internally to give variable dwell performance. So that the optical switch can be mounted in exactly the right position in the distributor, specifically engineered mounting plates and brackets have been developed to ensure perfect installation, and in the vast majority of cases without any permanent modification. Installation is also possible without any special tools.

The operation of the infra-red beam and chopper assemblies can be seen in this diagram. *(Courtesy Autocar Electrical Limited)*

The power module has to be mounted away from excess heat and moisture but close to the distributor for ease of wiring.

Losing this lot is no great loss at all! Fanatical classic owners can keep it in the boot, just in case.

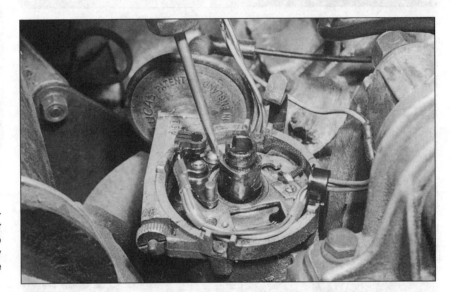

The optical switch is fitted in position – unlike points, adjustment is never required because there are no parts to wear out. Timing is set in the usual way by using a timing light and adjusting the position of the distributor.

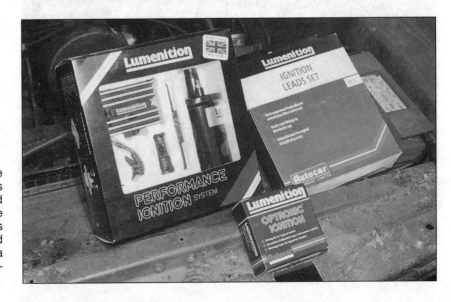

Lumenition offer a performance electronic ignition system, which is more suited to high-speed engines and performance drivers, particularly race and rally applications. This kit includes a more powerful module and matched high-performance coil. As well as a suitable distributor fitting kit, a suppressed HT lead set is also required.

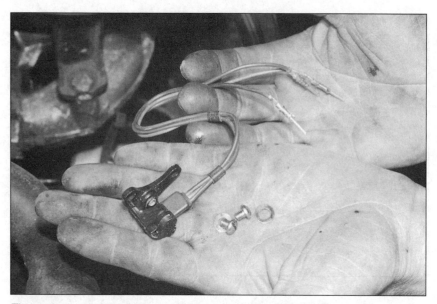

The optical switch is similar to the previous item and is fitted . . .

. . . to replace the points assembly. Here, the chopper is being installed, the rotor arm fits over the top in its usual position.

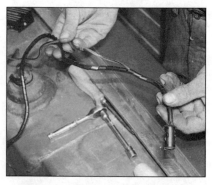

A suitable length of spiral binding is included for neatening the new loom section. Note the use of a three-pin plug to link the distributor wiring.

The suppressed silicone leads are an integral part of the kit, essential to get the best from the new components.

Ignition system fault-finding

Meter note

Checks involving your multimeter should be carried out with it set on 'DC/Volts', readings up to 20V or automatic (where applicable) unless noted otherwise.

Before checking ignition components, ensure the battery is fully charged and holding the charge correctly. Then check all the ignition components to ensure that they are physically sound and connected correctly. Look for obvious cracks or splits in the cabling and bared wires making unwelcome earth contacts. Check particularly the spark plug HT leads and the coil-to-distributor HT lead – even the slightest deterioration in these could result in ignition problems, such as poor starting, rough running, etc. Your visual checks should be as follows:

- Distributor cover (outside)
  Clean, dry, no 'tracking' marks.
- Distributor cover (inside)
  Clean, dry, no 'tracking' marks.
- Rotor arm
  Clean top contact, not fouling inside cap.
- Coil top
  Clean, dry, no 'tracking' marks.
- HT cable insulation
  No cracks, chafes or perishing.
- HT cable continuity
  Must not be open circuit.
- Spark plugs
  Clean and dry, gap correct.

Before you get too carried away, it's wise to do a few basic checks to avoid wasting time. An ignition fault can either be on the low tension (LT) or high tension (HT) side of the coil. The contact breaker points are a regular source of ignition problems on classic cars. With ignition off, prise apart the points with a small screwdriver and examine the faces. They should be clean and free from any pitting. Minor damage can be cleaned up using a small file or carborundum stone, but serious pitting requires new points to be fitted –

they're cheap enough. Make sure that the gap is as recommended in your handbook or Haynes manual.

Make sure your spark plugs are up to scratch – they're often ignored by owners for too long. Replace if required and, whatever, clean them up and ensure that the gap is correct.

When the capacitor fails (or worse, partly fails) it can cause all manner of trouble. It pays to replace your capacitor on a regular basis, and if you've a tricky ignition fault, it's wise to replace this before starting the checking procedure.

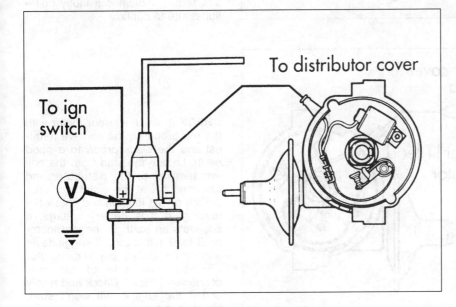

CHECK 1. Remove the distributor cap and ensure that the points are closed. Connect your meter with the red probe to the +ve of the coil (the positive terminal leading to the ignition switch) and the black lead to a good earth (the battery, if it's close enough). The reading should be battery voltage (or 6V–7V on a ballasted system). If there is no reading, there is no power down the wire from the ignition. Check this and the ballast resistor if applicable.

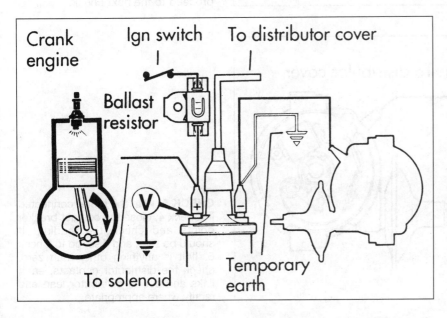

CHECK 2. (Ballasted systems only.) Connect your meter as Check 1 and add a small jumper lead between the –ve of the coil (the negative terminal leading to the distributor) and a good earth. Crank the engine and check that the meter reading is higher than obtained in the previous test. If this does not increase, check the voltage at the starter motor solenoid at the terminal which leads to the coil while cranking the engine. Remember to remove the temporary jumper lead before proceeding.

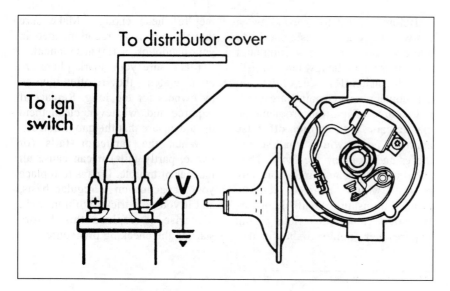

CHECK 3. Remove the distributor cap and connect the red meter probe to the –ve terminal of the coil and the black probe to a good earth. With ignition on and the points open, check the meter reading; if it is battery voltage, go to Check 5. If there is a zero reading, remove the –ve lead from the coil (which goes to the distributor) and check the reading again, which should be battery voltage – if so, go on to Check 4. If it is still zero, it indicates a faulty coil – substitute to confirm.

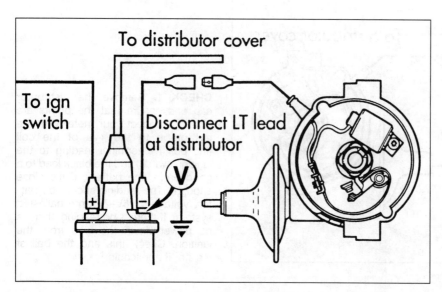

CHECK 4. Connect your meter with the red probe on the coil –ve terminal and the black probe to a good earth. Locate the lead from the coil –ve terminal to the distributor and disconnect it at the distributor end. Switch on the ignition and check the reading; if it is battery voltage, it suggests an earth in the distributor or LT lead. If it is zero, it suggests an earth in the ignition coil to distributor LT lead, coil side of the disconnected LT lead. Check and rectify and if the engine still won't start, proceed to the next check.

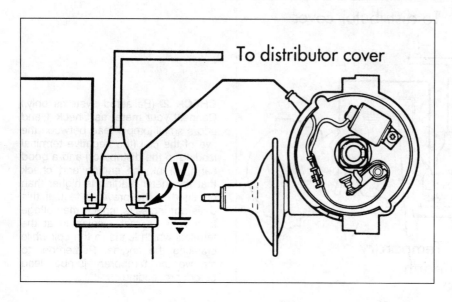

CHECK 5. With the meter connected in Check 4, close the contact breaker points and check the reading. It should be zero, and if so, go to Check 6. If it is anything other than zero, check the distributor contacts, earth links and coil to distributor lead and rectify where appropriate.

CHECK 6. With the distributor cap off, take out the HT lead from its centre and remove the HT lead from the centre of the cap. Hold it – using insulated pliers, NOT your fingers – about 6mm (¼in) from the engine block. Switch on the ignition and operate the starter motor. A bright, clean, regular spark between the lead and the block is a good sign and you can pass on to Check 7.If there is no spark or it is only weak, substitute the HT lead and repeat the test. If it is still weak, go to Check 7.

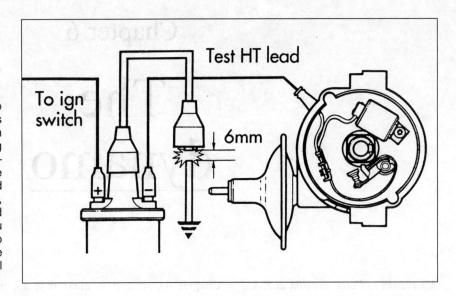

CHECK 7. Remove the distributor cap and visually check the top of the rotor arm to ensure that it is clean, and do the same around the 'arm' itself. It always pays to clean up both these brass areas, regardless. Remove the HT lead from the centre of the distributor and, using insulated pliers, hold it about 6mm (¼in) from the rotor arm contact. Crank the engine and watch the rotor arm – if there is a spark, it suggests that the arm is earthing and is faulty. Replace it, if this is the case.

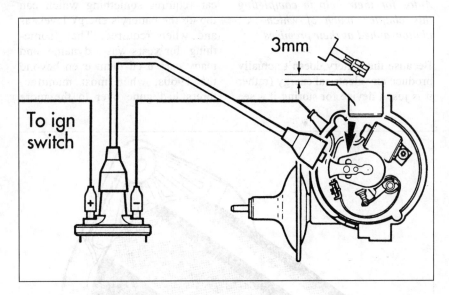

Final

If the ignition system checks out completely, then it's time to go back to square one. Have you missed something obvious? Is there petrol in the tank? Certainly, it would point to a fuel-related problem, or something more serious, perhaps.

Chapter 6

The dynamo

My thanks to Peter and Jim at P & J Autos for their help in completing this chapter, much of which was photographed at their premises.)

Because the battery doesn't actually produce any electrical energy (rather it is just a device for storing it – see Chapter 4), then it is clear that a car requires something which can top up the battery's energy levels as and when required. That 'something' for years was a dynamo, and many cars used them even beyond the 1960s, when most manufacturers had gone over to the more efficient alternator. A dynamo is a device which converts mechanical energy – the turning of a pulley via the engine – into electrical energy. It is often called the generator, although, strictly speaking, both alternators and a dynamos are generators of sorts.

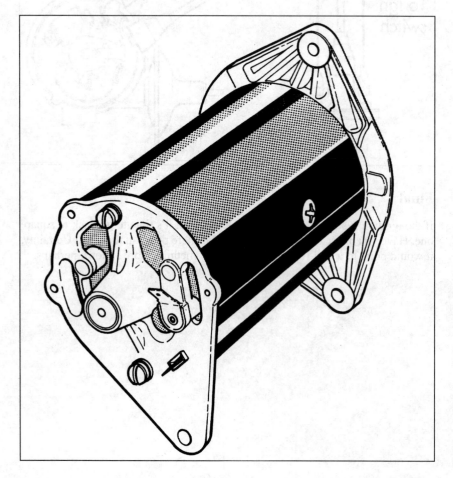

Basically, a dynamo is a glorified electric motor, with an armature spinning inside a set of field windings and the whole lot being enclosed in a steel case. The spinning motion is created by the belt which links the engine flywheel to a pulley on the drive end of the dynamo. The field coils consists of a pair of coils (occasionally four), each comprising several hundred turns of insulated copper wire, the original insulation being a cotton tape. This tape has a great resilience, but as we're dealing with classic cars, any original dynamo will now be very old, and the odds are that this tape has deteriorated badly. Low output, or none at all, could be the result of this.

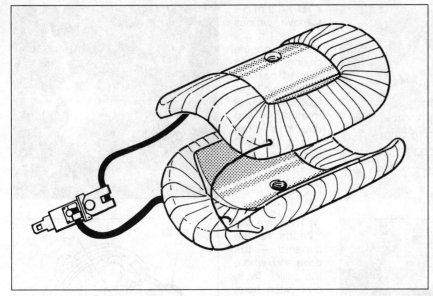

Two ends of the coils are joined to connect the field coils in series, whilst the other two ends are connected to the Lucar terminal assembly which protrudes from the end of the dynamo. At this point, one of the wires goes to earth because the assembly is riveted to the dynamo casing, whilst the other is connected to the field ('F') Lucar connector – insulation within the assembly ensures that the two do not meet. The coils are held in place by pole shoes, blocks of soft iron which have been magnetised during the dynamo production process. As the current flows through the coils, the magnetic flux surrounding the shoes is increased still further.

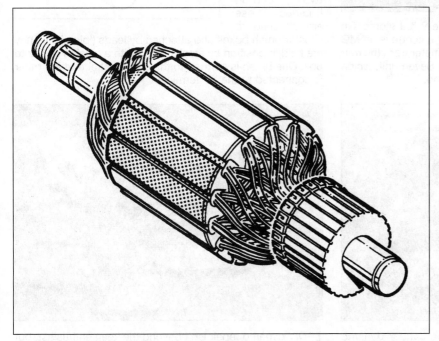

The armature rotates in the magnetic field between the two poles. The armature comprises a number of copper conductors which are wound on a soft iron core, which in turn is mounted on to the spindle. The ends of the armature coils are soldered to the segments of the commutator, which in turn is fitted to the end of the spindle. The job of the commutator is to change (or 'commute') the alternating current of the dynamo into the direct current required by the car.

Buying a used dynamo

When buying a used dynamo, say, from an auto jumble, you'll be buying either one that works or one that it useless – there's nothing in-between, unless you're buying something incredibly rare. Most popular UK classics used similar dynamos, millions of which were made and for which obtaining exchange units or parts to rebuild your own is easy. Make sure you have access to a battery because, though you can't test that a dynamo is actually charging, you can test whether it works as a motor by putting an earth (negative or positive – take care to get the polarity correct) and applying the live wire to the two terminals on the end plate. The simplest way to do this is to clip the live terminal firmly to a hefty (and well-insulated) screwdriver and then put the shank across the two terminals. The dynamo in each case should spin. It will also allow you to listen for rumbly, worn bearings. Clearly, you can't tell whether a dynamo is charging, but it's better than nothing and can prevent you buying a unit that is totally useless.

Oil – where it shouldn't be and where it should

Got an engine oil leak? Most classics have, but oil on the commutator means less charge getting to the battery. Best solve the leak, or at least stop the oil getting at the dynamo. Conversely, some dynamos, typically early '60s models, had a requirement for oiling the rear bush. Do you have one? Check around the commutator end plate (opposite the drive end) and look for either a small 'plug' or cover which is protecting an oil hole or, in some cases, just the hole. If you haven't got one of these, you've got a sealed bearing dynamo and need worry no more. If you have, apply a little light machine oil at regular intervals – it would probably state in the handbook 5/6,000 miles or so but, as ever, a low-mileage classic owner would be best halving that.

Continued on page 85

THE DYNAMO

Simple in principle and not entirely unapproachable on a DIY basis, the dynamo comprises many components. It's a subject area best tackled in a calm atmosphere with plenty of time on hand.

3 Dynamos have various markings stamped on the casing to help identification, notably voltage, type, direction of rotation and date. In this case, it is a 12V C40 dynamo made in February 1973 as denoted by '02–73'.

1 Three very different dynamos from the P & J stores. On the left is the popular Lucas C40; in the centre is an MG TF unit, which runs a cable driven tachometer from the rear of the unit; and on the right is an Austin Seven unit, which runs its distributor at 90° from the dynamo.

4 There are two ends to the dynamo – the drive end, where the pulley lives, and (seen here) the commutator end, which has the various electrical connections on it and which houses the brushes. The current is collected from the commutator by two carbon brushes. These are attached to clips or brush boxes and attached by leads ('pigtails'). They are held in position by steel springs with a tension of 6oz to 8oz. One brush is earthed to the end-bracket and the other is connected to the 'D' terminal.

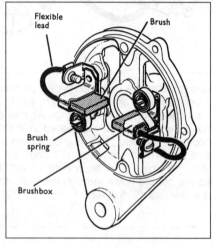

2 On the left at the back is an S-Type Jaguar dynamo (the power steering pump bolts to the rear); in the centre is a CAV model as fitted to some Alvis models and could run a water pump; and on the right is a dynamo with a 90° drive to run an hour clock. At the front this dynamo would sit between the crank and the cam on Triple M MGs.

5 DIY dynamo repair isn't beyond the keen enthusiast, but there are an awful lot of bits and pieces to put back together again! Non-serviceable items will have to be replaced, which adds to the cost and makes total dynamo restoration (as opposed to just replacing the brushes) a real labour of love. This is the Lucas C40 dynamo used by P & J Autos as the test example.

Keep a weather eye on the drive belt tension – it should typically be around ⅜in (10mm) between pulleys, although your car-specific handbook will be more precise. A slack belt will mean less charge going to the battery, with the associated poor electrical performance and ultimately a flat battery. If the belt is too tight, charging performance will be OK, but you'll pretty soon wear out the bearing. Make sure you also check the condition of the drive belt itself. If it has any cuts or signs of fraying, replace it as soon as possible or you could find yourself in a whole heap of trouble, minus dynamo, water pump, cooling fan, etc.

If you ever need to remove the nut securing the pulley on the end of the dynamo, hold the pulley in the vice to prevent it turning – do not stick screwdrivers or other objects inside the unit, or you could do irreparable damage. According to Jim at P & J, this is a common mistake, one which they often find themselves sorting out.

Dynamo and regulator fault-finding

If you have a repeatedly flat battery and/or are suffering from other electrical maladies such as dim lights, slow wipers, etc., it's natural to point the finger at the dynamo. But before you remove and dismantle your dynamo, make a few simple checks. If your system is not charging at all, then the red dashboard warning light should illuminate, but if the system is simply undercharging this won't necessarily be the case. Moreover, it could be a blown bulb, so it's worth starting from scratch to check –

switch off the ignition, turn it to the 'on' position and make sure the red warning light illuminates.

If you have an ammeter, it should tell you if your battery is receiving a charge. If it appears to be showing a discharge, it is good sense to use your multimeter to double check the reading – after all, the ammeter could be faulty. You can't trust anything in a classic!

Basic checks
Check the battery condition first – use your meter or a hydrometer. Check all battery, regulator and dynamo terminals for solidity, especially those

going to earth. Grab hold of the terminals on the ends of the wiring and give them a (gentle) wiggle – it's often the case that a connection that looks solid is actually broken and it's only the insulation keeping it in place. Make sure the drive belt tension is correct – it should typically be around ⅜in between pulleys – check your handbook.

Use your multimeter to check manually the extent of the charge. Remove the two wires from the regulator which lead to the dynamo – that's those to the 'D' and 'F' terminals – and bridge them using the lead you made up in Chapter 2. Select

Symptom	Probable cause
No reading at all, at any engine speed	Brushes
Reading of around 6V-12V	Armature
Less than 6V	Field circuit

'DC/Volts' on your multimeter and put the black lead to a known good earth and the red wire to the bridged leads. Start the engine and check the reading which should be 14.5V/15V at a fairly fast idle speed – up to 1,000rpm. If you get anything much different from that, the results can generally be interpreted as above:

Light work
The red 'ignition' warning light on the dashboard is there to tell you that there is an under-charging situation and should always come on as you turn the ignition key as proof that it is working and that the bulb hasn't blown. As the engine starts, it should go out, certainly as the throttle pedal is blipped. What can you glean from a simple light when it starts misbehaving?
● If it doesn't come on at all – even without the engine running but with the ignition 'on' – the most obvious cause is a blown bulb and you should assume this before you start dismantling your car. But, if replacement (with a bulb checked and known to be sound) doesn't cure the problem, you should first check the wiring to the bulb, making sure there is a power supply and good earth. Failing that, it points to the possibility of an internal dynamo fault and a job for the specialist.
● If the bulb stays illuminated regardless of engine speed, it could indicate a possible dynamo failure and a total non-charge situation. However, it's worth checking the

regulator first, as sticking contacts (see next section) on the cut-out could cause this symptom.
● If the warning light stays on as above, but is really very bright to the point where it actually blows the bulb, then the cut-out switch probably needs cleaning (see next section).
● Probably most serious of all is when the red light stays on even when the ignition key is switched 'off'. This is potentially a very nasty situation, as it points to a regulator with, once again, sticking cut-out points, jammed in the 'closed' position. The upshot would be that the battery would try to download its charge back into the dynamo wire, with overheating and fire always a possibility. The answer is to remove the battery leads in double-quick time and make a thorough examination of all relevant wiring to ensure nothing unpleasant has occurred. When everything has cooled down (and with the leads still off the battery) open up the regulator and check the cut-out switch. If it is sticking closed, it should be quite obvious. If you are unsure, consult a specialist.

How to change polarity

Dynamos can be either positive or negative earth. If there's one already on your car, it will already have been polarised to suit your particular electrical system. But if you buy one from an autojumble, you may not be sure. Equally, you may change your

car from positive to negative earth. Re-polarising a dynamo is simple.
To change a *positive* earth unit to *negative* earth, connect a **negative** lead from the battery to the dynamo case. Take a **positive** lead from battery and touch it briefly on the dynamo small terminal and then on the large terminal – you'll get a harmless blue spark from each. And that's that! For positive earth, reverse these instructions.

Control boxes
Control boxes are specifically positive or negative earth and cannot be changed in this way. As such, if you re-polarised a dynamo, then you must change the regulator box.

The control box (regulator)

If you've ever ridden a bicycle with a dynamo lighting system, you'll know the inherent problem – the current produced by a dynamo (whether pedal or engine-powered!) is directly related to its speed. On a bicycle, the effect is instant – slow down and the lights dim instantly. In a car, the current stored in the battery provides a buffer against this kind of instant reaction, but if there is already a heavy loading on the battery (driving in the dark and rain, with wipers, heater, heated rear window and lights on) the effect can be the same.
There's another problem for the car-mounted dynamo, in that if left unchecked, it could produce far too much current for the battery to handle. Clearly, with no control at all, there would fairly soon be trouble, as batteries boiled and bulbs burst. As such, the regulator (often called the control box) is a necessity to make sure that whilst the battery is always topped up, it is not actually blown up!
The typical control box comprises two or three 'bobbins' (actually wire-coil electromagnets) which operate by means of simple contact breaker points, which open and close

Like the dynamos themselves, the control boxes have changed over the years – the selection seen here are part of the P & J stock and, of course, are seen without their covers. On the far left is a simple cut-out as used on a three-brush dynamo, as found on many vehicles up to around 1950. Second left is a Lucas RB106, circa 1962, as used on sit-up-and-beg Fords, etc., and the next is more or less the same unit, but a later version where the screw terminals were replaced by more modern Lucar versions. Finally, on the far right is the RB340, which is the most common control box to be found on everyday classics. Note that the first three could be either 6V or 12V and positive or negative earth, and will be marked as such. The RB340 was only ever available in 12V negative earth.

many times during the average journey. The cut-out points open when the engine is running slowly and the dynamo is producing less voltage than the battery, otherwise, the dynamo would have the effect of draining the battery rather than charging it! So, the regulator monitors the state of the battery; the lower the state of charge, the more charge it is allowed to receive from the dynamo, via the regulator, of which there are two basic types.

Compensated voltage control regulators

Early regulators were known as two-bobbin units or, more precisely, compensated voltage control regulators, the 'bobbins' actually being electro-magnetic relays. Charging current is limited, usually to 16V, on a 12V system. The cut-out acts as an automatic on/off switch, allowing the battery to charge when needed and disconnecting the charging circuit between dynamo and battery when

required. As a general rule, it stops charging at around 13V and cuts in again when the voltage falls below 11V.

Current voltage control regulators

With the advent of more complex charging systems, a new system was introduced. This type of regulator is easily recognised by the fact that it has three, rather than two, electro-magnetic relays, these being a cut-out and voltage regulator as previously, with the addition of a current regulator. The first two operate as previously described, but the current and voltage regulators work together to control the electrical supply more accurately. When the maximum current is required from the dynamo, the voltage regulator stops working. Conversely, when the battery charge state is good and/or there is little or no electrical loading, the dynamo control is passed to the voltage regulator and the current regulator stops working.

Maintenance

If you are examining your regulator, always remove **both** battery terminals before removing the regulator cover. The points suffer like the contact points in your distributor, in that they can get pitted and burned over the years, which inhibits their performance. The points should be wiped clean with a little methylated spirits (work in a well-ventilated area). A simple way to make sure you get the points faces really clean is to moisten a piece of thin card with the spirits and push it in-between the points. Use *silicone carbide* paper to remove burns and rough spots on all the points (on each bobbin) except the cut-out contacts; because these are made of silver, rather than tungsten, you need to use a *fine sandpaper* – and carefully, too, otherwise you'll soon have nothing left! Take great care not to accidentally 'adjust' the points settings as you're working, or you'll end up with trouble and expense on the horizon.

Typical regulator problems include:
● Poor earth connections.
● Incorrect settings on the voltage/current relays and/or . . .
● Incorrect setting on the cut-out relay, faulty or damaged wiring to/from the regulator.
● Dirty/worn contacts within the regulator.

P & J usually recommend that *adjusting* the regulator is not really for the DIY enthusiast. Indeed, it's often the case that regulator troubles have been caused by an overenthusiastic owner getting carried away with a screwdriver and bending contacts too far. It's a simple job for a professional to test a regulator, and that's the best idea at this stage.

P & J tip

Dirt can build up on the points over a period of time, and when there is a lot of condensation around (if a car is parked out overnight and the

Continued on page 89

THE REGULATOR

The regulator tends to live in a world of extremes; either it's ignored when it comes to problem solving or it's unjustly accused for all manner of ills, the culprits for which are hiding elsewhere. Whatever, checking a regulator's performance is a different thing from actually adjusting it, which is something which should not be undertaken lightly.

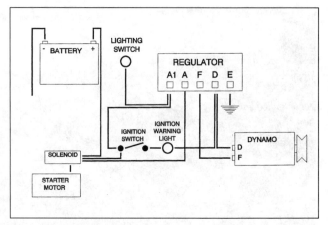

3 The wiring for a '2-bobbin', compensated voltage control regulator would be as shown in this diagram.

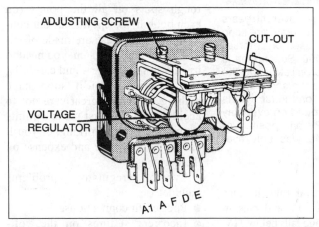

1 A typical Lucas compensated voltage regulator. At left is the voltage regulator and at right is a voltage-sensitive cut-out. *(Courtesy Lucas Automotive Ltd)*

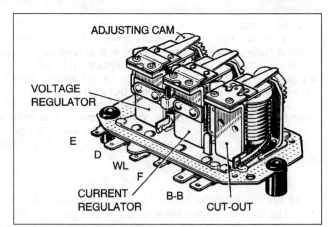

4 This diagram shows the various terminal references for a typical current voltage control, '3-bobbin' regulator. *(Courtesy Lucas Automotive Ltd)*

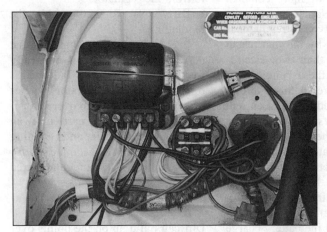

2 A 1961 Morris Minor with bulkhead-mounted regulator. Note screw-in connections and contact positions labelled on top of the Bakelite cover.

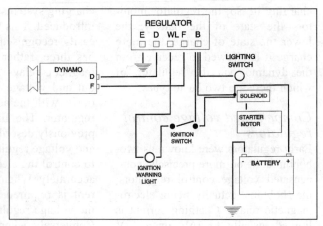

5 This diagram shows the more complex wiring for a typical '3-bobbin regulator', the benefits coming from more accurate control of the electrical supply.

warmth of the day gives way to a
cold night) there could be problems.
The moisture can form a 'resistance'
which effectively keeps the contact
that the points are trying to break.
It's not usually a dire problem and is
typified by the ignition warning light
staying on longer than normal. It
will probably go off after a short
while as the heat generated inside
the box makes the moisture evapo-
rate and restores the *status quo*.

Simple regulator check
Note that the performance of a regu-
lator/dynamo will depend on the
state of battery charge at the time.
Using your car's ammeter, or by

Battery charge *(Specific gravity reading)*	Amperage charge rate
1.270	Less than 5A
1.250	6A-12A
1.200	12A and above

connecting your multimeter across
the battery with 'Amps' mode
selected, check for the following
typical readings with the engine running at a fast idle speed. Then take a

reading with the headlamps on main
beam and the engine turning over at
approximately 3,000rpm. There
should be a charge, typically of
around 4A.

It's reassuring to find that just about all popular classic regulators can either be rebuilt or purchased as new. Left to right
there's a nine-post screw-fitting regulator, a screw-fitting Lucas RB106 and a Lucar-fitting RB310.
(Courtesy Holden Vintage & Classic)

The RB340 regulator is probably the most common version to be found on what could be classified as 'everyday' classics. Unlike earlier models, which were available as 6v or 12v, negative or positive earth, this one reflects the sign of the times by being only available in negative earth. Seen here without its cover, left to right is the cut-out, the current regulator and the voltage regulator. Note the three eccentric adjusting cams. The professional will have a special tool for adjusting these, though a carefully-wielded screwdriver will do the job - if you're competent and justifiably confident. Overall, adjustment is not recommended for the amateur, especially bearing in mind the kind of 'fry-up' that can result from inaccurate adjustment!

The current and voltage regulators both feature contact breaker points exactly like those found in the distributor (it's the voltage regulator shown here). Like standard ignition points, the faces can wear and the typical problem of a pit on one face and a point on the other often occurs. Clearly, if the faces are anything but clean and flat, they aren't doing their job properly. They can be cleaned up by using a small file to smooth the faces and methylated spirit on a cotton bud to clean them properly. They can be adjusted using a screwdriver, but again, it is not recommended for the DIY owner, as getting it right isn't as easy as it looks. Equally, once the points start to give trouble, it's probably time to look at a new control box.

DYNAMO STRIPDOWN

In this section, Jim from P & J Autos guides us through the stripdown and rebuild of a Lucas C40 dynamo, a popular model typically found on such cars as Minis and MGBs.

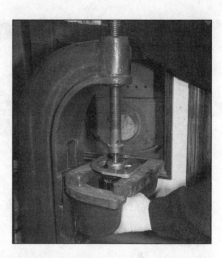

3 In this way, it will come off easily. At P & J there's a special press which makes removal particularly simple. The alternative is to use a copper-faced mallet, but great care has to be taken to avoid damaging the shaft and/or bruising over the end of the shaft and ruining the thread.

1 He started by removing the two through bolts which hold the end plates together. These can seize because of electrolytic reaction and may require some force – damaging them isn't a problem as new bolts are readily available. He used a copper-faced mallet to tap the commutator end-plate off, and then tapped the armature spindle to release the drive end-plate from the dynamo casing.

4 Inside the drive end-plate is a circlip which holds the bearing in place. The ends have to be tapped around until they are in the special access slot before it can be removed. When performing this kind of procedure think about your safety – wear eye protection in case the circlip flies out suddenly and watch out for your fingers lest the screwdriver slips.

2 Having got the assembly off, he tapped out the Woodruff key from the armature spindle using a cold chisel and hammer. It's important at this stage to check the condition of the key slot – if it is damaged it will allow the key to slop around and, in cases like this, the dynamo is effectively scrap, as it costs around twice as much to replace the shaft as it does to have the unit rewound. Jim buffed the end of the shaft, with the end-plate in place, in order to remove any rust and burrs.

5 After the bearing retaining plate has been eased out, the bearing itself can be removed. The bearing should never be re-used, so Jim could afford to be quite brutal when knocking it out with a hammer and cold chisel. This also knocks out the oil seal and oil seal retaining plate.

6 Some bearings are secured by plates riveted in place, as here.

7 He removed the two brushes. In this case they were secured by 4BA setscrews, but sometimes slotted-head screws are used.

8 There's a phosphor bronze bush in the commutator end-plate which has to be destroyed to remove it. This will be very brittle so, again, the eyes must be protected. There's also an oil reservoir pad and a star-shaped shim which protects the pad from rubbing away. The pad retains a small amount of oil which lubricates the bush throughout its life.

9 Examination of the casing revealed to Jim that there had been a problem with this dynamo. The white line around the inside (shown below the screwdriver) is actually where solder has melted from the commutator and been thrown outward. The probable cause was a regulator box fault allowing too much voltage to be produced, and the device to get too hot. This casing can be cleaned up, but the armature was scrap.

10 Jim removed the 'F' terminal from the dynamo case. This was secured by a rivet which has to be punched out. The pole shoes (two in this case) were held by two large crosshead screws. These are always extremely tight and Jim always starts by hitting the casing at the side of the screws in order to 'shock' the threads free – they tend to rust up over the years. He then used an impact

screwdriver to start them turning. Clearly, it's important to hold the casing extremely firmly, use exactly the right size screwdriver bit and protect the eyes during this operation. Some dynamos have four shoes, which have to go back in exactly the right order; to help, some have numbers cast into them or are marked with a series of punched dots. The numbering starts at the top and goes clockwise.

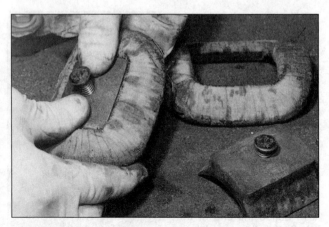

11 You can see here how the pole shoes fit inside the field windings. The shoes should press out easily, as shown here.

12 At this point, Jim made a thorough examination of the windings. The one from this particular dynamo was OK, but the one seen below in this photo is a particularly bad example, showing just what can happen in time. The covering material (which is cloth) has deteriorated to the point where the windings are exposed and would be shorting out against the case. Where this has happened, the (usually) copper-coloured windings go grey (this can be seen about half way up the lower windings) and would lead to low or no output.

15 This small 'butterfly' is made from cartridge paper and is vitally important. It is held in place by the field windings and prevents the through bolts shorting out on the winding/field coils.

13 Jim was then able to check the brush insulation – a multimeter can be used for continuity. One brush is live, the other is not. There should be continuity from the casing to the earth terminal, but no continuity from the casing to the other terminal. (The live brush goes through the casing to the outer terminal and is either screw or Lucar type). He also checked the mounting hole in the end bracket – any sign of elongation means that it should be discarded.

16 Having replaced the riveted terminal (this is an earth, so a good connection here is essential), Jim then fitted a new phosphor bronze bush into the commutator end-plate using a wooden handle from a long-dead screwdriver. It's important that the new bush be soaked in light oil for at least 24 hours before fitting.

14 The field windings in this case were re-usable, so he washed them in paraffin and dipped them in shellac; when left overnight to set, it protects the windings, waterproofs them and is a natural insulator. This is part of the overall attention to detail that allows P & J to offer a one-year warranty with all their service exchange dynamos. He then cleaned the case, using a wire brush on the inside, to remove pieces of rust or solder which could conceivably cause tracking problems in the future. P & J always paint the insides of their dynamos light green, largely for identification purposes, but it does help prevent corrosion.

17 When he fitted the new brushes, Jim put the spring to one side rather than the back of the brush, which keeps the brushes back out of the way so that installation of the armature spindle is simpler.

18 P & J are able to test armatures on a machine called a Growler. By holding something metal above each segment (in this case a broken hacksaw blade) they can tell if it is OK. If the insulation has broken down it will create a magnetic field and the blade will 'stick' to the armature. Obviously, if this is the case the armature is dead and a new one is required

21 After cleaning up the end of the shaft, using emery paper, Jim used the press to push the shaft into the newly-fitted bearing in the end-plate. After refitting the collar, the Woodruff key was tapped into place. Now is the time to apply the washer and nut to ensure that thread is clean – use a die or a special thread-cleaning nut if it 'sticks'.

19 The brushes run on the commutator which should be perfectly smooth, but they never are. It is sometimes enough to use emery paper to smooth them out, but at P & J it's simpler and more accurate to use a lathe – no more than ⅟₁₆in is removed. If it isn't totally smooth the brushes will just bounce off. A tip from Jim relates that leaking engine oil getting on to the commutator/brushes will lower the output of any dynamo.

22 To ensure that assembly is foolproof, there is a small locating peg in the drive end bracket which lines up with a notch on the case. Line them up and you can't go wrong.

20 The commutator has mica in-fills, which should be below the level of the copper. However, the copper wears over the years and ultimately wears level with the mica. At this point, the mica starts to eat into the brushes, wearing them out far more quickly than normal. Consequently the ridges have to be re-cut. The DIY method is to use a hacksaw blade very carefully, but P & J have a special electronic machine (an undercutter) which 'saws' the ridges exactly true. The most important aspect here is that the ridges should be exactly square, not 'V' shaped. Jim usually puts it back into the lathe to emery cloth away any slight burrs that may have been formed.

23 The commutator end-plate can't be installed incorrectly because the terminals only fit one way. The bolts should go under butterflies as shown earlier. Jim checked that the armature was free running, then used a screwdriver to (carefully) flick the springs into the correct position behind the brushes, which allowed them to pop forward into position on the commutator. P & J always check rebuilt dynamos and, on their rig, they should give anything up to 20V, depending on the unit. DIY testing with the dynamo *in situ* requires care to avoid all those moving parts.

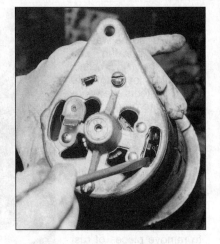

Chapter 7

Alternators

(My thanks to P & J Autos for their help with this chapter. There are many shapes and sizes of alternator, all of which differ in part but all of which use the basic principles shown here.)

By the mid 1960s, car manufacturers had already started to load up their products with ever more electrical items (electric windows, heated rear screens, etc.) and the poor old dynamo was looking decidedly old hat and unable to cope. The answer was to fit an alternator instead. In some respects they are very similar; both are engine-driven by a drive belt and both produce AC current which has to be commuted (or rectified) to DC for vehicle use.

The two main components of an alternator are the stator and the rotor. The stator is a circular laminated iron core on which three separate windings are wound. As the name

This diagram shows an exploded ACR alternator of the type found on many classics and used for the strip-down and rebuild section later in this chapter. There is a basic design difference in the alternator because the current is produced by the field coils rotating inside static main current windings – the opposite way round to the dynamo. *(Courtesy Lucas Automotive)*

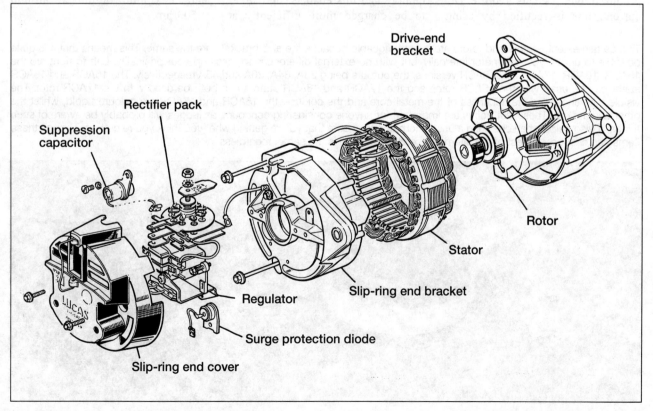

Suppression capacitor

Rectifier pack

Regulator

Surge protection diode

Slip-ring end cover

Slip-ring end bracket

Stator

Drive-end bracket

Rotor

Here are just a few Lucas variants from the P & J storeroom. On the left is a 15AC as fitted to the Triumph TR4. In the centre, the 11AC, available in positive or negative earth and designed for use in bigger cars, such as Humbers and Jaguars, and on the right is an E-Type alternator, again 11AC negative earth but with a different mounting bracket. At the front on the left is a regulator, and on the right is the relay for the dash warning light. With an 'AC' alternator, both these would be required.

suggests, it remains static in the case. The rotor is a coil of wire wound on an iron core pressed on to a shaft. When current is passed through the winding, the assembly becomes an electromagnet. Iron claws are situated on both sides of the coil. The ends of the rotor coil are connected to slip rings mounted on the shaft. Current is supplied from the battery through the brushes and slip rings to energise the rotor field winding and produce a magnetic field.

As the rotor revolves inside the alternator, an AC voltage is produced but, as cars require DC current, this is rectified by using diodes – semi-conductor devices which allow current to flow in one direction only, a bit like a one-way valve in a hosepipe. (The dynamo uses a commutator and brush gear to achieve the same result.) Because the current produced is three-phase, six diodes are required (two per winding) for the conversion process.

An alternator can be driven more quickly and this enables the battery to be charged more efficiently at lower engine speeds. A typical alternator will start to produce useful output at around 1,500rpm with the maximum at around 7,000rpm.

Most are driven at twice engine speed (although this is decided by the manufacturer and can be varied depending on the application) which means that useful output starts with the engine turning at around 750rpm and maximum output at around 3,500rpm.

To a certain extent, stators and rotors are interchangeable because the end-brackets are the same. This means that it is quite possible to uprate your alternator internally, but with no external differences to mess up your originality. Left to right are the 15ACR, 16ACR, 17ACR and 18ACR versions, the outputs being 28A, 34A, 36A and 45A respectively. The 15ACR and 16ACR stator can be used with the 15ACR rotor, and the 17ACR and 18ACR stators can both be used with the 17ACR rotor. The visible differences are the thickness of the metal core and the colour – the 15ACR and 17ACR are coloured gold, whilst the other two are red. These last points are important for anyone considering concours, as judges will probably be aware of such things. It also helps when checking a used alternator, to ensure that you're getting what you think you're getting. Though these items can change, the rest of the alternator service package is the same, regardless.

A whole load of bits! This is the alternator after Jim had dismantled it. It's important to check that the holes in the end mounting bracket have not elongated. If they have, the unit is useless – unless you happen to have a spare one in your parts bin.

Alternators come in all shapes and sizes, and though most units featured built-in regulators, there were quite a few that didn't. As such, their model designation is just 'AC' rather than 'ACR' (the latter denoting the regulator's presence).

Checking your alternator

Before getting carried away removing and stripping your alternator, make the obvious checks first. Make sure the battery and its connections are sound, and that the drive belt is in good condition and at the correct tension. You can use your multimeter to check the charge rate; select the suitable 'DC/Volts' scale and connect the red lead to the positive battery terminal and the black lead to the negative. Start the engine and check the reading – Gunson's Testune moves a needle in the green or red band, depending on the result. A standard digital/analogue meter should be around 13.5V. With the engine still running, switch on some heavy electrical loads – headlamps, heated rear screen, heater fan, etc. Expect an initial dip in charge, but

this should pull back almost all the way to the original reading as the alternator 'takes up the slack'.

Voltage checking

You can make sure that the alternator is getting its voltage quite easily. Set your meter to 'DC/Volts' and remove the multi-plug from the back of the alternator – don't wiggle it or you could cause damage to the rectifier. Switch on the ignition (don't start the engine) and with the black meter lead connected to earth, put the red meter lead to each of the three terminals inside the plug (not the alternator) in turn. You should get battery voltage on each. Remember that the thin wire goes to the warning light on the dash, and if there's no voltage reading here, it could mean a failed bulb.

If your battery is OK and the various terminals are getting the volts they should be, it looks like an alternator fault. The final test is to deliberately part flatten the battery – by putting on the fan/headlamps for five minutes or so – then start the engine and run it at a high idle speed (not in an enclosed space, of course). Put your meter ('DC Volts') across the

battery and check the reading. It should only take a few minutes for the battery to reach 13.5V. If it doesn't, your alternator trouble is confirmed.

No charge

If you decide your alternator isn't charging, there's no need to panic – initially at least! The larger and more expensive alternator components – the rotor and stator – seldom give trouble. Problems are likely to be associated with the cheaper bits, such as the rectifier, the bearing, the slip rings and the brushes. For most popular models, these are available from Lucas dealers or specialists such as P & J.

Important hints and tips from P & J

● If you don't want to pop the diodes like pea pods, DON'T run the alternator without ALL the wiring connected.

● It's interesting to note that alternator end-plates can be positioned in one of two ways depending on whether you want a right-hand or left-hand fitment. The former is usually British Leyland (or BLMC, etc.) whereas Ford usually opted for the latter.

● Never charge the battery without first disconnecting (at least) the earth lead.

● Never weld a vehicle with the alternator connected (remove the multi-plug beforehand) or the battery connected/installed.

● Keeping the drive belt tight will ensure that your battery is always properly charged – but if it's too tight, you'll wreck the alternator bearings. Check your handbook or Haynes manual for details.

● In general, if the red dashboard charging warning light comes on and stays on, it's a rectifier fault. If it doesn't come on (when ignition is turned on) it's either regulator or low brushes or internal fault.

● When changing from a dynamo to an alternator, most companies work on an exchange basis – it may be cost-effective to buy an old alternator from a scrap yard to exchange, rather than buying outright.

● When routing the wiring for a dynamo/alternator swap, take great care to keep it away from the exhaust, moving parts and sources of moisture.

Changing from dynamo to alternator – basic requirements

● Alternator
● 14/0.010in and 80/0.012in wire – lengths to suit your particular vehicle
● Multi-plug kit
● Brackets (right/left handed – check before you buy)
● New drive belt

With a negative earth vehicle, changing from a dynamo to an alter-nator is fairly simple. In fact, the biggest difficulty is likely to be physically fitting the alternator – it's smaller, so you'll need to consider the mounting brackets and their posi-tions. It's a good idea to contact your owners' club at this point – there's bound to be someone who's been there and done that. Equally, many car-makers fitted both dynamos and alternators at different points in a particular model's lifespan, so it may be possible to uprate using O/E fittings (either from a scrapyard or new parts where available). Alternatively, there is a pukka Lucas conversion kit available for certain models, although, being based on new parts, it's not as cheap as using second-hand stuff. P & J often advise owners as to which particular model alternator is best suited to a specific application, something you should consider, especially if you're planning to add electrical accessories. The most obvious point is that the new unit should be secured properly and that the pulley should be in-line with the drive belt.

Talking of belts, it's probable that your original drive belt will be too long for the alternator, as a smaller pulley is used. Where applicable, you can just buy a belt specified for a later, alternator-equipped version of your car. Alternatively, use a piece of string as a makeshift belt, and use the measurement as a guide when you go to buy a new belt from a specialist. Remember to set the alternator adjustment about halfway along its travel, otherwise you'll have either too much slack or not enough.

This diagram shows the basics of wiring up a new alternator. Note that new cable (1) should be 14/0.010in and new cable (2), 80/0.012in. The 'dotted line' cables should be removed, or at least be carefully taped up out of harm's way.

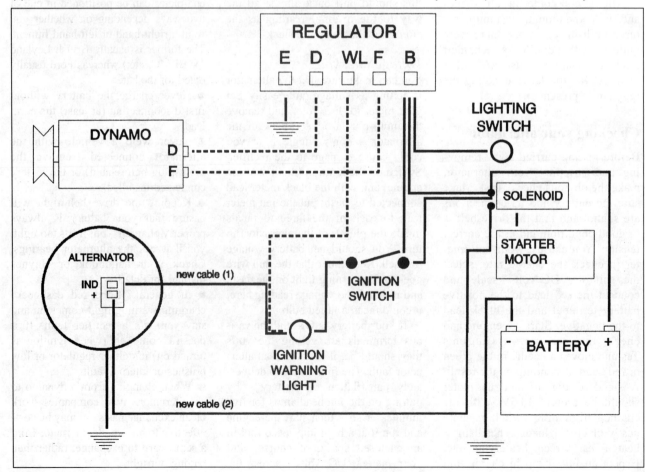

These are the basic components that P & J always install in a rebuilt alternator, and they are available as a service package for the DIY owner.

Electrically, the conversion requires that you take your time and double check the connections (and dis-connections) as you go, and remove both battery connections before you start. It's advisable to solder (as well as crimp) the connections. The control box for the dynamo can be removed altogether, although it's simpler and neater to leave it where it is. For making the connections on the alternator, buy a proprietary Lucas plug kit to neaten the job and reduce the options for making mistakes. There are ways to use existing cables, but it's usually easier to make up some new ones.

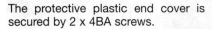
The protective plastic end cover is secured by 2 x 4BA screws.

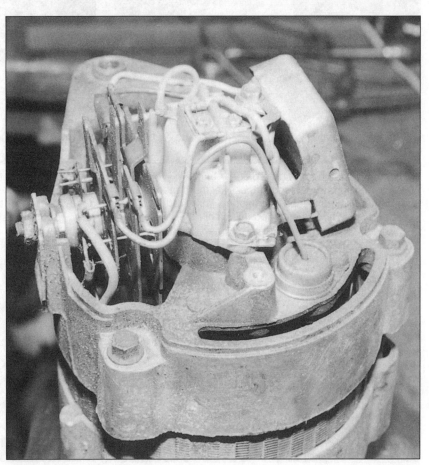
Identification time. On the left, the thing with the wires coming off it is the rectifier; the white plastic lump in the centre is the brush box, and on the right, the small aluminium box is the regulator.

ALTERNATOR STRIPDOWN

In this section, Jim from P & J Autos guides us through the stripdown and rebuild of a Lucas 17ACR, a common unit as used on such classics as the MGB and Cortina, among others. His first tip concerns removing the alternator from the car – when removing the three-pin plug resist the temptation to 'waggle' it free, rather pull it out square-on. If you don't, you could damage the rectifier terminals or, conceivably, a diode.

3 He then loosened the rectifier securing nut but didn't actually remove the rectifier at this point. Then he . . .

1 Jim removed the anti-surge diode – the item in the front left in this photo, looking rather like the capacitor in a distributor. Miniaturisation techniques improved over the years and later models included this within the regulator.

4 . . . removed the brush box retaining bolts. With the protective cover taken away you can check out the condition of the brushes themselves. Poor performance often requires just a change of brushes to remedy.

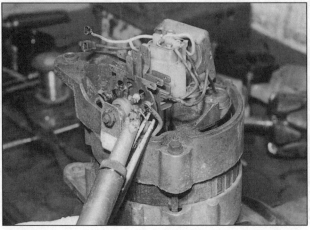

2 Jim un-soldered the three rectifier wires using a 200W iron. There's two wires on the right (they go either way round) and one on the left.

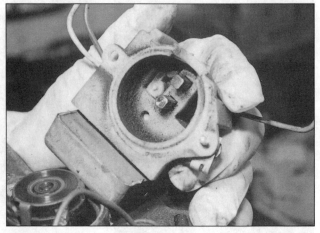

5 Looking into the inside of the brush box shows worn brushes and a carbon build-up (which looks like brake dust).

6 The rectifier was unbolted and removed from the unit. Note that the small rubber cap should be removed and put to one side – it's very rare to find they're beyond re-using.

9 The casing is secured by three 2BA screws and, having removed these, Jim carefully prised the stator out of the case. Note that you should prise UP, not from the top part of the case.

7 Each rectifier has nine diodes. On the right is a new rectifier, and on the left, 'our' rectifier. The fault with this one was that one of the diodes had broken – it can clearly be seen second from the left.

10 If you damage the stator coils, the alternator is scrap, so you've not only wasted your time and effort so far, but now you've got some more expense on your hands; time and patience will be rewarded.

8 This is the built-in interference capacitor. Whilst it may still be working OK, it's a real pain to replace on its own and cheap enough to throw away every time and replace.

11 At the drive end, the Woodruff key has to be tapped out, and it is followed by a collar. There is always rust on the shaft and it's important to clean this off before the rotor is tapped off, otherwise the bearing may stick on the shaft.

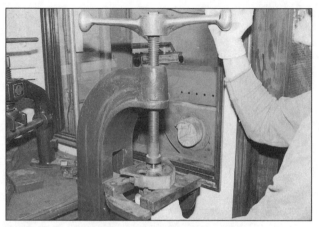

12 At P & J there's a special press to push out the rotor. It can be tapped out, but great care must be taken not to damage the alloy end-plates, which can crack very easily and gets more brittle with age.

15 Underneath, there should be a felt pad, rubber seal and metal washer. (The bits and pieces are only necessary when it's an older type 'open' bearing, but are still used for spacing purposes with the more modern sealed unit.) It's important to check the condition of the bearing housing. Being in the alloy end-bracket, it's quite soft and can be easily damaged.

13 The bearing in the drive-end bracket is held by a circlip. This should be tapped round so that the open ends align with the cut-out so it can be prised out. Take care to protect your eyes in case it comes out in a hurry!

16 Jim un-soldered the two wires – 180° apart – from the slip ring.

14 After the metal seal, the bearing can be tapped out using an impact socket of a suitable size.

17 The wires were flattened, and long-nose pliers used to prise the slip ring gently off the shaft.

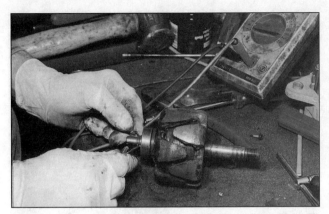

18 Use your multimeter (set to 'Resistance/Ohms') to check that there is continuity between the two wires on the rotor and that there is NO continuity between either of the wires and the outside of the rotor casing (in which case it would indicate a short circuit).

19 At P & J there's a special machine to remove the bearing without damaging the shaft or the rotor. It can be done with a ball-joint separator, but great care is required. Make sure that the separating action doesn't damage the two wires as it removes the bearing. They also have this machine to press the new bearing into place. The DIY method is to use

a suitably sized impact socket, making sure that it applies its pressure to the outside edge of the bearing to avoid damaging the ball race. Make sure that the bearing isn't pushed all the way down on to the plastic insulator, otherwise it will effectively act as a brake.

20 The new (left) and the old slip rings. Note the wear pattern around the centre of the old one which has just one locating pin in the centre hole for locating into the shaft. The new one is a later version which has two pins which makes for more positive location.

21 Jim added a drop of Loctite's Lock 'n' Seal to make absolutely sure there would be no untoward movement, and slotted the slip ring firmly into place. He then soldered the two wires back into place.

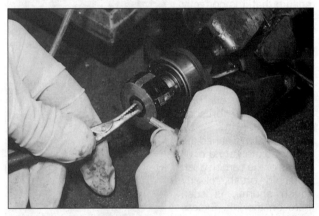

22 You can check the accuracy of your soldering by using your multimeter (set to 'Resistance/Ohms') to do a continuity check; you need continuity between the two faces of the slip ring (i.e. the centre and the outer edge) NOT between the centre and the bearing or rotor.

23 Jim thoroughly cleaned up the stator (you can use paraffin or proprietary degreasant) and tested it for continuity. There should be NO continuity with the core (the large lump of metal going around the wires) but there should be continuity between the

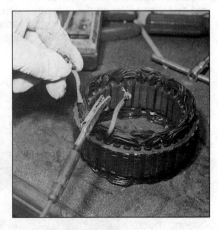

three wires shown here. Jim reckons that stators rarely give trouble unless there have been bearing problems, when the rotor runs out of true causing it to 'kick' and damage the inside of the stator.

24 After putting in the 'O' ring and spacer, Jim tapped the bearing into its housing using the ball end of a ball-pein hammer and a copper-faced mallet. It's important not to damage the seals. He added the bearing retaining plate and circlip, placed the two ends of the large circlip away from the opening and pushed them into the slot. Use a screwdriver positioned in the opening to lever the two ends together and the circlip into place. It's vital to tap the circlip all the way round the groove to ensure that it is correctly seated. The drive end-

bracket was pressed back on to the rotor shaft using the special machine shown earlier. It's important to check the two slip ring wires aren't damaged at any point.

25 The brushes are held by four 6BA screws. The brushes should always be replaced. Jim cleaned the brush box to get rid of all traces of the carbon dust. The old brush, clearly much shorter, is seen here on the left. Excess wear was caused by a worn slip ring, the

grooves in which we've already seen. Make sure that the brushes are free to move in and out and that they aren't sticking at any point. The whole assembly – brush box, brushes, regulator – was then loosely rebuilt. Jim re-used the old collar and Woodruff key (neither was worn or damaged) and made sure that the shaft nut threads were OK. If they're not, use a wire brush and thread-cleaner to spruce them up before going any further.

26 The stator is a tight fit and should be pushed or tapped gently into place. It's important to spin the rotor to make sure there is no bearing noise – don't confuse it with a little drag from the bushes.

27 Before fitting the rectifier, the brush box/regulator assembly was removed so that they didn't distort the rubber cap making it foul on the slip ring soldered joins. Jim tapped the end-bracket into place and tightened the three bolts a little at a time so that the cover came down square. With the brush box/regulator replaced, the stator-to-rectifier wiring was completed; loop the ring of the wire over the diodes

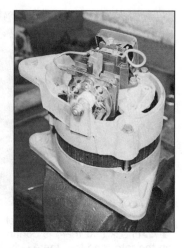

and then bend over ends of diodes – if you don't, the protective plastic end cap won't fit. Make sure you don't damage the diodes doing this.

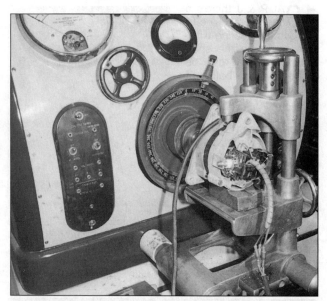

28 Having taken this much trouble to rebuild the unit, it's unlikely it won't work, but P & J test all their rebuilt units under load in order to offer a 12-month warranty.

29 The final procedure is to fit the fan over the Woodruff key. Hold the pulley in the vice and tighten the nut, but don't put a screwdriver inside the alternator to prevent it turning!

Chapter 8

Starter motors

Unless you've ever had the dubious pleasure of having to start a car using a cranking handle on a regular basis, you're unlikely to truly appreciate what a wonderful device the electric starter motor is. If nothing else, it doesn't offer a daily opportunity to have your thumb broken!

Like many other aspects of the typical classic car, the starter motor is largely ignored until the fateful day comes when you turn the ignition key and find yourself listening to the sound of silence rather than a harsh mechanical whirring noise followed by the firing of the engine on all cylinders. It's tempting just to wander off and buy a new starter (or service exchange unit) but like the dynamo, there's plenty you can do yourself, given a little patience. And you'll save yourself lots of cash if the unit isn't totally duff.

Types and description

There are two types of starter motor; the inertia drive, which was used by most companies up to the end of the 1960s and the pre-engaged type, which has been used almost universally since. Both types are activated

The P & J store is a wonderland for the classic car owner, with an incredible range of electrical items for just about every obscure model you've ever heard of – as well as more mainstream classics, of course.

The starter motor – any type – is almost invariably situated where it's awkward to get at. Very often it's necessary to remove it from underneath the vehicle, so take plenty of precautions to avoid injury (see Chapter 1). It's always at the back of the engine bay and usually hidden beneath a raft of exhaust headers or complex carburation. If you've a rear-engined car, like this Imp, you don't get off with it, either; it's still tricky to get at and you'd have to like pain to try it with a hot engine!

by a solenoid which takes a low current trigger from the ignition switch to put some very high current from the battery to the starter motor itself. The starter motor is earthed through its casing to the engine (which in turn is earthed directly to the battery).

The starter will typically have to turn an engine at around 80rpm to 120rpm in order to get it to fire. This requires in the region of 200A to 300A, which is no small amount of current, and this is why a down-on-power battery just won't be able to cope with starting a car. It should also be remembered that an increased load is placed on battery and starter when the weather is cold and the engine oil thick, causing a 'drag' on the mechanical components.

Changing inertia for pre-engaged

It is possible in most cases for a pre-engaged starter to be fitted where an inertia was previously fitted. However, a requirement is that the car ring gear

can be matched up, because the starters are different in their basic *modus operandi* – one *pushes* and one *pulls* and the ring gears are chamfered in different directions. It is also necessary for the pre-engaged nose of the front drive bracket to match up with the car in question. P & J can usually advise which fits what and, more important, what can be made to fit what.

SAFETY NOTE: When you're removing a starter and/or solenoid, make sure you remove the battery earth lead beforehand – there's too much current to mess around with, especially as you're likely to be rolling around under the car and close to fuel lines, etc.

Buying a used starter motor

Peter from P & J is quite firm about buying a used starter motor, say from an autojumble. He points out that you'll be buying either one that works or one that is useless – with nothing in-between, unless you're

buying something incredibly rare. Most popular UK classics used common starter motors, of which millions were made, and it is easy to obtain exchange units, or the necessary parts if you plan to rebuild your own. When buying, make sure you have access to a battery so that you can perform a simple test. For an inertia type, connect cables from the battery to the motor casing and the main terminal. For pre-engaged types extra care is required as they give a powerful 'kick' when energised. Connect the cables as before, to the casing and main terminal, and then use an insulated screwdriver to bridge the main terminal and the solenoid terminal that would normally be connected to the ignition switch.

Solenoids

A starter solenoid works like a relay, in that a small wire from the ignition switch triggers the unit which can cope with the massive currents – upwards of 250A – to the starter motor. On later classics with pre-engaged starter motors, the solenoid tends to be mounted on top of the starter motor itself, whereas inertia starters had a separate solenoid, often fitted to the front bulkhead. The latter often had the advantage of having a small button which enabled the owner to start the car from the engine bay. The obvious potential problems here are those of starting the car in gear and getting caught up in the fan belt, etc., so care must be taken.

Technicalities

A solenoid is made up of a coil of wire (windings) with a spring-loaded, soft iron rod floating in its centre, the rod being attached to one pole of a heavy-duty switch. When the solenoid is energised, by passing a relatively small electrical current through the windings, the magnetic field set up around the windings attracts the iron rod (or plunger) and pulls it in towards the centre of the coil, against the pressure of a spring.

Solenoids come in various shapes and sizes, this being a very popular type used on many British classics of the '50s and '60s. It has Lucar terminals and a central push-button which enables the user to start the engine from under the bonnet . . .
(Courtesy Holden Vintage & Classic)

Short of nothing, P & J Autos seem to have a solenoid for every occasion, from the Roaring Twenties to the Swinging Sixties!

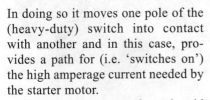

. . . as does this one which looks totally different but which does exactly the same job. Happily, most solenoids are still available off the shelf.
(Courtesy Holden Vintage & Classic)

In doing so it moves one pole of the (heavy-duty) switch into contact with another and in this case, provides a path for (i.e. 'switches on') the high amperage current needed by the starter motor.

Once the power to the solenoid windings is switched off, the magnetic field collapses and the plunger is forced back by the spring, so separating the heavy-duty switch contacts and interrupting the circuit

Over the years, P & J realised that certain cars were more prone than others to wrecking their solenoids. This is because some models, the MGB V8, for example, site the solenoid precariously close to the exhaust system, the answer being to fit a heat shield; this is one Peter made earlier for a (now) happy customer.

to the starter motor. One of the most obvious uses of this kind of arrangement is the starter solenoid. Depending upon the type of starter

motor fitted, this may be either a relatively simple magnetic switch, or the same kind of switch combined with a mechanical lever arrangement.

Stripping and rebuilding a starter motor solenoid

At P & J Autos, Peter stripped, examined and rebuilt a solenoid as part of the pre-engaged starter section later in this chapter.

Peter removed the large wire from the starter motor itself to the solenoid – this is called the jump lead – and then . . .

The two screws holding the end-cap were removed, then the terminals were un-soldered. Note the size of the iron, a hefty 200W is required for this kind of heavy-duty work. In this case there are two terminals, but some units have three.

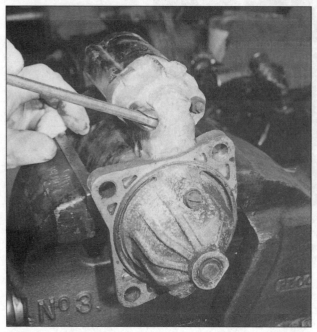

. . . removed the two bolts from the solenoid, whence it simply slid off.

The solenoid's component parts. On the right is the end-plate, in the centre is the moving contact and on the left is the body.

The massive current involved in starting the engine ultimately causes 'wear patches' in the moving contact, as can be seen on the right hand example (the effect is rather like the wear on contact breaker points). Don't bother attempting to repair or clean up this sort of wear. On the left are new components for comparison.

With the field winding shellacked and the casing cleaned-up and resprayed, Peter replaced the cap, making sure that the wires (two one side, one on the other) went through the correct holes. Note the white plastic insulators, which are essential.

The solenoid field winding (centre) is extremely reliable, and Peter says it's very rare to find one that has failed. Like the dynamo, this winding is covered with paper which can rot over time. P & J always strip this off, clean up and re-wrap the windings and then dip them in shellac, which sets overnight to provide a good layer of protective insulation.

The end-cap has to be lined-up with the moving contact and the holes for the three wires, too. Note the new 'O' ring in the end-cap which has been temporarily held in place by a small blob of grease.

Having tightened up the securing screws, Peter then tested it to ensure its complete operation.

Inertia drive starter motors

This type of starter is simple in its basic operation. A pinion is mounted to a helical thread on a shaft which, when turned at speed by the starter motor itself, is 'thrown' along the shaft. (This movement is actually caused by inertia, hence the name.) Fitted to the pinion are teeth which match those in the engine flywheel so that, as the pinion is thrown forward, the teeth in the flywheel/pinion engage and the engine turns over and (it is hoped) fires into life. When it does so, the driver stops operating the starter motor, the shaft stops turning and the pinion retracts.

Inertia drive starter motors are generally reliable, but as they get old and tired, a common fault is to find that they jam when engaged with the flywheel. This does the starter motor no good at all, and even worse is the possibility of damage to the flywheel, which means gearbox removal to replace it. So, whilst a starter motor overhaul is often looked at as a distress task (and occasionally, a distressing task!) it's a good idea to look on it as routine maintenance, and if your engine has done many years/miles of service, then servicing it as shown here may well be a very good idea indeed.

Many owners drive by the adage 'if it ain't broke, don't fix it'. The trouble is that when it does break, it could cost an awful lot more to replace a flywheel than service your starter. You choose!

Removal

There are only two bolts securing the starter motor to the engine, so it shouldn't be too much of a problem. Rusted bolts are a possibility, although as most classic engines have at least the odd weep of oil, there's the likelihood of inadvertent regular lubrication! Perhaps the biggest problem is likely to

Always recognisable because of the huge spring sticking out of the end, there are various styles of inertia starter motor. On the left is a 1950s M35G (with a cast-iron bracket) as fitted to cars such as the MG TD/TF. In the centre is another M35G, but this time a later (1960s) version with an alloy bracket. On the right is an M35J as fitted to cars such as the Triumph Spitfire and Hillman Imp.

be access on certain cars (it's often the exhaust system and/or manifold to blame) and in some cases, it might be simpler to raise the car to get at it. If this is your problem, remember to take great care when working under your car – always chock and block the wheels on the ground and remember that when applying large amounts of torque, you could pull the car off a jack (or stands). In this case, it's best to go for ramps where you can. Don't forget that there will be the wiring to remove as well.

As with dynamos, inertia starters have their casings marked with such information as model number, voltage, date and direction of drive. As ever, this is more important than ever for concours entrants, where a wrong date on a casing could cost points! This one was originally made in 1970 and rebuilt by P & J in 1999 – now that's recycling for you, and it cements the argument against those who reckon we should buy new cars because older cars are wasting resources.

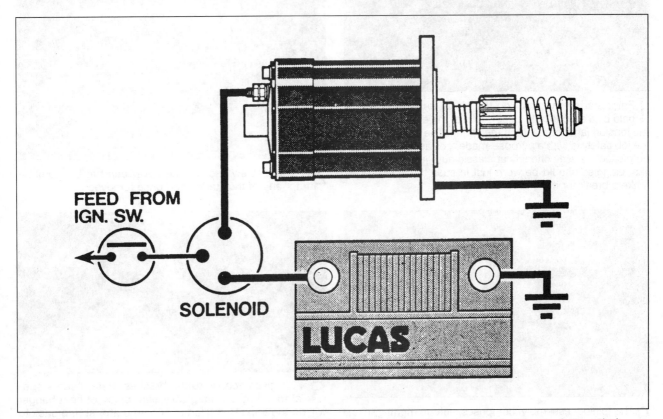

The inertia starter motor circuit is inherently simple, as can be seen from this diagram. *(Courtesy Lucas Automotive)*

INERTIA STARTER MOTOR STRIPDOWN

In this section, Peter from P & J Autos guides us through the stripdown and rebuild of a Lucas M35G inertia starter motor. Note that where new phosphor bronze bushes are used, they should be soaked in engine oil for at least 24 hours before fitting.

3 On this starter, the spring – on the right – had broken (not instantly obvious at first glance and a reason why you should always carefully examine any second-hand starter you buy), the result being that it would be loathe to disengage and this in turn would probably have contributed to the terrible state of the pinion teeth.

1 Peter started by removing the pinion assembly. This is held by a surprisingly small circlip at the end which holds the tension (and lots of it) on the spring. The best way to do the job safely is with a purpose-made tool, as here. This can be picked up fairly cheaply at classic auto jumbles and the like. Goggles should be worn just in case the spring does make a break for it!

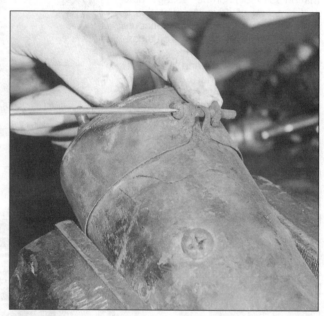

4 A single screw secures the cover band at the commutator end of the starter, and once removed . . .

2 The pinion assembly comprises, left to right; pinion, pinion sleeve, spacer, spring, collar and circlip.

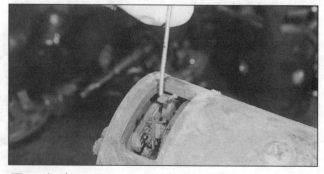

5 . . . it gives access to the brushes. Peter used a special tool, but a strategically bent piece of coat hanger will do the trick. He pulled the commutator spring back to release the brushes.

6 The live terminal post nut was removed, along with its collar and fibre washer, followed by the through-bolts holding the ends and casing together. These usually have slotted heads and, because they have to be tight, are likely to be chewed up. Apply Plus Gas, patience and the right size screwdriver. If you really have trouble, use a 'driver that can be turned by a ring spanner, allowing you to put maximum pressure on to the bolt.

9 Peter then took out the pole shoes. They're usually held by four crosshead screws, although in odd cases they are slotted heads, and on really big starters there are eight of them. They will be (or should be) extremely tight, and it will not be possible to remove them without a good impact 'driver and the right bit. Always wear goggles for this operation. Peter 'shocked' the screw threads first by hitting the casing at either side of the screws.

7 Peter was then able to remove the commutator end-plate.

10 The field coils were in a terrible condition and headed for the P & J waste bin. Where possible, they are cleaned up and shellacked.

8 This casing looks particularly rough – and it is! It has alloy coils and, because the post was also ruined, the whole casing had to be binned (alloy soldering is especially difficult and repairing such a casing is time-consuming and pointless considering the number of this type of starter motor there are).

11 Replacing the end plate/brush assembly is simple and, though it must go in the correct way round, thanks to an excellent design feature, it is not possible to get it wrong; there is a 'peg' in the end plate which must line-up directly with the slot in the edge of the starter motor casing – it's seen here at the five o'clock position. With peg and slot lined up, it simply must be the right way round.

12 Peter replaced the brushes as a matter of course – the old brush is the lower one in this photo.

15 . . . they should be re-soldered. Note, as ever, the heavy-duty soldering iron.

13 The brush braids are soldered to the end caps and then physically secured by a metal clip. This clip should be 'unrolled', as shown here, and the join un-soldered.

16 The phosphor bronze bush was knocked out – damage is OK, because it can't be re-used. Tap from the outside in. Wear goggles whilst doing this operation.

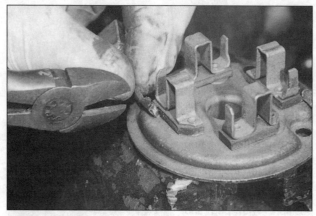

14 The new ones should be fed into the metal clip and then, after they have been crimped firmly into place . . .

17 Peter replaced the bush using the wooden handle of a long-dead screwdriver. Waste not, want not!

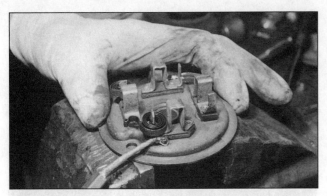

18 The brush spring has to be replaced. Peter's basic lore is to put it on the post at a point where it isn't correct and then turn it through 180° to hook it into place. The pressure on the springs should be at minimum 8oz, which can be measured with a simple spring balance, available from hardware stores.

21 The commutator should be smooth, and to this end Peter put it in the lathe and resurfaced the commutator with a cutting tool, and finished off using emery cloth.

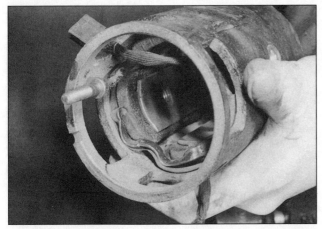

19 As with dynamos, it is important to ensure that the thick paper/card insulator is intact and in place, to prevent the through bolts from shorting out on the windings (field coils).

22 Peter put the drive end-bracket in place complete with two shims. It may need more, but any further adjustment can be achieved far more easily at the other end of the starter.

20 The commutator should be smooth, and to this end Peter put it in the lathe and resurfaced the commutator with a cutting tool, and finished off using emery cloth.

23 Check out the chewed, bent and battered original pinion at right - not untypical, as they take a real battering on inertia starters. Not surprisingly, a new one was fitted.

24 The plastic insulator was put over the post, and the end-plate, complete with brushes, was fitted into the casing. The collar, fibre washer and nut were fitted to the post.

27 Having tested the amount of float, he determined that another three shims were required – the float should be no more than 25 thou.

25 The pinion assembly was replaced in a reversal of the removal procedure. It's vital to ensure that the circlip is a firm fit in its groove before releasing (slowly) the pressure off the spring.

28 With the end float checked and correct, Peter then popped the brushes into place using a special tool to 'flick' the springs off. The final practical task is to refit the cover band before . . .

26 When replacing the commutator end-bracket, ensure that the notch in the casing aligns with the protuberance in the casing. Peter fitted one shim before replacing the plate.

29 . . . taking the newly-built unit off to the test rig – quite an expensive rarity in itself – to check the performance. This includes a locking torque test, something not possible without this kind of specialist equipment. This one worked to perfection, as one would expect, but then nothing is allowed to leave the workshops unless it is 100 per cent.

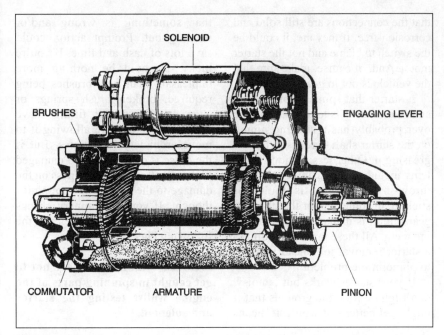

SOLENOID

BRUSHES

ENGAGING LEVER

COMMUTATOR ARMATURE PINION

The pre-engaged starter is visibly more complex than the inertia version, not least because it has the solenoid along for the ride. *(Courtesy Lucas Automotive)*

Pre-engaged starter motors

The second type of starter motor is pre-engaged, fitted to most cars from the late 1960s onwards. It's inherently more reliable but, as ever, there's a price to pay, and this time it's cost (of repair and/or replacement) and complexity. Nevertheless, it's not beyond the reach of the competent DIY enthusiast.

The pre-engaged (as the name suggests) engages the pinion with the flywheel before the starter motor itself starts to turn. As such it is much kinder to all parties concerned, in particular the teeth on the flywheel. Once the engine is firing and the pinion is being driven at high speed by the flywheel, the armature is protected against over-speeding by the freewheel action of a roller or clutch plate.

A pinion on the starter engages on the vehicle flywheel and turns to start the engine. Where the inertia pinion is pulled back onto the flywheel, the pre-engaged version pushes the pinion into battle.

When the solenoid is triggered, it pulls back a lever which pushes the whole assembly, pinion and all, forward into the starting position. Compare with the previous photo where the pinion was at rest.

If you're a real classic car enthusiast, you'll have to curb your natural tendency to apply standard grease to metal moving parts – if you do this on your starter motor it's a sure thing that it will start to stick. Peter always puts a dab (not a tube full!) of heat-resistant copper grease on the armature splines before the pinion is refitted.

Starter motors – basic fault finding

Starter problems tend to be quite limited, and a reluctant starter motor can often be traced to an even more reluctant battery. Both types of starter need enormous amounts of current to make them function correctly. A slow or non-functioning motor could be down to a flat or insufficiently charged battery or, as is common with classics, dirty or ill-fitting electrical connections.

Check that the earth terminal to the body/chassis/engine is solid and clean. Check the electrical connections to the starter motor in the same way. Check, also, the wiring and solidity of connections to and from the solenoid (see later in this chapter). Remember to physically get hold of the connections (ignition off) and give them a wiggle, as they can often break or be loose but look sound.

If you've got an automatic car, remember that it will have a starter inhibitor switch to prevent the starter turning when the car is in gear. Check

that the connections are still solid and corrosion-free. If they are, it could be the switch to blame and not the starter motor. And, of course, make sure that the vehicle is not in gear!

A starter that spins happily round and round but fails to turn the engine over probably has a sticking pinion on the starter shaft – a reason for *not* greasing it. Other less obvious problems include the possibility that the throw-in mechanism is faulty or sticking in some way or that the ring gear/pinion is damaged or has missing teeth. All these problems point to a starter removal job ahead in order to pinpoint the problem.

If your starter works but is noisy, don't ignore it on the grounds that it might get better – it won't. It means that something is wrong and/or wearing out. Prompt action could save lots of cash and time. If you're lucky, it could be nothing more unpleasant than new brushes being required, broken brush springs or even that the starter fittings have worked loose and are allowing it to move around as it operates. But if the noise is coming from a damaged pinion, pretty soon it will pass on the damage to the ring gear – not a nice thought. If your preliminary checks reveal nothing obvious, then run the following checks.

SAFETY NOTE: Take care not to get caught in spinning parts of the engine whilst testing the starter and solenoid.

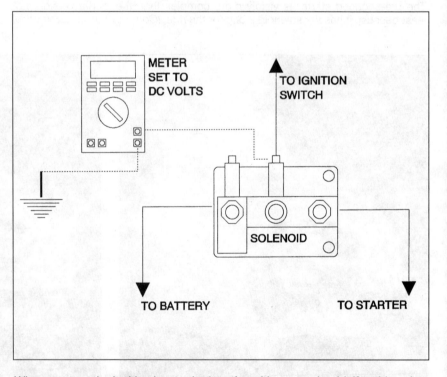

When you turn the ignition key to the 'start' position, you should, if nothing else, hear a click as the solenoid operates. If you don't, this is your first clue, and you can use your multimeter to ensure that a power supply is reaching the solenoid. Locate the solenoid and note that there are two thick wires and a thin wire connected to it. The two thick wires go to the starter motor and battery respectively, the thin wire is the feed from the ignition switch. Set your meter to 'DC/Volts' and put the black lead to a good earth and the red lead to the thin wire to the solenoid (leave the wiring connected). Have an assistant turn the key to 'start' and note the reading. If it is battery voltage, then it shows that the ignition switch and the wiring from it are sound and that the solenoid is suspect. If there is no voltage present, check the wiring from the switch for breaks or loose connections and the switch itself.

Set your meter to 'Current/amps' and disconnect the thin wire from the ignition switch at the solenoid. Connect the meter in line with the thin wire, i.e. connect one end to the wire and the other to the solenoid terminal. Again, have your assistant operate the ignition switch and, if all is well, the meter should show a reading of around 4-6A. This shows that the solenoid is sound internally. No reading indicates a faulty solenoid, which should be replaced.

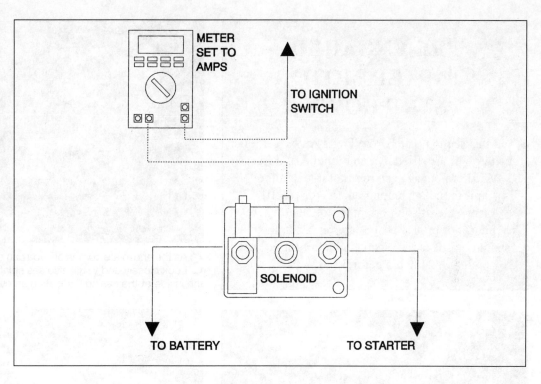

METER
SET TO
AMPS

TO IGNITION
SWITCH

SOLENOID

TO BATTERY   TO STARTER

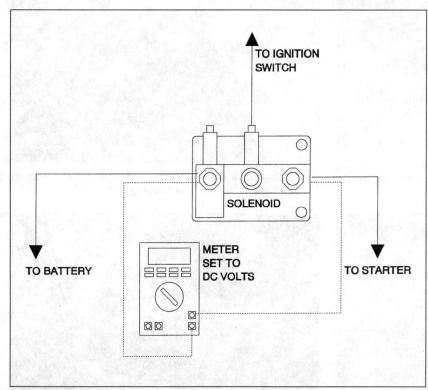

TO IGNITION
SWITCH

SOLENOID

TO BATTERY

METER
SET TO
DC VOLTS

TO STARTER

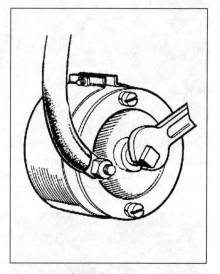

Reset your meter to 'DC/Volts' and connect it across the two terminals which have the thick wires leading from them (one from the battery and one to the starter). The initial reading should be battery voltage dropping to zero as your assistant operates the ignition key as previously. Anything other than this indicates faulty points inside the solenoid. If your solenoid passes all these tests, it would appear that the starter is getting all the current it needs, so the problem must be internal. There's one more problem area, namely that . . .

. . . sometimes inertia starters can jam. You can free it off by turning the square shaft end (sticking out of the back of the starter) with a suitable spanner. Alternatively, with the car in a high gear, try rocking it slightly to free it off. If you can't reach the square shaft end (or you're dressed in your Sunday best and don't want to roll around on the ground) you could try tapping the side of the starter with a hammer. Use some discretion here – what you're aiming for is a sharp shock to free off the pinion, not a demolition blow to crack the case!

PRE-ENGAGED STARTER MOTOR STRIPDOWN

In this section, Peter from P & J Autos guides us through the stripdown and rebuild of a Lucas M35J pre-engaged starter motor, a common unit found on, among others, the MKIII Cortina, etc. It's important to note that where phosphor bronze bushes are replaced, they should be soaked in clean engine oil for at least 24 hours beforehand.

3 As the end-plate comes off, you can see the rotted gasket. Look closely and you'll also see splatters of solder around the inside of the casing, indicating an overheating problem.

1 This is the commutator end of the starter (i.e. the bit without the pinion) and Peter removed the star washer by tapping it down to release the tension.

4 Looking back down into the end plate, Peter removed the brushes by simply unclipping them.

2 Four screws secure the end plate but they often seize, so an earlier application of Plus Gas is recommended. If they break, they can be drilled out, but it's tricky because they're so small.

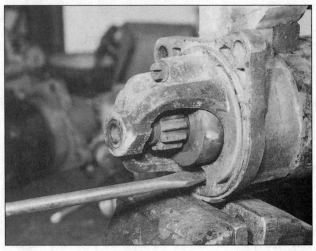

5 At the drive end fixing bracket, Peter removed two long bolts – take note here, because they're different lengths.

6 The casing just slides off – note the locating peg to the lower right of the casing. There's a piece of sponge which sits between the starter motor and the solenoid and which prevents detritus getting into the delicate innards. If it's missing, it points to an earlier (and unprofessional) rebuild.

9 Peter tapped the collar toward the pinion to reveal that underneath is a circlip sitting in a groove. After the circlip had been prised off the shaft, the collar and pinion were slid off. It's a good idea at this point to check the clutch mechanism; the pinion should turn easily one way, but not the other. It's usually, but not always, clockwise.

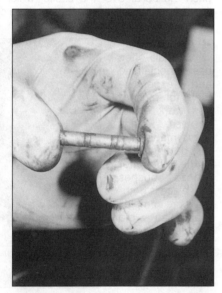

7 The fulcrum is held by a large aluminium rivet which has to be tapped out. As can be seen here, this one had developed two groves in it, whereas it should be smooth. This would inhibit the fork from operating properly as it threw the pinion forward. This was wear from usage over time and lack of lubrication – see next caption.

10 To the rear is a new commutator, and in front is 'our' unit. As you can see, the brass end on the older unit is considerably shallower than the new one, indicating that it had already been overhauled, and possibly more than once. Peter reckons that removing half the original depth is a maximum for reliable starting and a long-life.

8 Peter removed the armature assembly. Note here the small piece of sponge inside the fork. This has to be lubricated on rebuild to provide a constant source of oil for the pin. It's not uncommon to find the sponge missing altogether.

11 There's a phosphor bronze bush in the drive end, which has to be removed, using a suitably sized *impact* socket – a standard socket could easily shatter. Don't worry about damage, because it has to be thrown away. There's another one at the commutator end, which should be removed in the same manner.

12 Where the commutator has not been too badly worn or cut back already, it's generally sufficient to emery paper the end in the lathe, and the same technique is applied to the shafts. Because they run in phosphor bronze bushes, it's more important than ever that they should be totally smooth.

15 Peter pushed the pinion assembly on to the shaft, then added the collar and crimped the circlip back into its grove. Then he used self-grip pliers on the pinion to push the collar over the circlip, which has to be tapped lightly into the collar from the opposite side.

13 Here, Peter is linking the solenoid and operating fork. This is tailor-made for an easy error if you're not totally awake, as it can be fitted in one of two ways. It's not the end of the world if you get it wrong, but it can slip off, which means the engine won't turn over and you've got some more work to do.

16 Professionals often use specialised and expensive tools for renovation work – but not here. Peter's home-made tool for getting new brittle phosphor bronze bushes into place is nothing more complex than an old wooden screwdriver handle! This is the drive end bracket into which . . .

14 The brass bush in the centre of the pinion should always be replaced. Look closely down its centre and you'll see it's full of lubrication holes.

17 . . . the armature was fitted and the new pivot pin installed. It should be tapped through the alloy casing and the matching holes in the fork before being spread at the opposite end using a centre punch. Don't forget to replace that oil-soaked sponge.

18 As a general rule, any starter after 1960 will have aluminium windings – prior to that, copper windings were mostly used. Aluminium windings can be a problem for the DIY enthusiast, as special solder is required to solder on new brush tails to the windings. Therefore, it is important when cutting them off, to leave some brush tail remaining on which to solder the new brushes. There's a long and a short wire, and if you put them back cross-hobbled, the motor will run backwards!

21 Peter oiled the shaft lightly before fitting the whole assembly back into the casing. Note the locating lug in the end-plate which lines up with the cut-out in the casing. Can't go wrong, really! The retaining bolts were then fitted – they actually screw into the field pole shoes rather than the opposite end bracket. He used an impact socket to tap on the

new star retaining clip to the end plate. The motor can be tested by putting an earth lead to the case and a live lead to the jump lead post. The motor should spin, although it clearly cannot engage anything at this point.

19 Here, the new brushes have been soldered into place – again Peter's 200W iron was essential to do this heavy duty job. Note the paper insulator beneath the brush wiring, which is important as it prevents them earthing to the case.

22 Peter clipped the plunger around the fork and then put the spring over. He used light oil over the plunger and then fitted the solenoid. It's hard to get this wrong – the writing on the case usually goes to the top, although, contrarily, not in this case. More important, the larger terminal with solder on it must go close to the jump lead on the starter.

20 Peter discovered that this commutator end was for the bin. Excess heat had caused the plastic assembly to become brittle and snap. He fitted a new end-plate and brushes, which come all-of-a-piece complete with the post, and require no soldering. Because of the screw-spacing, it is impossible to fit them the wrong way round.

23 The finished article. As ever, P & J have the facility for testing both the motor and that the solenoid is engaging correctly.

Chapter 9

Windscreen wipers

Ways of making bits of rubber travel back and forth across the windscreen have varied over the years. Up to the '50s, most cars had either vacuum wipers, which breathed air from the induction manifold or were driven from the camshaft. There are two basic types of electrical windscreen wiper; there is a direct-acting system which uses a cam type arrangement linked to steel arms, so rotary action is turned into a to-and-fro motion. Attached to the arms are the wiper spindles, and this kind of set-up is more common on later cars.

The alternative is a more complex flexible spiral rack, fitted into a ferrule (a steel tube which keeps trouble out and grease in) and directed to the wiper spindles. On the ends of those are wheel boxes which engage with the flexible shaft and convert the circular motion of the rack into the back-and-forth motion required by the wiper blades.

The motor itself (under the case) resembles a starter motor or dynamo, as seen in previous chapters, and the repair/replacement procedures are consequently very similar. It uses a gearbox to reduce the speed to a reasonable level.

Early wiper motors were relatively simple devices, being single speed and with no parking mechanism – unless you count being very accurate with the on/off switch! As years and cars progressed, these two very welcome features were added, though in doing so life was made more complicated for the DIY electrician.

MoT requirements

Correctly functioning windscreen wipers are an MoT requirement, regardless of the age of the car. The wipers must be capable of wiping constantly. The exceptions to this are where the vehicle has an opening windscreen or where there are other means of providing the driver with an adequate view; the *Tester's Manual* doesn't elaborate on what this might be – the mind boggles! (See Chapter 12 for electric windscreen washers.)

A typical rack type wiper application in a Triumph TR4. Positioned neatly up against the bulkhead, the drive rack goes almost directly to the wiper arms, but on some cars . . .

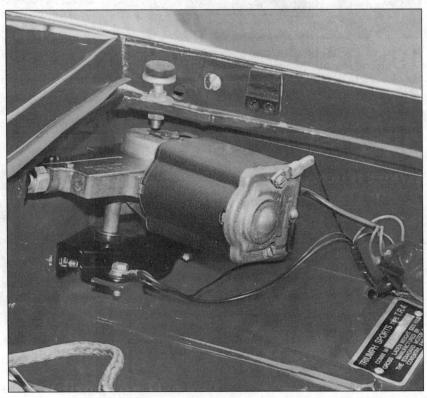

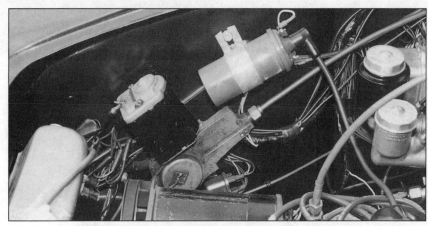

... such as this Lotus Elite, there wasn't room to put the motor in the most obvious position. This shows the benefit of the flexible drive system, because the motor can be positioned almost anywhere in the engine bay, as long as the drive doesn't pass through too tight a turn.

Diagrams such as that overleaf are invaluable when you look at how little you can actually see when you get to look at it in the metal.

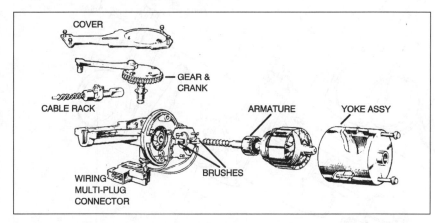

Schematic of typical flexible drive type wiper motor. This is a two-speed.

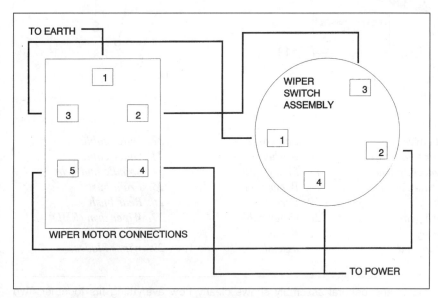

A simplified schematic wiring diagram of the above assembly.

Parking

Self-parking wipers include a switch (called a limit switch) which short circuits the brushes to stop the wiper motor working once the 'off' switch has been operated.

The wiper motor and its mechanism is remarkably robust, given that it has to work in the worst conditions and usually receives absolutely nothing in the way of maintenance. In the general way of things, most will last well into the car's first or even second restoration, but one thing guaranteed to give it a hard time is to switch on the wipers whilst the blades are stuck to the screen by frost. Although most of us would switch them off as soon as we realised the blades weren't moving, if the mechanism has gone past the parking position, the motor will still be trying to move the wipers. You'll need to dive out quickly and free the blades by hand – even if they then run 'dry' over a frosted windscreen, a pair of damaged rubber blades will be much easier and cheaper to replace than an electric motor. The answer here is to clear the screen, at least in part before using the wipers.

Wipers don't work

You switch on the wipers and nothing happens – what next? (We will assume

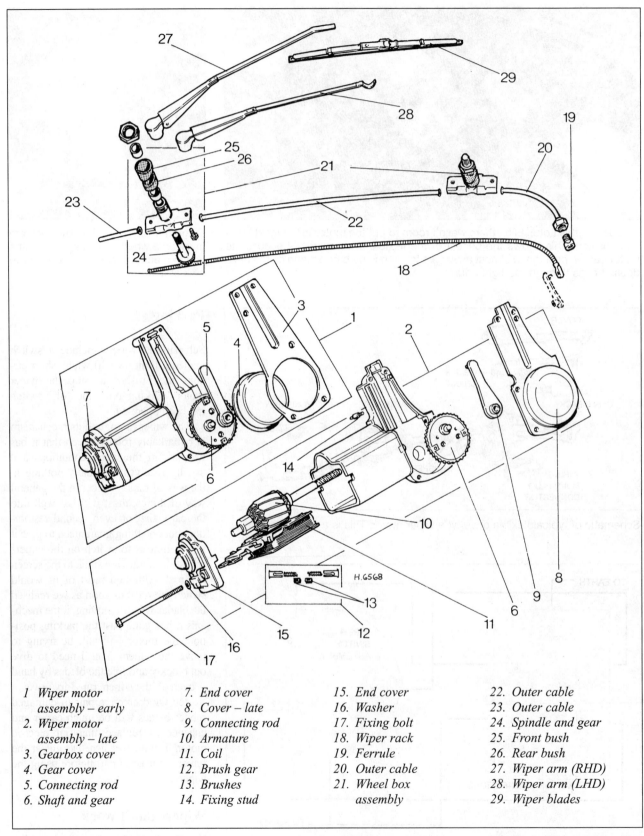

1 Wiper motor assembly – early	7. End cover	15. End cover	22. Outer cable
2. Wiper motor assembly – late	8. Cover – late	16. Washer	23. Outer cable
3. Gearbox cover	9. Connecting rod	17. Fixing bolt	24. Spindle and gear
4. Gear cover	10. Armature	18. Wiper rack	25. Front bush
5. Connecting rod	11. Coil	19. Ferrule	26. Rear bush
6. Shaft and gear	12. Brush gear	20. Outer cable	27. Wiper arm (RHD)
	13. Brushes	21. Wheel box assembly	28. Wiper arm (LHD)
	14. Fixing stud		29. Wiper blades

This exploded diagram of a Mini wiper motor and general assembly shows clearly how everything fits together. Two different motor types are shown.

Holden Vintage & Classic can provide a wide variety of motors for most popular applications, as well as . . .

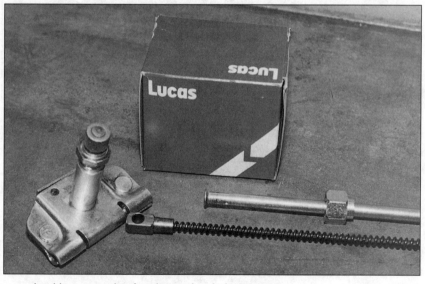

. . . wheel boxes, racks, ferrules and switchgear, etc.

Though not electrical, dragging wiper arms/ blades and sticking spindles can put extra strain on the motor and cause it to slow or wear out prematurely. Make sure your wipers are always operating smoothly, with no sign of drag.

they aren't frosted solid to the windscreen!) If the engine starts and runs properly and other electrical items are functioning correctly, the battery should be OK. So, the first possible culprit is a fuse. If this is intact, then either there is no power to the wiper motor, the motor itself is faulty or something is physically inhibiting the wiping motion. (If you have a wiper motor with a thermostatic cut-out, then you will need to wait – typically around 15 minutes – and then try the motor once more before progressing through the test sequence.)

Use your 12V test light or multimeter to confirm that power is reaching the switch, and then that the feed from the switch is taking the power out again when it is turned to 'on'. If there is no 12V out, then the switch is faulty. Like many switches, these are prone to internal heat problems which, over the years, can cause burning of the contacts and/or melting of the plastic innards causing a lack of contact (or intermittent contact). Sometimes, it is possible to dismantle the switch, although repair is seldom possible or practical: even when it is, it's usually not long before the trouble recurs.

If the switch is found to be working, locate the electrical connections on the wiper motor and make sure that there is a 12V feed in – don't forget that the ignition will need to be 'on'. If there is no feed, then there is probably a break in the wiring between the switch and the wiper motor, so it's a question of patient sleuthing to find it.

If there is power to the motor but it just won't work, then it's time to remove it and investigate further or seek a replacement unit. Which choice you make will depend on your abilities, equipment available and, in many cases, the availability of new/reconditioned motors. Where motors are available 'off the shelf' for your car, it is often the wisest move to take. After all, if your classic is still running its original motor, it hardly owes you anything and is likely to need a complete rebuild rather than a few running repairs. And if the new motor lasts another 25 years, it won't be bad value!

Motor problems

It's ironic that, in many cases, a damaged or burned out motor is not caused by electrical problems, rather a physical problem of the wiper mechanism seizing up, usually due to lack of lubrication. When acti-vated by the switch, the motor will continue to try to work the mechanism, even though it has jammed solid.

Slowing down

Where the wiper action has slowed, this is most commonly because of lack of lubrication in the drive linkage. You should attend to this as soon as possible to prevent excess wear on the motor. It could be that the brushes are wearing out and need replacing. They're usually pretty easy to get at, although, in general, you'll need to remove the motor from the car, first.

On older classics, the sheer age of the wiring and switchgear could create enough electrical resistance to slow down the motor. If this is the case, then there are good odds that the rest of the car is going the same way, and possibly a complete rewire is on the cards – see Chapter 15.

Splineless behaviour

An odd wiper problem (but it happened to me) is one where the wiper switch operates normally and the motor can be heard functioning as it should, but the wipers don't move. In my case the splines on the wiper arms (it could be spindles as well) had worn out and just wouldn't grip each other. It usually occurs where a securing nut hasn't been tight enough and has allowed some amount of 'slop' over a long period of time. Eventually, the splines are worn away until – oh dear, a new wiper assembly is required.

Maintenance

There is little electrical maintenance possible, but there are other aspects of windscreen wiping that can prevent or delay the presence of electrical troubles.

● Replace the blade rubbers at regular intervals to prevent dragging or chattering across the screen.
● Make sure the rack mechanism is well oiled/greased to prevent excess wear on the motor.
● Keep the wiper arms tight to the spindles so they can't work loose.
● Don't use the wipers on a totally frozen screen – scrape at least the area around the blade rubbers and preferably the whole screen.

Wiper motor examination

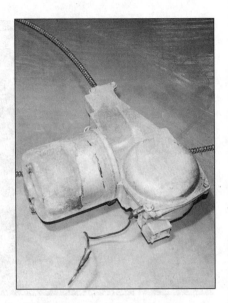

This Lucas motor is typical of that found on many classics. In this case it has seen service on a Jaguar XJ6.

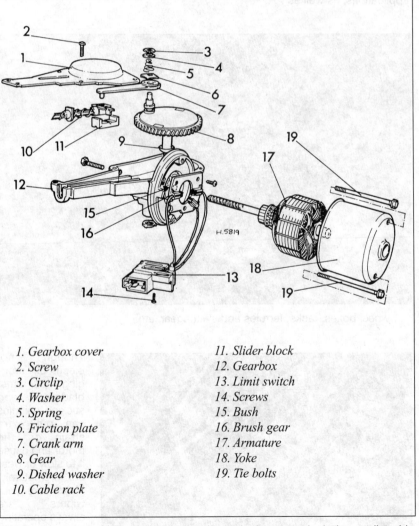

1. Gearbox cover	11. Slider block
2. Screw	12. Gearbox
3. Circlip	13. Limit switch
4. Washer	14. Screws
5. Spring	15. Bush
6. Friction plate	16. Brush gear
7. Crank arm	17. Armature
8. Gear	18. Yoke
9. Dished washer	19. Tie bolts
10. Cable rack	

This is an exploded diagram of what this particular motor includes, as listed in the key.

WIPER MOTOR STRIPDOWN

Stripping down the wiper motor is usually a fairly simple task (seized fasteners not withstanding) but beware, as ever, of small springs, nuts and bolts which develop a mind of their own and leap into a darkened corner of the workshop if you let your concentration slip for a second. Equally, make sure you grasp the inter-relationship between all the parts BEFORE you pull them apart. If you haven't already got a diagram to follow, make a clear sketch as you progress.

3 Once the cover and motor have been pulled away, it is easy to see that the three sets of brushes (for this twin-speed motor) are getting towards their sell-by date. Spin the rotor and listen for the rumbly noise that signals bearing wear – replace where necessary.

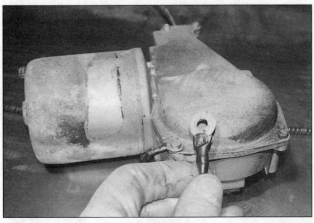

1 As ever, a good earth is essential – this model has a separate earth lead connected, using a ring terminal under one of the case screws and a ring terminal for connecting to the vehicle bodywork at the other end.

4 Most wiper motors have at least one multi-plug connection, especially where twin-speed is a feature. You can check power feeds and switching using your meter on the plug itself. It's always worth checking the contacts (as here) for corrosion or other signs of deterioration. A spray with WD40 or electrical cleaner never goes amiss.

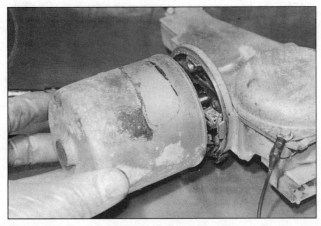

2 The motor lives behind this cover, which is secured by two long bolts. Scribe a mark on the cover and wiper body to ensure you get it back the right way round – otherwise, the motor could run backwards.

5 The top cover protecting the gear mechanisms was secured by five small screws. It's important to use the right size socket on items like this, which will probably never have been apart in 20 years or more.

6 The mechanism in all its glory. Though it looks a little complicated, it's actually quite simple. The large cog is the final gear and it is connected by a rod to the flexible rack. With the wheel moved through 180° . . .

8 This in-and-out movement is created as the motor spins and the pinion on the end turns the final gear wheel. The teeth on the wheel are plastic, so check carefully for signs of damage.

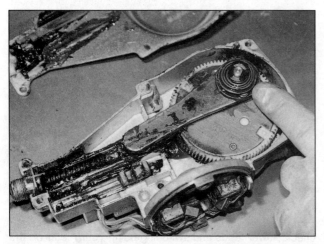

7 . . . you can see that the rod has pulled the rack into the motor casing. Note the use of vinyl gloves to avoid getting that unpleasant grease on the hands.

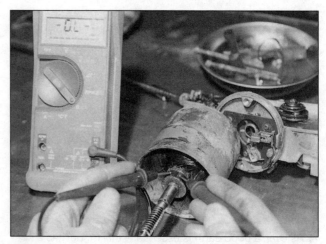

9 The commutator segments can be tested in the same way as those on a dynamo or starter motor. Look for continuity between them. If the copper segments have worn down too far, the mica in-between will have started to cut into the brushes and will be wearing them out at a rate of knots. Make sure that the gaps between the segments are positive and square. You can sometimes use an old hacksaw blade to cut down carefully into the gaps but you may find it too large for smaller motors like these.

Chapter 10

Lighting

(My thanks to Holden Vintage & Classic for their help with this chapter.)

Bulbs

Essentially, a bulb is just a long piece of thin wire (the filament) coiled many times to fit into a small sealed vacuum-filled space within a glass envelope. When connected into the lighting circuit and switched on, the current from the vehicle battery passing through the filament causes it to get very hot, and the by-product is, of course, light. Far more heat than light is produced, though, and in terms of energy usage it's actually very inefficient.

Typical bulb wattages

Head lamp (BPF)	50/40W
Head lamp (UEC/sealed beam)	60/40W/60/45W
Head lamp (halogen)	60/55W
Indicator lamps	21W
Brake lamps	21W
Side lamps (front/rear)	5W
Number plate lamps	5W
Interior lamps	3W

Take care when removing bulbs; most are bayonet fitting which require a press-and-turn action, but corrosion between the metal base and its holder can make the bulb stick. Use a rag to protect your fingers. If the glass does break, it may be possible to remove the base using pliers, but it's generally better to remove the holder assembly

(where possible) to work on it from the rear. Whenever you replace or check a bulb, it pays to squirt a little WD40, not just to keep good electrical contacts, but also to ward off corrosion.

Headlamps

The basics of the car headlamp have remained virtually the same since the days when electric lighting took over from the naked flame. Each lamp typically comprises a steel (or plastic) back shell in which a reflector is

fitted, and over which a glass lens provides protection and a method of directing the light. Small long-reach screws were fitted for fine adjustment. There were a few differences between UK and European systems, and the sealed beam lamps of the mid-'60s made a mercifully brief showing. Today, the choice of replacement and upgrade lamps is almost unlimited, as Holden's can provide uprate kits to convert most types of fitment to most others! The choice, as ever, is down to the individual.

Unmistakably E-Type, but it's only the wing design that makes it individual – the basic lamp was used on many different cars. Better still . . .

. . . just about all types of classic headlamp, bulbs or accessories are still available.
(Courtesy Holden Vintage & Classic)

British pre-focus (BPF) and Unified European (UEC)

From 1945-1963, most headlamps used BPF bulbs, which are generally rated at 50/40W, or 24/30W for 6V systems. The bulb is two-contact (main beam and dip), bayonet style, and the earth contact is made separately at the loom plug. The Continental equivalent was the UEC bulb, which was essentially the same, apart from the plug/socket arrangement and the shape/power of the bulbs. They were rated at 60/40W for standard bulbs and 60/45W for the sealed beam variants.

Sealed beam headlamps

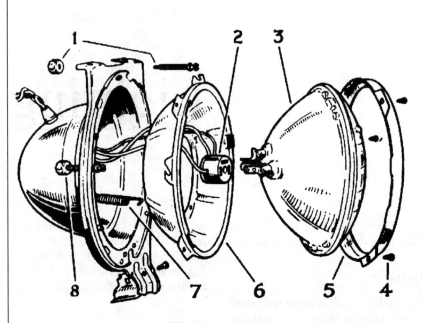

1. Vertical beam vertical adjusting screw
2. Cable connector plug
3. Sealed beam light unit
4. Rim retaining screw
5. Front rim
6. Seating rim
7. Tensioning spring
8. Horizontal beam adjusting screw

The sealed beam headlamp was hailed as the best thing since sliced bread, but it turned out to be a bit stale. Whilst a reasonable idea in principle, it offered little, if anything, in the way of improved illumination despite being more expensive to make and, of course, to buy. Worse still from the consumer's point of view, when a bulb failed, the whole assembly – the reflector, bulb and glass – had to be thrown away and replaced. Wasteful *and* expensive.

The connections on the back of the sealed beam unit are the familiar three-pin variety.

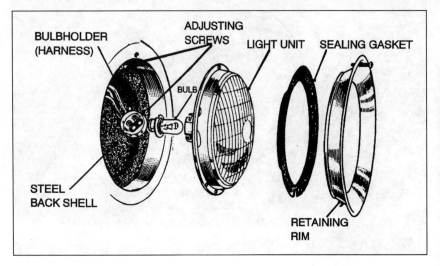

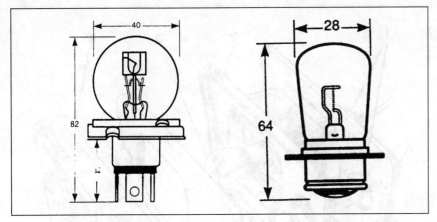

This diagram shows the difference between the Euro UEC three-pin bulb (left) and the BPF bulb.

Getting brighter

Halogen bulbs are filled with a halogen-based gas which enables the filament to reach higher temperatures and thus produce more light. The glass has to be strengthened for this purpose, and if you touch it with your fingers it will affect the performance and life of the bulb, so touch it only using a rag or, better still, touch only the metal base of the bulb.

Halogen bulbs are prefixed by the letter 'H'. Differences lie in the filament and base design and they are not interchangeable. H1–H3 are all single-filament units used for spot/fog lamps. H4 are double filament units used for headlamp applications.

The most popular wattage for H1–H3 is 55W, and most headlamp bulbs are 60/55W. It is possible to substitute different wattage bulbs as long as the 'H' reference is the same. HOWEVER, when uprating in this way, bear in mind that an increase in wattage means more current, which may require the wiring to be uprated (with thicker wire) in order to prevent overheating problems, and possibly even a fire.

The latest in bulb technology is the so-called 'blue' bulb, which produces up to 30 per cent more light by using xenon instead of tungsten. Where available, they can be used as direct replacements for conventional 'H' bulbs without altering the wiring or switchgear. They must be used in pairs, of course. If you want to see in the dark more than you want originality, there are kits available to convert both sealed beam and bulb lamps (even the 2-pin BPF) to full halogen units.

All new. On the left there's an H1 halogen bulb, with its H4 headlamp equivalent alongside.

Pattern

The beam pattern, i.e. where and which direction the light goes after it has left the car, is mainly determined by the pattern of lines on the headlamp glass (some bulbs have 'shields' over them to direct the light in a particular way). This has been the case until very recently; but now, because of the availability of incredibly complex computer technology, it is possible to construct the reflector bowl with a myriad angles in it so that the pattern is created there and the glass lens (in some cases, the plastic lens) is clear. At the time of writing, aftermarket retro fit headlamps of this nature are not available for classics, although there are several fog and spot lamps that could easily be fitted to a classic.

It is not strictly an MoT failure for a lens to be cracked, but the beam pattern should not be affected. A cracked lens can often allow condensation, which could distort the beam and, eventually, it will cause the reflector to rust.

Front sidelamps which show white are a legal requirement and are either included as a push-in bulb holder within the headlamp reflector or mounted elsewhere on the front of the car (either separately or within an indicator/sidelamp cluster). Where fitted in a headlamp, access is from the rear of the assembly (typically from inside the engine bay) where the holder can be released. Where fitted elsewhere, access is either from the rear of the assembly or cluster, or, more likely, by unscrewing the lens cover and twisting the bayonet-fixing bulb. This diagram is of a typical lamps cluster, with the larger part being the indicator lens and the inner section being the sidelamp.

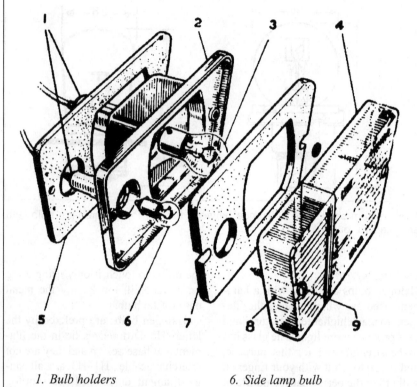

1. *Bulb holders*
2. *Diecast metal lamp body*
3. *Indicator bulb (single filament)*
4. *Indicator lens (amber)*
5. *Rubber mounting gasket*
6. *Side lamp bulb (single filament)*
7. *Rubber lens seal*
8. *Side lamp lens (clear)*
9. *Lens fixing screw*

At the rear of the car, there must be a red reflector, a sidelamp and a stop lamp at each side. Some classics have the whole lot contained in one cluster, others have them divided in various ways. Designs and fitments have changed over the years, with the layout becoming more adventurous with the increasing legal requirements and the advances in technological design.

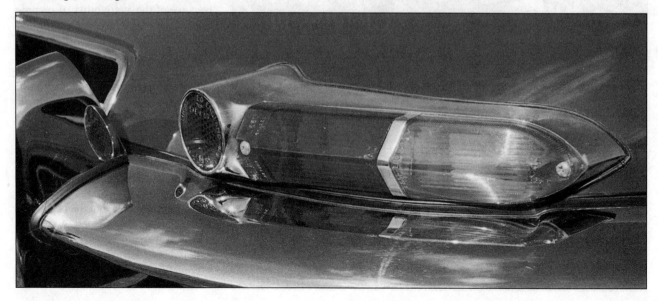

A huge number of classic lamp clusters are still available off-the-shelf from specialists. *(Courtesy Holden Vintage & Classic)*

Here, the reflector is fitted separately, whilst the stop, tail and indicator lamps are in two housings which are secured by two screws each.

The stop and tail light are often combined, the result being a twin filament bulb which, by definition, needs twin contacts, as seen at top. Below is the single filament indicator bulb.

Brake lamps

All classics are legally required to be fitted with rear brake lamps. Technically, there must be (at least) two lamps, spaced equidistantly shining through red lenses. The bulbs must be 21W (which produce a markedly brighter light than the side lamps, which are typically 5W). The circuit is simple, in that a feed to the lamps passes through a pin-switch, positioned at or near the brake pedal. As the pedal is pressed the circuit is made and the bulbs illuminate. Non-functioning lamps can be checked using the general fault-finding procedures, the most usual problems being blown bulbs and, of course, corrosion-related bad earths. In addition, the switch itself can be a source of trouble; ensure that it is mounted securely and the wiring connectors are sound. Some switches can be adjusted and this should be checked/amended as required.

THE LIGHTING CIRCUIT

The lighting circuit, bulbs and holders, is almost universally ignored until something doesn't work, when it's seen as a curse. Bearing in mind that those small pieces of glass and twisted wire have to perform (often for years) in extremes of heat, cold and damp whilst being vibrated and bumped around the roads, it's a wonder they work at all! Check your lights regularly for operation, spray inside holders and snap-connectors with WD40 and check for wiring integrity.

3 All light assemblies have anti-moisture gaskets which become hard and brittle over time – check and replace to prevent corrosion problems. Water can also get in via cracks in the lens which can be caused by stones thrown up from the road or simply tightening the securing screws too much. A smear of petroleum jelly around the edge of the lens cover will help keep water at bay.

Remember that dirt build-up on the inside of the lens can really dim your lighting power. A wash with clean soapy water will help you see the light.

1 The filaments can be seen clearly through the glass; twin at left and single at right. It is usually possible to see a broken filament, but not always. Check for continuity (i.e. a sound filament) . . .

4 Festoon bulbs are typically used for classic interior lights or, as here, in a period manually-operated reversing lamp. This one didn't work, so the checks were made. Power was reaching the bulb, the earth was good and the bulb appeared sound. But when removed . . .

2 . . . by setting the meter to resistance (Ohms) and touching one probe to the bulb casing (earth) and the other to the contact (or contacts on a twin filament bulb). You might need to emery paper the surfaces for a good connection. If the circuit remains open, the bulb is duff; if a resistance is recorded, it is sound. (You should never use your meter in this mode on a circuit with power in it.)

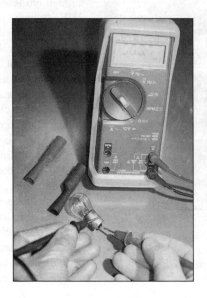

5 . . . the end-cap dropped away revealing plenty of corrosion and the reason for the failure.

Reversing lights

It was well into the 1970s before manufacturers started fitting reversing lights as standard on popular cars. Prior to that, they were either not fitted or fitted to top models only. However, they were a popular aftermarket accessory during the '60s.

Original equipment reversing lights usually have the advantage of being built into the design of the car and being linked electrically to a small switch (usually in the gearbox itself) so that the lights come on automatically as reverse gear is selected (more important, they go off when another gear is selected). In some cases, it is possible to retro fit an O/E style fitment; for example,

the VW Beetle 1303S had rear lenses with white reversing lamp sections fitted and a gearbox operated switch. Its smaller engined brother (a mere 1303) didn't have the switch or the bulb, but the white lens was still in the rear clusters. It was relatively simple to obtain the switch from a main dealer and with a little wiring, O/E style reversing lamps were fitted.

See Chapter 12 for details on fitting an aftermarket reversing lamp.

Indicators

Most practical classics are fitted with flashing electric indicators rather than semaphore signals. These have to be regulated to flash at between 60-120 times per minute,

and the bulbs must be 21W front and rear. The control switch has to be self-cancelling, and the lamps are energised by a flasher unit, usually positioned under the dashboard – you'll find it by activating the indicators and listening for the on/off click from the unit. They are quite small units, and two common types are in use – an oblong version and a cylindrical type.

Hazard flashers became gradually more common throughout the 1960s, and involved either using a special type of flasher unit or an extra flasher unit in tandem to make the front/rear lamps flash alternately. This unit is a non-serviceable item, i.e. if it is faulty it must be replaced. Fortunately, just about all are still available at reasonable prices.

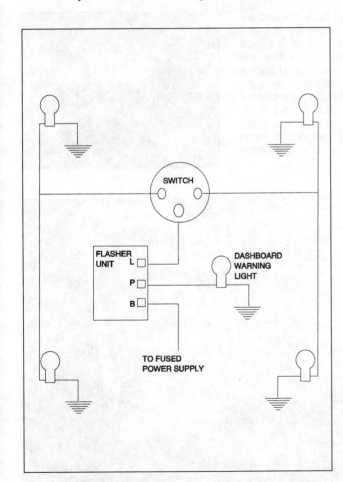

This wiring diagram shows how simple life used to be. Based around the early type of Lucas cylindrical flasher unit, there's a separate terminal on it specifically for the dashboard warning lamp.

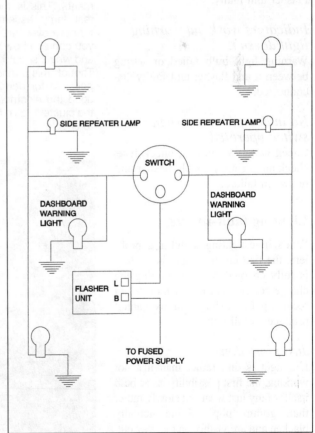

Many classics will have a flat oblong type of flasher unit whereby both the dash lights and the optional side repeater lamps were wired in parallel to the control switch.

Indicator faults

Unlike brake lamps, most indicator faults are obvious from behind the wheel. Fault-checking, other than non-functioning lights, should start with ensuring that the battery is fully charged and holding the charge properly.

Flashing too slow:
Wrong wattage bulbs, very bad contacts at bulbs, old and worn wiring with too much resistance, faulty flasher unit.

Flashing too fast:
On only one side suggests that a bulb (front or rear) has failed. Otherwise, wrong wattage bulbs.

Indicators come on continuously (i.e. do not flash):
Flasher unit faulty.

Indicators work but warning light doesn't:
Warning light bulb failed or wiring between it and flasher unit faulty/disconnected.

No indicators work when switch operated:
Check battery condition, check fuse, check all wiring; possible flasher unit or switch failure.

Lighting fault-finding

When investigating a lighting problem, the first check is that the battery is fully charged AND is holding the charge correctly. A bulb which is not receiving full voltage simply cannot produce its full light.

Just plain dim
If a light is dim rather than just not working, the first possibility is the bulb itself. Many just wear out slowly rather than going 'pop'. Some actually blacken and are visibly on the way out. Whatever, swapping the bulb for one known to be good is the first step.

If this reveals nothing, check all the connections for soundness, espe-cially the earth. Wire wool the base of the bulb and make sure the bulb holder isn't showing signs of corrosion. Look at the lens cover – these are universally ignored and often build up a film of dirt and moisture which can hinder the light to an amazing extent. Removing the lens and giving it a good clean with an alloy wheel brush and soapy water mix could make a great difference.

A light which flickers between off and full on suggests intermittent electrical contact, the most probable being the bulb itself. Check also the wiring to the bulb holder and the earth.

No light?
Check the bulb. Sometimes it's obviously dead – you'll see or hear the filament is broken – sometimes you'll need to check it with the meter.

Check the fuse – remember, some cars have different fuses for different lighting circuits/sides.

Check that power is reaching the bulb socket.

If there is no power, work back through the wiring system to the switch and the fusebox to see at which point it is lost. It could be a broken wire, for example.

Check that the earth to the socket is sound and that bulb earth/live are corrosion-free.

Only on rare occasions is the switch itself faulty, but as most classics are 25–40 years old, it's possible that an original switch has eventually given up the ghost.

Lamp clusters and bulb holders are attacked from all sides by the elements. This is the back of a typical rear lamp assembly. Note that the rubber cover has been pulled back – you can see how well it's done its job and why it should always be replaced. Though this connection looks OK, it's possible for corrosion to have damaged the electrical connection within the cluster – give the wire a gentle tug to check.

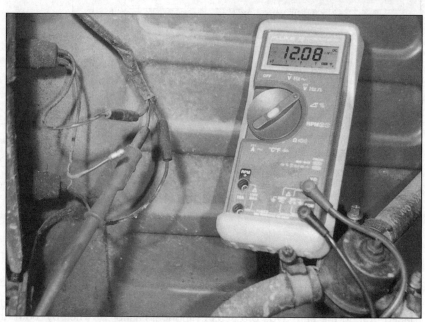

Check that power is getting to the faulty lamp/cluster. A meter is better because it tells you how many volts are getting there – too few volts equals too little light.

Chapter 11

Horns

There are two main types of horn used on most classics – the wind tone (WT) and the high frequency (HF) – but both work on the same basic principles.

SAFETY NOTE: When working under the car, take the usual precautions with regard to lifting the vehicle and protecting your eyes from falling dirt, etc. Where the horn is in the engine bay, do it with a cold engine to prevent getting burned – remember that electric fans can come on after the ignition has been turned off.

Modes of operation

The two basic methods of sounding the horn are *positive* or *earth* activation. To check yours, use your test lamp with the following instructions:

1 Turn on the ignition if it is required for the horn to operate.
2 Connect the crocodile clip to a good earth and put the test point to the wire on the original horn.
3 If the lamp lights up, the horn is EARTH ACTIVATED.
4 If it doesn't light, then the horn is POSITIVE ACTIVATED.

This is a pair of fancy, chrome-plated HF horns. When the horn push is pressed, current flows through an electromagnet. Thus energised, it attracts the armature to the point where the contact breaker points are pulled open, which then releases the armature and allows the points to close once more, causing the diaphragm to vibrate. The vibration is at a set frequency, as is the horn tone.

In the WT horn the operation is very similar except that a solenoid is used, rather than an electromagnet, to operate the contacts and cause motion in the diaphragm. This pair of wind tone horns would typically be fitted to cars like the MG TD and TF and Triumph TR2 and TR3. *(Courtesy Holden Vintage & Classic)*

This is a later style single unit. *(Courtesy Holden Vintage & Classic)*

Wiring

This series of diagrams shows the basic wiring for twin horn set-ups, which is essentially the same for a single horn installation.

POSITIVE ACTIVATED. The standard wiring layout for twin horns with the horn push in the power feed wire. The horns are earthed at their mounting points and have a live wire leading to the horn push button. The connection is normally open until the horn push is pressed, when the circuit is completed and the horn sounds. *(Courtesy Ring Automotive)*

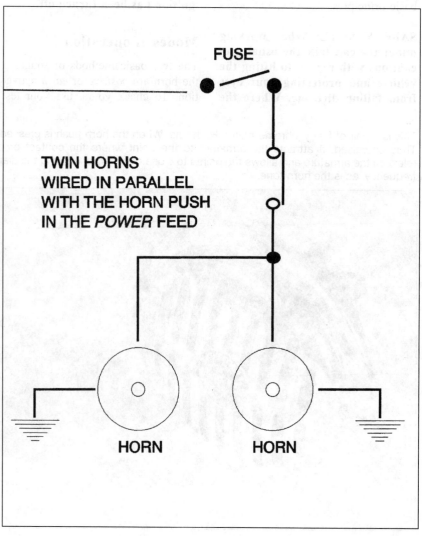

FUSE

TWIN HORNS
WIRED IN PARALLEL
WITH THE HORN PUSH
IN THE *POWER* FEED

HORN   HORN

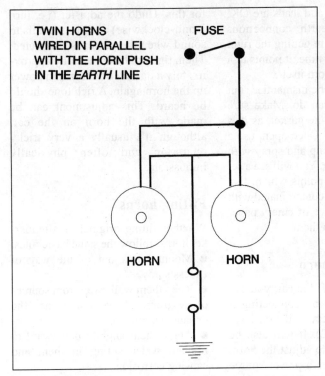

TWIN HORNS WIRED IN PARALLEL WITH THE HORN PUSH IN THE *EARTH* LINE

FUSE

HORN   HORN

EARTH ACTIVATED. Put the horn push in the earth line, as here, where there are two wires to the horn(s), one directly from the (fused) power feed and the other to the horn button. When the horn button is pressed, it connects this wire to earth, completing the circuit. *(Courtesy Ring Automotive)*

Horn maintenance

Remove the connectors occasionally, clean off any 'furring' and smear on copper grease. Make sure that the connectors (almost univers-ally the Lucar or spade type) are a snug fit and not likely to work loose with vibration. The horn terminals often corrode so badly they break off – you'll then need a new horn. Check the mounting nuts and bolts for security and also that they are not rusting solid – use copper grease again. Check the wiring to and from the horn is smooth running, not kinked at any point and not chafing on sharp edges. Brush out any road dirt which could mute the sound and/or clog the contacts. Always remove the battery earth lead before removing the horn. Expect the fasteners to shear so have suitable drill bits and taps/dies etc. on hand. When replacing the horn, use copper grease on all the fasteners to guard against corrosion in the future.

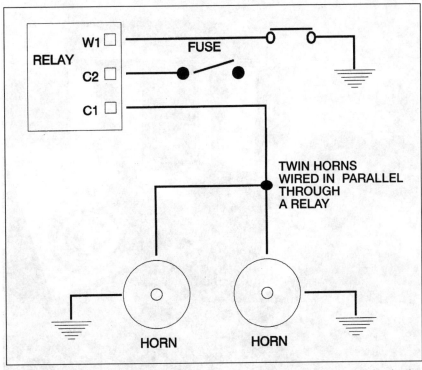

RELAY

W1

C2

C1

FUSE

TWIN HORNS WIRED IN PARALLEL THROUGH A RELAY

HORN   HORN

Twin-tone horns often require up to 10A of current, so a relay will be in the system, as here. *(Courtesy Ring Automotive)*

MoT

All vehicles must have a method of providing an audible warning to another road user, so a dead horn makes your car illegal! Vehicles manufactured after 1 August 1973 must not make a 'harsh or grating sound' – and your guess is as good as mine! You can have two-tone horns on your classic, and many manufacturers fitted them as standard. However, they MUST sound at the same time so they're not confused with the emergency services.

Vehicles designed before 1 January 1905 and built before 31 December 1905 are allowed to have a bell, gong or siren their sole means of audible warning.

When the horn stops working

● Check battery voltage and condition.
● Check the fuse is sound.
● Check that the horn connections are sound and not corroded.

Multimeter Checking

With the ignition on (where required) set your multimeter to 'DC/Volts' and put the red lead to one of the terminals and the black lead to the other. Have a helper press the horn-push, and check the meter reading, which should be just about battery voltage. (Be prepared for the horn to sound suddenly!) If it is lower by much more than 0.5V, then you can check the power feed by connecting the meter between the horn supply lead and the battery terminal. Have your helper press the horn push, and again you're looking for a voltage figure within 0.5V–0.75V of battery voltage. Low figures indicate wiring problems, which are usually bad or corroded connections or, occasionally, problems with the wiring itself – for example, a chafed wire where some of the copper strands have been cut, leaving a much thinner wire than the original. In extreme cases, where the wiring is very, very old, there could be just so much resistance in the wire that enough current can't get through. Replacing the horn wiring should solve this particular problem, although it indicates trouble ahead in other electrical areas.

If the wiring seems intact, connect the multimeter between the horn earth terminal and the earth terminal on the battery. When the horn push is pressed, you should get battery voltage as previously. If not, check out the wire feed in the same way as the power feed.

If the terminals and leads are OK, the power and earth connections check out and you're getting the right voltage at the right time, it points to a problem with the horn itself.

Most horns can be dismantled, but there's little you can do. Make sure you don't damage the gasket, as it is an essential spacer. Once open, use a soft brush to clean up and spray with an electrical cleaner. You will see a set of contact breaker points which, like ignition points, get contaminated with carbon. Slide a piece of emery paper in-between to clean them.

Adjusting the horn

Once the horn is off the car, you can test it periodically by connecting it to your slave battery – if you have one (see Chapter 2). It will also be handy if you need to adjust the horn, as the horn requires a power source for this. Undo the adjuster (i.e. turn it anti-clockwise) until it just fails to sound when the power is connected. Then, tighten the adjuster by approximately a quarter of a turn and power up the horn again. A rich tone should be heard. This adjustment can be made with the horn on the car, although it's usually a very tricky operation and often physically impossible.

Fitting horns

Whether fitting original or aftermarket horns, follow the same basic rules:
● Mount horns out of the way of excess spray.
● Keep them well away from sources of extreme heat (such as the exhaust manifold).
● Angle them slightly downward to prevent water sitting in them and causing corrosion.

Companies such as Ring and Holden's offer a wide variety of different horn types, with most classic style horns readily available, complete with brackets, etc.

Air horns

Aftermarket air horns (usually two, but can be as many as five) are fed by a small compressor, and these have a fairly prodigious appetite for current, so a relay is required to switch them on (see Chapter 3). Operating the horn button works the compressor, which in turn pumps air down the twin plastic tubes to the horns themselves. The wiring is simple and basically the same as for conventional horns, though the horns cannot be 'tuned' in the same way.

If your air horns don't work, the same fault-finding principles apply, with the extra check that the plastic air pipe is connected to the horns/compressor and is not leaking.

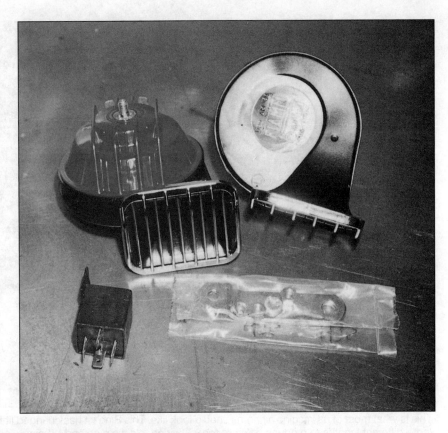

The twin electromagnetic horn package has been designed to look a little more chic. It's really a shame to put them out of sight.

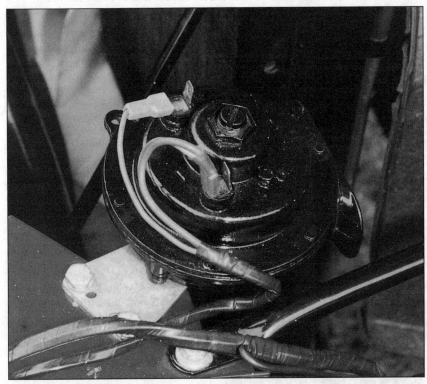

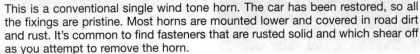

This is a conventional single wind tone horn. The car has been restored, so all the fixings are pristine. Most horns are mounted lower and covered in road dirt and rust. It's common to find fasteners that are rusted solid and which shear off as you attempt to remove the horn.

If you need one of these, you've got some car! This is a French-made Cicca air horn which was produced as a 'must have' accessory in the 1920s. (Courtesy P & J Autos)

This is what most of us imagine air horns should look like. This Ring kit has changed little in 30 years, comprising the twin horns (note different lengths to produce different tones), wiring, plastic pipe and 'Y' piece, compressor and all-important relay.

Seen on an Austin Healey Sprite, the horns have to be positioned slightly downward to prevent them filling with water but not so low they would fill with dirt and mud from the road. The compressor should always be mounted vertically (as here) with the relay close by for ease of wiring. All electrical components should be kept out of any direct spray and away from moving objects, such as the fan belt, and sources of heat, particularly the exhaust manifold. Consider also that there has to be a small diameter plastic pipe from the compressor to the air horns (with at least one 'T' piece) so the closer the better. Remove the battery earth lead before starting the job. Make good solid connections when joining the terminals to the wires (see Chapter 3) and route the various wires with some thought; preferably loom them using shrink-wrap and try to make them blend in with the general layout of the engine bay.

Chapter 12

Fitting accessories

Extra lighting

If the rest of your electrical system is up to it, there's no reason why your classic shouldn't run some extra lighting. In general terms, fog lamps are the most useful form of extra lighting in the UK, driving lamps being more useful for those with particularly fast cars who travel on quieter roads as a habit. In truth, most driving lamps are fitted more for their daytime appearance than their night-time effectiveness. See at the end of this section for rules and regulations relating to foglamp mounting positions, etc.

Which wattage?

Check that the technical specification of your lamps, wiring and switchgear match. By using the principles in Chapter 3 we can work out the power consumption using $I = W/V$ (current = watts divided by voltage). If we assume there are two lamps each rated at 55W, then the current requirement is 9.16A. Use the wire size table in Chapter 2 to choose the correct thickness – opt for larger rather than smaller where there isn't a wire size at exactly the right current rating. If you buy lamps as part of a kit, then the wiring supplied will be exactly right for the job in hand.

Make sure that your dynamo/alternator and battery can cope with the extra load (in this case 110W). Check out the typical power consumption figures in Appendix 2 and list the likely totals your car will take for any given journey. If the figure you get is much more than your system can handle, you'll get poor performance from your new lamps and, ultimately, a flat battery!

General hints and tips
● Never touch the glass part of a halogen bulb.
● Take the trouble to set-up your lamps correctly.
● Always use a grommet where wiring passes through a hole in the bodywork.
● *Always* use a relay with extra lamps.

Before you buy your lamps, check that they will physically fit – especially in terms of depth, as some lamps could foul the radiator grille or wing. It can be difficult to get proprietary suitable brackets for many classics, with the trend for 'plastic' bumpers meaning that most fixings are designed with them in mind, so ponder how to mount them before buying.

Preparations
Prevent moisture by smearing Vaseline around the edges of the two lamp halves. Check the lamps at reg-

Fog and spotlamps are far from being a new idea and so can be fitted with a clean conscience to any classic. These Cibié Oscars are classic lamps in their own right, fitted in this case to a Rochdale Olympic.

Foglamps are best placed beneath the bumper to shine under the fog blanket and angled slightly 'toe-out' so as to illuminate the hedge-bottom/kerb and centre white line. Driving lamps should be aimed in the same general way as the standard main beam. Take time to set your lamps correctly. Beams too high won't help your vision and will dazzle oncoming traffic.

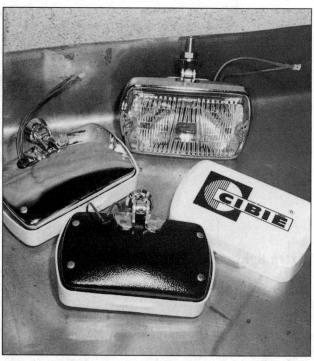

Period classic lamps, such as these Cibié Airport 35 models, are still available and look superb with those chrome backs. Who's for a spot of forest rallying?

ular intervals to make sure that condensation inside the lens is not forming pools of water in the lamp – eventually, this will cause rust on the reflector and ruin the light pattern. Coat the securing screw threads with a copper grease or Vaseline so they don't seize. Vaseline can also be used on exposed metal surfaces during the autumn/winter months to prevent unsightly surface rust appearing. In dryer weather, it can easily be removed, along with all the dirt and grime that will have collected there.

Most lamp sets come complete with protective covers for use during the daytime. It's wise to fit these to prevent expensive lens damage, especially in summer, and even more so for foglamps.

The simplest way to add some lamps is to buy a complete package like this one which comes complete with wire, brackets and fasteners, switch with bracket and tell-tale lamp, covers and daytime protective shields and relay.

Some lamps come with a wiring kit and a relay, others with nothing other than an instruction sheet. Regardless, the simplest way to install extra lamps is to use a pre-wired kit like this Fast Fit Kit. All the wiring is ready-fitted with connectors of the relevant sort (ring for earth connections, etc.), with an in-line fuse and everything fitted to the correct terminals on the relay. If you like an easy life, it comes no easier than this.

Lighting rules and regulations

Driving lamps
● Should be positioned symmetrically; the same height from the road and the same distance from the side of the vehicle.
● They can only be used in conjunction with the main beam and MUST be extinguished when dipped beam is selected.

Fog lamps
● Should be positioned symmetrically; the same height from the road and the same distance from the side of the vehicle.
● The outer edges of the lamps should be no more than 400mm from the outer edges of the car.
● The maximum height above ground is 1,200mm.
● Fog lamps must be wired to come on with the vehicle's side lights.
● Fog lamps can be used without the headlamp main/dip beam if required.
● They can be used when visibility is seriously reduced, not just in actual fog.
(Courtesy Ring plc)

Make sure that there's a good, tight fit where the wire goes through the grommet into the lamp. Apply Waxoyl/Vaseline around the hole before fitting the grommet. On the back of the lamp (NOT the lens), smear all the electrical connections with copper grease before fitting, which will help prevent corrosion-related problems at a later date.

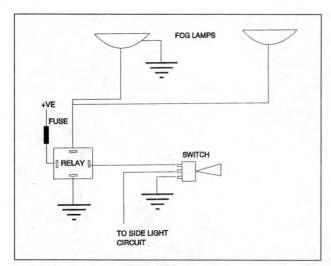

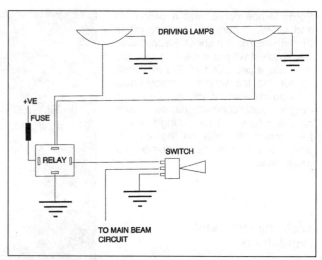

Foglamps have to be wired to come on only with side-lamps, so a wire from the switch has to be linked to the wire which is 'live' with the sidelamps illuminated. Most instructions advise the use of self-stripping connectors, but it's more reliable to splice a soldered join.

Driving lamps are wired in a similar manner except that the switch has to be linked to the main beam feed, as shown here. This is important legally, as driving lamps should *never* be used on their own or with just side lamps. Align to ensure they don't dazzle other traffic.

Fitting an electric fan conversion

Most classics have engines which are constantly running a large, heavy metal (sometimes plastic) fan blade, whether it's needed or not, being wasteful of fuel and power. The viscous fan (which turned at low revs, but 'slipped' at higher engine speeds) was more efficient, but the best answer is a thermostatically controlled electric fan. Kenlowe has all sorts of kits for all sorts of cars and all sizes of engine – the bigger the engine, the more cooling is required. By removing the original fan, the engine has slightly less work to do. Then, by allowing the engine to get to a reasonable working temperature before the electric fan cuts in, it runs more efficiently, has a quicker warm-up time (with less engine wear), does more mpg and produces more power.

Installation

Refer to your Haynes workshop manual for details of removing the original fan – don't forget to work with a cold engine and with the ignition key in your pocket for safety. Keep the fan and any spare fasteners

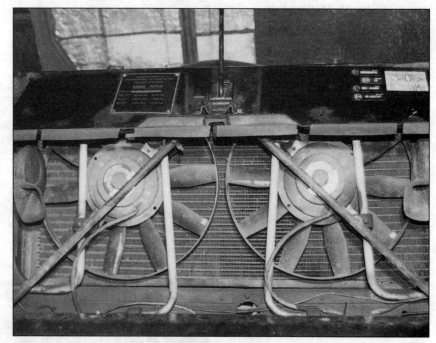

The Kenlowe fan comes with a collection of brackets and adaptors which enable the fan to be mounted in a whole host of different ways, so it's up to you to find the best method for your particular classic – ingenuity is a characteristic common in most classic car enthusiasts. The Range Rover with its 3.5 litre V8 requires two fans to keep cool.

in case you sell the car and want to put it back to standard for the new owner (and so you can swap your electric fan to your next classic).

Check how efficient your temperature gauge is before starting – if it's giving a false reading, this will effect how well the new fan works.

The thermostat relies on a sensor which is inserted into the hose where it goes into the top of the radiator. Leaks are prevented by Kenlowe's patented seal. The capillary tube, which is connected to the thermostat, is then carefully bent to shape so that it is out of the way and unlikely to get snagged by moving parts, or the owner during servicing.

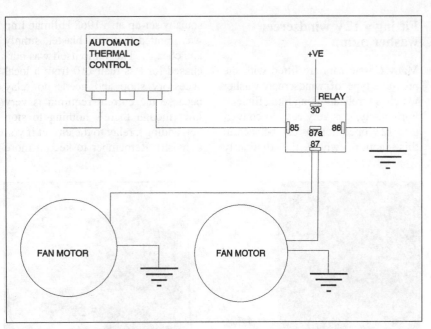

The wiring isn't difficult and requires only that you can make a few good terminal connections and route the wiring out of harm's way. *(Courtesy Kenlowe Limited)*

The thermostat has a wide range of adjustment, but the instructions recommend you set it to cut in when the dashboard temperature gauge reaches about three-quarters of the way up the scale. When dealing with classics, it's probably best to err on the side of safety and start by setting it around half way up the scale; after all, the gauge could be faulty. Kenlowe offer a manual override switch which could be useful for drivers who make their engines work hard for a living (serious off-roaders, for example) or as a plain belt-and-braces measure in case the thermostat fails.

Hot start

Another Kenlowe innovation is the Hotstart, again aimed at reducing your petrol costs, exhaust emissions and, more important, your engine wear. Most engine wear – around 80 per cent – occurs on cold start-up, so if you always start with a hot engine, you must benefit.

The Hotstart main unit is a 3kW heater complete with an integral pump, which is fitted into the cooling system and then plugged into a mains 240V electricity source. When operational, the coolant is heated and pumped around until a temperature of 85°C(185°F) is reached. This typically takes around 15 minutes. The inbuilt thermostat then holds this temperature for as long as the device is switched on.

The socket for the mains plug (both specially waterproofed) can be installed under the bonnet or, in some cases, under the bumper for easier access. For regular use, a simple timer is ideal – trot out to your garage on a frosty morning, unplug the mains from the Hotstart and turn the ignition key; you can see a temperature gauge reading which tells you that when you spin the starter, your engine will be starting without the choke or the excess wear associated with it.

Fitting a 12V windscreen washer pump

Many classic cars are fitted with the pressure type of windscreen washer which is rarely anything like efficient. Fortunately, it is very easy to convert it to 12V operation, as can be seen in this section, where the distinctly squishy set-up on a 1968 Hillman Imp was uprated to a real blaster, simply and cheaply. The pump itself was purchased for less than £10 from a local accessory shop and needs no relay because the current required is very low (though there's nothing to stop you adding a relay to the circuit if you so wish). Remember to keep a more regular eye on the washer bottle level, as you'll use more fluid once you've gone all-electric. If you have a positive earth car, then your choice is more limited. The most realistic option is to try to salvage a pump from a scrapped positive earth car – not exactly easy, but owners will be used to it!

A universal pump can be purchased from any accessory shop. It works very simply, sucking the water from the pump via one pipe and pushing on to the windscreen washer jets from the other.

Cut the water pipe from the original reservoir close to the point where you want to mount the new pump (which has to sit vertically). Check the condition of the pipe, because plastic goes brittle and cracks over time, and the pipe connections. One terminal is connected to the 12V via the switch in the car and the other is connected to an earth – the easiest way is to fit a ring terminal to a short lead and make the earth at the pump mounting screw.

The switch has to be a 'momentary' type, i.e. it works only while depressed, available at all motor spares shops. This diagram shows the simplicity of the wiring. Fitting requires no great skill, and no need to solder if you don't want to. It's a good idea to fit an in-line fuse, not least because you're dealing with water and electrics, however obtuse the connection.

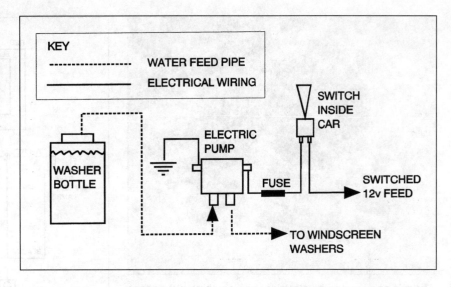

Trailer electrics

(Thanks to Indespension for their help in preparing the information and diagrams included in this section.)

Lots of classic owners use a trailer, either with or for their classic car. Trailer electrics are legendary for working badly, but they're easy to wire and check – the single biggest source of problems is poor earth connections. Always connect the earth lead directly through the plug/socket and to a good solid earth in the towing vehicle.

The basic wiring of a towing socket and plug has become standardised and should present no problem for the keen

DIY'er. If you already have a tow bar, updating and/or replacing the electrical bits and pieces is simple – virtually every corner motoring spares shop carries various towing accessories.

Always disconnect the battery earth lead when fitting a trailer/caravan socket.

Dip all the stripped wire ends into copper grease before fitting and do the same with the small screws which hold them in position. Six of the wires can be the same length but (depending on the design of the plug/socket) with less distance to travel, the centre (black) wire will need to be a little shorter. Remember to fit the plug top, sealing rubber, etc. before you wire the plug –

and smear Vaseline around the edges to keep water at bay.

Special seven-core cable is used for wiring in standard trailer lighting. This will come as part of a complete kit, or it can by purchased by the metre. It's usual to link into the vehicle's wiring loom inside the rear wing, just behind one of the rear lamp clusters. Towing kits usually include self-stripping connectors for this task, but it's far better and more reliable to splice or fit screw-type terminal blocks.

Lights

All lights should be 'E' marked. This table shows the basic requirements:

Item	Number required	Colour
Rear reflecting triangles	2	Red
Rear marker lights	2	Red
Stop lights	2	Red
Direction indicators	2	Amber
Number plate light	1	White
Rear fog light*	1	Red
Front reflectors**	2	White

* Not required if the trailer is less than 1.3 metres wide.

** Required on trailers more than 1.6 metres wide but not those less then 2.3 metres long and manufactured before October 1985.

There is no need for the electrics to be anything but perfect – the wiring and plugs/sockets are available from just about anywhere, very cheaply. Both the plug and socket seen here cost less than a fiver the pair from VWP.

All standard plugs/sockets have the terminals marked (numbered 1–7) so it's difficult to cross-hobble them. They're also marked with their wiring loom designations (shown in diagram) which makes getting it wrong even harder.

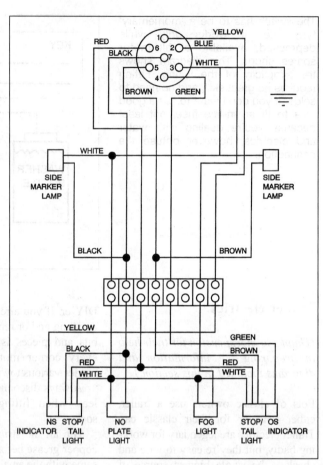

This diagram shows a schematic layout of a standard 12N trailer socket. The side-marker lamps tend to be used only on larger trailers – if that's not yours, simply ignore the relevant areas.

Standard 12N Plug

1 L Yellow	Nearside indicator
2 54G Blue	Rear fog lamp(s)
3 31 White	Earth
4 R Green	Offside indicator
5 58R Brown	Offside tail lamp
6 54 Red	Stop lamps
7 58L Black	Nearside tail lamp and number plate lamp

When making wiring joins underneath the chassis, use a waterproof junction box. With screw terminals inside, it seals totally against the elements and has a tough rubberised construction to last for years. *(Courtesy Vehicle Wiring Products)*

When routing the wiring, use the right-sized cable clips to keep it out of trouble. This VWP box contains a selection of 250 black nylon clips in a variety of sizes – no excuse for cutting corners now!

Maintenance

● Squirt the socket and plug with WD40 on a regular basis, especially during the winter months.
● Remove the lamp lens covers then the bulbs and spray in the bulb holders.
● Clean up the bulb contacts.
● Check the wire routing to ensure it isn't trapped or damaged.
● With a helper, check all lights work correctly.

Caravan connections

Supplementary sockets for caravans are coloured grey (or at least, partly grey) and should be wired using grey-coloured cable. The socket should be fitted alongside the original socket, ideally on a double plate for neatness and ease of fitting. It is recommended that for the 12V feed, a 25/30A wire be taken directly from the battery to the boot area, with an in-line fuse fitted as close to the battery as possible.

Standard Grey 12S plug (Caravan)	
1 Yellow	Reversing lamp
2 Blue	Caravan battery
3 White	Earth
4 Green	12V power supply
5 Brown	Not allocated
6 Red	Refrigerator
7 Black	Not allocated

Caravan 12S socket in-vehicle connections	
1 Yellow	Reversing lamp
2 Blue	Spare (battery charging)
3 White	Earth
4 Green	Power supply (int. light)
5 Brown	Spare
6 Red	Power supply (fridge)
7 Black	Spare

Because some caravan 'accessories', such as a fridge, would flatten a standard battery, it is common practice to fit a split-charge relay which ensures that the accessory can only take current from the battery while the engine is running. The wiring should be as shown here.

Reversing lamps

When all things are considered, it makes as much sense to have a white light at the rear of the car for when you're reversing as it does to have headlamps at the front. Incredible, then, that it was well into the 1970s before manufacturers started fitting them as standard. Prior to that, they were either not fitted or fitted to top models only.

Original equipment reversing lights usually have the advantage of being built into the design of the car and being linked electrically to a small switch (usually in the gearbox itself) so that the lights come on automatically as reverse gear is selected (more important, they go off when another gear is selected). In some cases, it is possible to retro fit an O/E style fitment.

This Ring reversing lamp is inexpensive to buy and simple to fit. It comes complete with a small bracket for bumper or bodywork mounting.

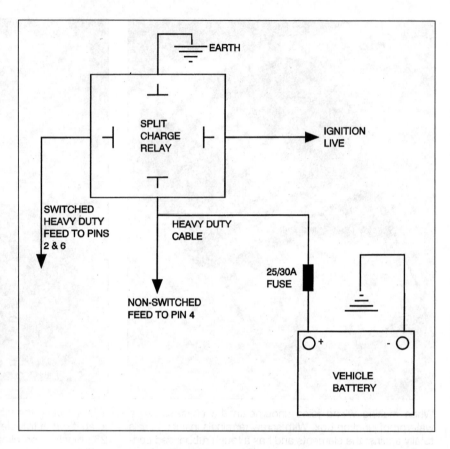

In most cases, however, reversing lamps have to be an add-on, which means finding somewhere to mount a separate lamp, routing wiring from the rear of the car to the front and installing a switch. It's important to make sure that there is a tell-tale light alongside the switch to prevent the lamp being inadvertently left on.

Basic rules
● No more than two reversing lamps should be fitted.

● A single lamp should be centred or fitted at the driver's side, no closer than 100mm to the rear brake lamp.
● When fitted in pairs, they should be fitted equidistant from the centre line.
● They should be no lower than 250mm from the ground and no higher than 1,000mm from the ground.
● An illuminated switch must be fitted.

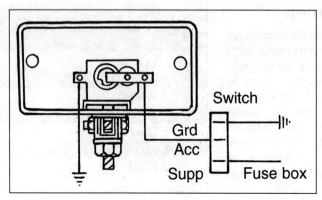

The wiring is just a matter of taking a wire from the positive side of the bulb to the operating switch and from the negative side of the bulb to earth. Note that the switch has three terminals because it must be illuminated.

Chapter 13

Classic in-car entertainment (ICE)

Buy a new car today and you'll be very unlucky to find that there is no radio/cassette deck in the dash, and speakers (usually four) fitted by the vehicle manufacturer. However, a radio (radio/cassette combined units didn't really take off until well into the '70s) was very much a luxury back in the 1950s and '60s.

A brief history of ICE flow

In-car entertainment started in the USA around 1932, when American companies were making 80 per cent of all car radios. Producers included Philco, Arvin and Crossley and American Bosch. In the UK, Ecko and Pye were among the pioneers.

All were valve sets, having either five or, more powerful, eight. To produce a good result and withstand the rigours of a car environment, meant that both build and sound quality were high. Many reckon that the best valve sets remain as good as modern decks, albeit with less overall power.

America was then, as now, far more affluent than Britain, and it was only the most upmarket UK cars that came with a radio. And no wonder – when the average car cost around £100, a good radio could easily cost £25, a quarter of the value of the car! Those lucky Americans also had the advantage of a huge choice of radio stations to listen to, whereas Britons had the BBC or nothing.

However, we did have a Long Wave band, which had to be added to Euro-spec, American radios, as only Medium Wave was used across the Atlantic.

The problem for mobile audio was not only one of cost, but also of size – in the age of the electrical valve, everything was built big. Most valves require high voltage to make them work – anything between 100V and 300V! Domestic 'wireless' sets of the time were almost as big as a sideboard, so packaging everything to fit unobtrusively into a car was difficult. Moreover, there was the not inconsiderable problem of radio interference – seldom a problem in a large set positioned permanently in the sitting room with a fixed aerial on the roof. But with a set fitted close up to an engine creating many thousands of volts for its ignition system, trying to receive a signal from a small aerial in a car, constantly changing speed and direction, was a whole different ball game.

Early solutions to these problems were unadventurous. Many manufacturers produced separate power supplies, amplifiers and tuners which were installed like an iceberg, where just the control unit/tuner would be on show and the rest hidden from view. Other solutions included putting everything in one box which could be mounted wherever was convenient and then linking the box via a series of Bowden

cables to levers on the dashboard, rather like a set of heater controls.

After the war (and to some extent *because* of the war and the need for electronics companies to progress technology at a faster rate than normal), valves became more advanced, getting smaller and more powerful, and fewer of them were needed for a given job. This enabled radio sets to be made more compact, which was ideal for in-car use. Speakers, too, were improved, with fader controls coming into fashion. However, the ability to fade between one speaker in the front of the car and one in the back should not be confused with stereo – the sound was still good old monophonic. The year 1946 saw the introduction of one of the most famous names in car audio (still around today), Radiomobile – a jointly funded company formed by HMV and Smiths.

One of Radiomobile's first sets was the 100 model, found on the options list for Rolls-Royce and Bentley. It was produced for around ten years and cost £40 when the average UK wage was a measly £8!

In the late 1940s, American legislation decreed that a driver should not take his hands off the wheel to tune the radio, hence self-seeking tuners. By the early 1950s, valves had become yet smaller and yet more powerful, and many radios were supplied as two-box models, with a separate power supply mounted remotely.

It was a long time before car manufacturers cottoned on to the fact that in-car audio was a good thing. In this Sunbeam Alpine, the owner has mounted his radio under the dash where it's easy for the driver to reach and not uncomfortable for the passenger.

1950 was made a landmark year by HMV introducing the first 7in x 2in radios for in-dash installation. This became the generally accepted size for radios until the European DIN E standard took over in the 1980s.

Towards the end of the '50s, the first transistors were to be found in radios; they were originally used as well as valves, but soon replaced them altogether, and by the mid-1960s, valve radios were no more.

Pieces of eight

The eight-track tape player, like the Edsel, seemed like a good idea at the time but was inherently flawed; the tapes were large and bulky and the decks themselves were larger than any standard aperture. Moreover, you could flick between the tracks but not rewind, so you had to go all the way round for a favourite track. You can still find them for sale at auto jumbles, though they shouldn't fetch too much money and are usually only purchased to give a period feel. They belong to the decade that taste forgot, which is probably where they are best left.

Restoring vintage radios

Several companies specialise in nothing but these old radios. Although old radios may be dated in some respects, they have an overriding advantage – it is possible to work on them! As a general rule, an expert will spend around 20 hours putting a historic deck back into full operating order. One of the main problems is that the wax capacitors deteriorate badly and have to be replaced, as does the rubber-covered wiring. The valves themselves are surprisingly resilient, and it is typical to find that up to six out of eight are perfectly usable, regardless of age – truly, they're not made like that anymore! A full restoration would usually also involve restoring the trim and shotblasting/enamelling the casing. At the time of writing, the finished job would cost roughly the same as a high-specification modern CD/tuner.

Unless you've specialist knowledge, it's more than a bit tricky to restore your own valve radio, not least because of the safety implications involved in dealing with electrics that frequently have 300V running around them. This said, most of the specialists offer a mail order spares service for those capable of doing the work safely.

SAFETY NOTE: When you're working on any radio, use only one hand so that you don't 'earth yourself' allowing a current to pass up one arm and down the other – via your chest. It takes only one thousandth of an amp to stop your heart!

This Series 1 E-Type has an aperture in the centre console for a 7in x 2in deck – the period fitment would be a radio-only – but little thought has been given to ergonomics. How would you operate the deck whilst in top (4th) gear?

The word 'radio' is used to denote a single box music-maker because, for the most part, classic ICE will be just a radio. However, the basic principles apply to a combined radio/cassette deck.

Choosing

Modern equipment is superb, and the only downside of fitting it into an old car is one of image and 'rightness'. If you're more concerned with what your ears tell you than getting the period right, then choose new.

Buying a period radio isn't as simple as buying a modern deck – there aren't dealers on every street corner offering discount prices and comprehensive warranties. The safest way to ensure you get just the right set for your car, and one which is guaranteed to work, is to use a specialist (see Appendix 1) and buy a fully reconditioned unit. It won't be cheap, and, as ever, you pays your money . . .

When buying privately or from a trader at one of the numerous auto jumbles/shows, ask to listen to the radio working; even with no aerial, you'll be able to see it light up and hear it make

Up to the mid-1960s, most cars were positive, rather than negative, earth, so ensure the radio you choose will operate on your car's electrical system. Some radios had a polarity switch, and if yours has one, make sure it's set correctly before you turn it on! All radios had a warning label, but over the years, most have peeled off, leaving no obvious markings.

A typical early Radiomobile radio/cassette deck, with push buttons for the waveband changes but still a manual rotary knob for specific station tuning. Note there's no FM band, not untypical for this vintage.

some noise. Buying a deck without testing it is a lottery and should be reflected in the price. Many trim pieces (knobs, dials, etc.) are unobtainable, so research beforehand. Paying a high price for a deck that hasn't been tried can only be justified by its rarity or its importance to you and your car.

Make sure:
● It works!
● It is the correct voltage for your car (6V, 12V or dual).
● It is the correct earth for your car – or has a swap-over switch.
● You have valve sets checked over before you use them because of the high voltages involved.

Radio

Probably the biggest bugbear with most older radios is that they operate on AM and LW wavebands only. With no FM (frequency modulated) waveband, you won't be able to get stereo transmissions, even if your deck is a stereo unit.

Installation

Fitting second-hand classic ICE usually has to be done without the original instructions, so more care than usual is required. First, identify what's what. Wires with in-line fuses must be power-carrying of some description and will usually be red, yellow or orange, and earth wires will usually be black or occasionally brown. Remember that a 30-year-old radio may have suffered the ministrations of 'the enthusiast', so treat wiring colours with mistrust. Speaker leads should be obviously different from the main power/earth connections. They are supplied as twin cable and there should be two wires per speaker, both the same colour but one having a stripe down it.

Many radios were designed to earth through the casing. There may be a male Lucar (spade) terminal on the back of the deck for a separate lead to be attached. Alternatively, make up a lead with a ring terminal so it can be attached to one of the casing screws.

Installing is fairly simple, with most early decks being made on the same principle. The twin knobs on the front of the deck were a push fit on to a splined rod and, when removed . . .

As a rule, there were threaded holes in the side of the deck for various mounting possibilities.

. . . the single nut holding the deck in situ could be removed. Use a long-reach socket to get this off, not, as many owners do, a pair of long-nose pliers!

Where the deck is to be mounted other than in a dash aperture, you can buy this kind of adaptor kit from major aftermarket suppliers. You'll need a similar kit if you're installing an early deck into a later style ISO DIN aperture (which is larger).

The complete front panel assembly. Take care here, because many trim pieces are now extremely rare and hard to get hold of.

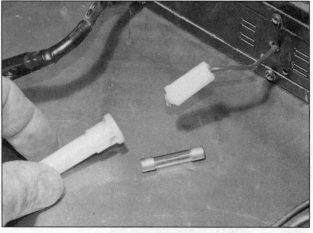

Power-carrying leads should always be equipped with an in-line fuse – don't uprate it if it keeps blowing; there must be a reason and it's better to blow fuses than decks!

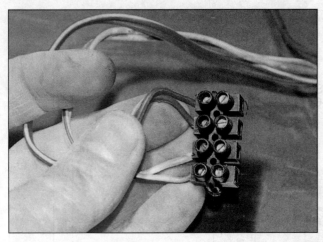

The wiring on this late '60s deck is simple – power, earth and four speaker leads (seen here). Compare with modern decks which . . .

. . . are considerably more complex. However, because they are now almost universally wired to the same type of plug, swapping and changing decks is actually the work of minutes. Progress, eh?

Wiring

It's wise to wire your radio through an ignition-switched live; i.e. a feed that is only live when the ignition switch is on. That way, you can't accidentally leave the radio on overnight to flatten your battery. Equally, taking it from a fuse in the vehicle fusebox is a good belt-and-braces safety measure – yours and the radio's.

Radio maintenance

There isn't much you can do in this department, but keeping the deck clean will always help. Use a photographer's blower to get dust from the intricate front panel. Removing the trim panel for access to the tuning/volume/tone controls is wise occasionally to spray the switches with WD40 or, better still, a purpose-made electrical cleaner – disconnect the power first, of course. The dirt and dust builds up over a period of time and causes crackling and spitting as the rotary controls are used.

If you've a cassette deck, use a proprietary cleaning cassette regularly to remove the build-up of magnetic particles from the playing head. Using quality tapes rather than cheap 'n' nasty Sunday market specials will help keep your heads clean. Eventually, the head will become dirty 'magnetically', which means you'll need a demagnetiser. These are available from specialist hi-fi shops, although they should be used with some care, following the instructions to the letter.

Basic fault-finding

So, you switch on the radio and nothing happens. Whether you've just fitted the deck or it was fitted to the car when you bought it, the same basic check procedures apply. As ever, assume nothing and start with the obvious.

1 Does the ignition need to be on for the deck to work? If so, is it on?
2 Is the deck switched on? Is it turned up? Obvious, but it's been overlooked before now.
3 Is the radio tuned to a broadcasting station?
4 If you're using a tape player, is there a tape in the deck?
5 Does the power lead come from the vehicle fuse box? If so, check the fuse.
6 Remove the deck and ensure that any in-line fuses are intact.
7 Use your meter to ensure that voltage is present in the power feed(s) before AND after the fuse.
8 Check the earth connection. Is it solid on the casing or terminal? Is it solid where it earths to the vehicle?

If the deck lights up and appears to the function correctly, but there is no sound, it points to a speaker problem.

1 Check the speaker connections at the back of the deck and at the speaker itself.
2 Connect the speaker to a different input to confirm it is working.
3 If so, check the wiring between speaker and deck for breaks, shorts, etc.
4 If it appears to be solid, it looks like deck trouble; confirm by running a new and separate lead from speaker to deck – if there's still no sound, it *is* a deck fault.

Stereo

1 If you have sound from one speaker only, confirm the solidity of all wiring and terminals.
2 If solid, swap over the speaker connections on the back of the deck.
3 If the sound moves, it indicates a deck failure (one of the two channels has gone down).
4 If the sound stays on the original channel, it points to a speaker failure.

Still no go?

When you've run the checks above, you're now at the point where expert knowledge is required. If you've got an early set with valves in, great care has to be taken because of the large voltages running around in the deck. And few of us have the electrical know-how to deal with transistors. You'll need to consider whether the deck itself is worth further investigation and/or repair, or whether it is better just to replace it. If you take the latter route, you'd be well-advised not to just throw the original away – someone, somewhere might be looking for just that set and be prepared to pay for its repair. Also, even if it is a fairly common unit, it's worth stripping off the trim, rotary knobs, etc., because these are becoming increasingly rare. Again, even if you don't need them, some-one might.

The hole story

As the 1980s drew to a close, just about all cars came complete with a DIN E size hole in the dash or centre console, a size which became a universally adopted size for radio/cassette decks. Picking a head unit for a modern car, therefore, is simple, as you can be certain it will fit. Classics are not so simple; many had no provision at all for a radio, and others had holes that were to a different standard (usually 7in x 2in) and thus modern decks are usually too large. To retro-fit a later deck to an earlier car in the original mounting aperture means enlarging the hole or, of course, mounting it elsewhere. Some cars just weren't designed to cope with the excesses of ICE – the Mini being one of the most obvious examples. For cars which have DIN E size holes, mounting an earlier size radio is much simpler – adaptor plates are available from any high street motoring store.

SAFETY NOTE: If you hang a head unit below the passenger side dash, will it became a danger to a luckless passenger in the event of an accident? Similarly, if it's placed there, how will you reach it whilst the car is in motion?

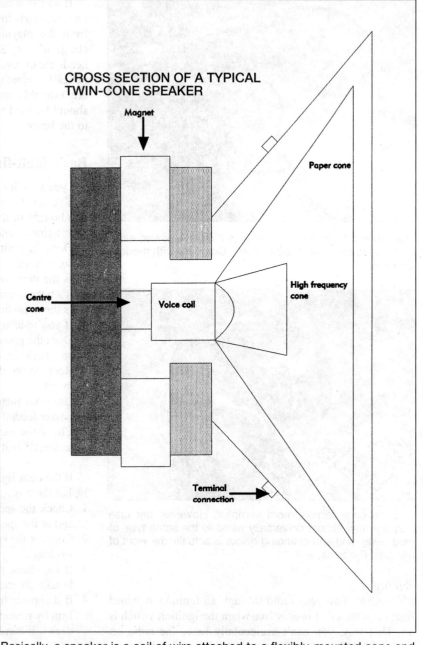

CROSS SECTION OF A TYPICAL TWIN-CONE SPEAKER

Magnet

Paper cone

High frequency cone

Centre cone

Voice coil

Terminal connection

Basically, a speaker is a coil of wire attached to a flexibly-mounted cone and most standard classic speakers will look something like the one in this diagram. The coil, which can move freely, is surrounded by a fixed magnet. The amplifier (whether a separate power amp or the one integral in the set) produces a variable alternating current which passes into the coil, generating a varying magnetic field. This interacts with the magnetic field produced by the fixed magnet and causes the speaker to move in and out, depending on the direction of the current. This in-and-out movement actually causes the air to move; the lower the frequency (or note) the more air there is to be moved. Consequently, speakers designed to reproduce very low, bass notes (woofers or sub-woofers) have to be much larger than those designed to handle only the highest frequencies (tweeters). The sound waves are produced to resemble the originals produced by the sound source (cassette deck, tuner, etc.). Because the direction in which the cone moves is dependent on the current, the wires must be connected the same way round on all speakers in the system. If this is not so, then 'phasing' will result.

Fuses

All power connections to a radio must feature an in-line fuse. However, unlike modern decks, with their complex 'I can sort it out myself' circuitry, the fuses used are likely to be rated higher than of old. Many moderns make do with low-rated fuses, 2A or even 1A, whereas 5A or 8A fuses were common. If you've bought an older set second-hand, it's your first port of call to ensure that (a) fuses are fitted and (b) they are of the correct amperage. If you're unsure and can't discover (from a manufacturer or specialist) the exact rating, err on the side of caution by fitting a LOWER rating fuse – it may blow prematurely, but it's better to lose a fuse than dump a deck!

Power

One of the most important aspects is power rating, which is measured in Watts (W). Older classic radios didn't produce that much by modern standards, but quality was often incre-

dibly high. An amplifier will usually have two power ratings on its official specification. For example, an amplifier marked 10W/30W, the lower figure will be the RMS or rated power and is the maximum continuous power that the speaker can handle. The higher figure is the MUSIC (or MAX) power and is the maximum power that the speaker can handle for short (sometimes very short) periods of time. Of the two, the RMS power is the more realistic, although clearly it's in the ICE-makers interests to lead on the max power ratings. The closer together the two power outputs are, the better the amplifier. When purchasing speakers to suit your deck or separate amplifier, it's important that you match the power output as well as the impedance (see later in this chapter).

Speakers

The importance of having suitable speakers in any audio system cannot be over-emphasised. All too often, they are regarded as an after-thought, even on complex and

expensive set-ups. But without good speakers, everything else in the system is wasted.

Polarity

Each speaker has two terminals on the back of it, a plus (+) and a minus (−), just like your car battery. In a mono (single speaker) system, it's not important which way round these go – some speakers have a large and a small terminal, so clearly you'll have to have matching terminals on your speaker lead.

However, where you have two speakers, and especially where stereo is possible (not necessarily the same thing), it is important to keep the polarity the same. That's why speaker leads have one of the wires with a stripe on it. It doesn't matter which you choose, whether to take the striped wires to the positive or negative terminals on the speakers, just as long as all speakers in the system are wired the same. Getting it wrong won't damage anything, but you will get an odd sound, as one speaker will be moving out as the other is moving in.

A typical speaker has one large cone, and handles all frequencies (notes) high and low. Splitting the sound between more than one speaker improves the quality. Two speakers in one enclosure, as here, is called a co-axial (the centre speaker handles only very high notes) and three speakers would be a tri-axial.

If you have a speaker with terminals which are not clearly marked, there is a simple way to check. Take an ordinary 1.5V (AA) battery and connect it briefly across the speaker terminals. Take note of which speaker terminal is connected to the positive terminal of the battery. If the cone moves outwards (as on the left), then you have touched the positive terminal of the speaker to the positive terminal of the battery. If it moves inward (as on the right), then you have touched the negative terminal of the speaker to the positive terminal of the battery. Having ascertained which is which, you should mark them accordingly and make sure you get the wiring matched up.

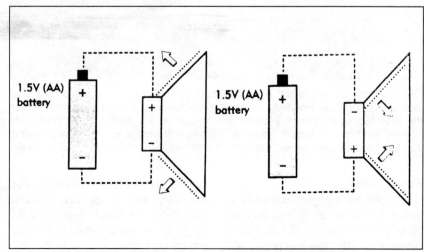

Later style speakers often have two different sizes of terminal on the back of the speaker which, when combined with speaker wiring fitted with matching connectors makes it impossible to cross-hobble the polarity.

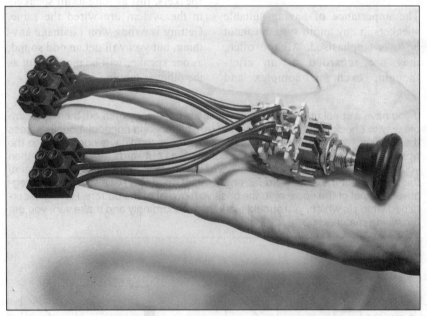

Though many classic radios are mono, as the '60s progressed stereo became increasingly popular. However, it was later still that four-way stereo systems (not the dreaded quadraphonic!) came into vogue where decks were fitted with internal front-to-rear faders. You can add two extra speakers if you wish and if you want full fading facilities, you can fit a separate fader like this, quite simply.

Power rating

One of the most important aspects is power rating, which is measured in Watts (W). A speaker, like an amplifier, will usually have two power rat-

ings on its official specification. For example, on a speaker marked 10W/30W, the lower figure will be the RMS or rated power and is the maximum continuous power that the

speaker can handle. The higher figure is the MUSIC (or MAX) power and is the maximum power that the speaker can handle for short (sometimes very short) periods of time. These figures must correspond with those of the amplification available. The closer together the two power outputs are, the better the speaker. For example, if a speaker can handle 100W MAX and 20W continuous, it's not as good as one which boasts 100W MAX and 60W continuous.

It is vital to obtain the correct specification speaker to match the rest of your audio system.

When choosing speakers, you should look to exceed the quoted power output of the amplifier by around 50 per cent, and remember to compare like with like when it comes to ways of defining power. So, if your amplifier delivers 20W per channel MAX, your speakers should be capable of handling 30W power channel MAX. Consider also the future; if you are planning an amplifier uprate in the foreseeable future, you will save money by installing suitable speakers now, rather than upgrading at a later date.

Impedance

Impedance is a term used to denote the amount of electrical resistance. The unit of measurement is the ohm, and speakers will usually be either 4 ohm or 8 ohm. It is important to match your speaker impedance to that of your set.

If you have a speaker impedance of, say, 8 ohms and the set is rated at 4 ohms, the speaker will lose some of its efficiency. However, if the impedance were mismatched the other way around, that is with the speaker impedance being the lower of the two figures, then not only will efficiency suffer, but there is also the possibility of damage to the unit. The wiring of the speakers can also result in differing impedances.

Older speakers were rated at 3 ohms, but it's hard work to find them, and 4 ohm speakers work just as well – moreover, they're available everywhere.

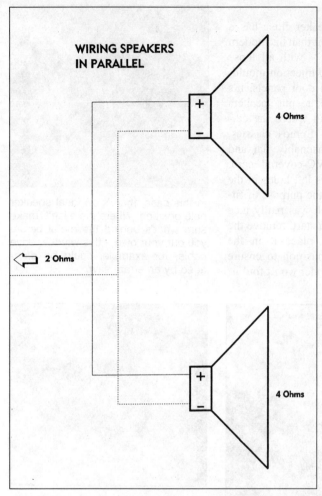

This diagram shows how wiring two speakers in parallel produces an impedance lower than the original, whereas . . .

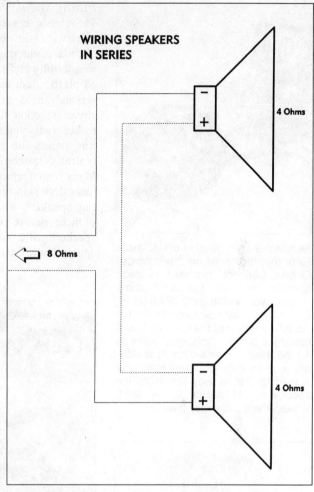

. . . wiring in series, doubles it.

Frequency response

The frequency response of a speaker is, simply, a denotation of the highest and the lowest frequencies (or notes) that it is capable of reproducing. Frequency response is measured in hertz (Hz) or thousands of hertz (kHz). Clearly, there has to be some overlap in terms of speaker capabilities; a tweeter will work between 2,000Hz and 25,000Hz, for example, but it will really only be at its best reproducing sounds in the 15,000Hz-plus range.

Speakers are divided into four main areas:

Tweeters. Very high frequencies, typically rated between 2,000Hz and 25,000Hz.

Mid Range (or mid-woofers). Mid-range frequencies typically rated between 300Hz and 12,000Hz.

Woofers. Low, bass frequencies, typically rated between 35Hz and 4,000Hz.

Sub-woofers. Extremely low frequencies, many of which are felt, rather than heard, typically rated below 200Hz.

Speaker safety

Never switch on a radio *without* the speaker(s) connected; if the bared wires touch, it could damage the output stage of the amplifier.

Checking speakers using a multimeter

Before you start checking the speaker, set the meter to 'Resistance/Ohms' and look for an initial reading of '1' or 'OC' (open circuit). Touch the probes together to get the inherent resistance in the leads themselves. This will be (or certainly should be) a very small figure. Make a note for future reference.

IMPORTANT NOTE: Never measure ohms (resistance) on a circuit which has power in it – at best you'll blow a fuse in the meter, at worst you'll ruin it altogether.

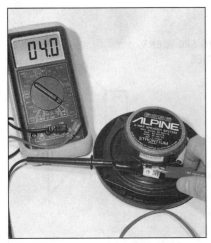

As speakers are rated in ohms, make sure the meter is on 'Resistance/ Ohms'. Connect one lead to each speaker terminal. For a 4 ohms speaker, you should get 3.0–4.5 ohms. Deduct the initial resistance to get the actual resistance of the speaker. This is reading 4 ohms which, even allowing for the resistance in the leads, is virtually spot-on. If you get a zero reading or a reading that is way too high, the speaker would appear to be dead. Replacement is the only answer.

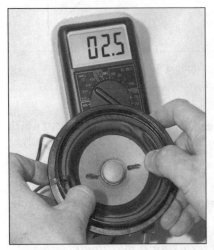

However, not all speaker problems are solved as simply. Sometimes, the speaker could be making a short circuit part way through the cone movement, so that the problem is sporadic. Check the lead resistance again and connect the leads as previously. Using your thumbs, GENTLY press the cone in as far as it will go and let it out again slowly. The reading should vary slightly but at no point should it go to zero – if it does, replacement is required.

Fitting speakers

The classic car speaker fitter has a much easier time of it than his modern tin box counterpart – with all those wonderfully stylish, injection-moulded plastic dash and door panels, it's seriously hard work to put speakers anywhere other than where the carmaker wants you to. In most classics, trim panels are reasonably flat and typically leather/PVC-covered card. Many manufacturers left holes in the inner door skin for the purpose of fitting speakers, which was really nice of them. Before you start, remove the speaker grille and place it in the approximate final position to ensure that the window winder won't foul it.

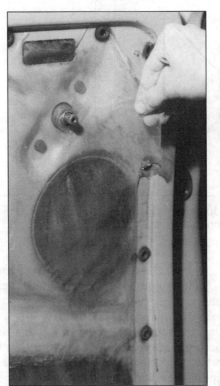

Remove the panel and any necessary door furniture (handle, armrest, window winder, etc.). Panels are usually secured around the edges by pop fasteners. These fasteners are easily replaced, but not necessarily the panel. If you're lucky, the original plastic membrane will still be intact – try to keep it that way. If it's not, cut a piece of plastic sheeting to size and stick in place when you've finished. It's there to stop damp from the inner door damaging the trim panel.

In this case, there's an ideal speaker hole position. Where there isn't, make sure what's behind the metal before you cut your own – this window drive cable, for example, could be damaged by an errant saw.

Mark the position of the speaker on the panel and start by drilling a pilot hole. Then use a small hand saw or a jig saw to make the hole. Take it steady and use a fine-toothed blade to prevent ripping the trim.

Most speaker kits come with a plastic ring like this, which is designed to put some strength into the mounting when fitting a speaker into a relatively thin card panel.

Use the grille and a felt tip pen to mark the positions of the fixing screws, and drill carefully through the panel and metal of the door. In order to prevent the speaker rattling (especially when producing bass sounds) try to get at least one of the fixing screws into some metal, rather than just the card.

When running the speaker leads into the cabin, make sure they go through holes fitted with grommets to prevent chafing and possible short circuits.

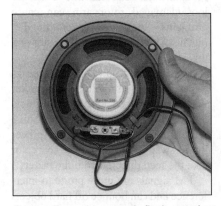

Route the wiring and fit it to the speaker *out of situ* for a test before final fitting. Make sure the terminals are a tight fit, and if there's a cable clip (as here) use it to prevent terminal damage should the wire get yanked accidentally.

Aerials

Even when fitting expensive modern, hi-tech head units, many owners still run them with £5 aerials and expect wonders from them. They won't work well like this, and older radios require even more attention to the aerial. True concours buffs will probably need to have exactly the right aerial for the car, but as aerials look much the same regardless of age, it's an area where you can go 'modern' without compromising the look and feel of the car. A good telescopic aerial from one of the quality makers (such as Hirschmann) will make a world of difference to your radio reception.

Aerial maintenance

It's always advisable to retract your aerial when you park/garage your car. Apart from keeping it out of the elements, it also removes an opportunity for mindless vandalism. Give it a squirt of WD or light oil occasionally and wipe it over with a cloth. If you don't use your aerial often, it pays to extend and retract it a few times and apply the lubricant to ensure that it doesn't get rusted in the 'down' position.

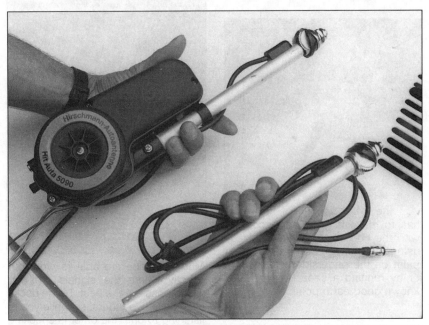

Classic or modern, the aerial choice is the same, with the most popular options being a manual telescopic or an electric version of the same unit. Either way, you'll need plenty of space beneath the wing (front or rear), more being required for the electric version's motor.

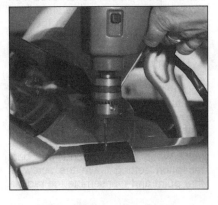

When fitting an aerial, try to position it as far away as possible from the dynamo/alternator to reduce interference problems. Check carefully under the wing to make sure nothing will be damaged by the drill. Before drilling, cover the area with masking tape, to prevent paintwork damage should the drill slip. Dot punch the position first, of course. If you're fitting at the rear of the car, you'll need an extension for the aerial wire which must be routed away from power-carrying looms.

Having made the hole, remove any burrs by using a round file. Touch-up where the paint has been removed to prevent the onset of rust. Remember that . . .

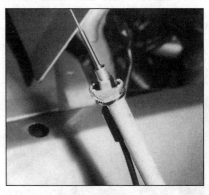

. . . the lower section of the aerial has to make a good earth contact with the bodywork. Achieve this by using copper grease rather than paint on the underside of the wing, or by running a separate wire to a known good earth point.

Having assembled the aerial in the wing correctly, tighten the top nut, but go easy – the aerial has to be a tight fit, but apply too much torque and you'll damage the top plastic piece and ruin everything.

Aerial tip
If you're replacing an aerial, before you pull the original lead out from the dash, tie a piece of string to it. That way, routing the new cable will be so much easier!

Getting in trim

Modern radios are able to work out exactly where the signals are and which ones are the best. Some decks even have two tuners, so while you're listening to one, the other is checking for a better signal! Classic radios don't (usually) have such luxuries, but most have an aerial trimmer screw. This will be found somewhere set into the casing of the radio. Sometimes the trim panel has to be removed first. Because the screw is very small (and often plastic) it's vital to use the right size 'driver to turn it – watchmakers' screwdrivers are ideal.

Power up the set, connect the aerial and tune in to a distant station with poor reception – 210/230 metres MW is often a good area to try. Turn the screw slowly and you'll hear the reception getting better or worse depending on the position of the trimmer. When you've found the best reception setting leave the screw at that point and reassemble the radio.

Dealing with interference

Modern car radios are extremely good at resisting interference, but classic radios in classic cars will usually be less so. The basic quality of the set is important; cheaper decks are generally more prone to atmospheric interference and crackling from such things as washer motors, whereas the better quality (and higher-priced) opposition suffered none of those problems.

A good quality aerial, correctly fitted and earthed is essential. Most forms of radio interference come from various electrical items already fitted to the car. In some cases (plug leads, for example) they could be faulty. In others, they may be working perfectly, but just need suppressing. Listed opposite are some of the most common sources of interference and the types of noise they are likely to make.

To isolate the culprit, park the car in an open space, otherwise confusing signals could get in the way. Close the doors and boot lid.

Interference with the ignition off is usually the clock. Switch on the ignition and turn on various electrical components one at a time, which will often nail down the offending item. No results? Run the engine and listen for the sounds given in the table. Internal spark plug cap suppressors fail over time, so replacement may be required. A distributor cap hairline crack or loose/damaged rotor arm can cause problems. Some car makers fitted a metal shield around the distributor and this is worth a try.

Interference from only one speaker/pair of speakers could be the speaker wiring routed too close to the vehicle loom – re-route and try again. Some radios are fussy about their power input; swap the fused power source or take the feed directly from the battery.

FM signals are more prone to interference and can bounce off hard objects resulting in 'ghost' sounds.

Plug leads are subject to wear, so changing yours for a set of silicon replacements may do the trick. To check, disconnect the lead at both ends, set your meter to 'Resistance/Ohms'

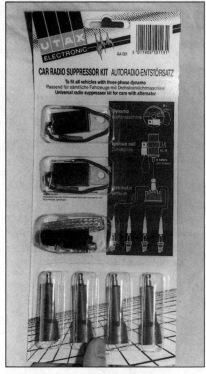

This kit comprises suppressors for four spark plug caps, HT lead, distributor cap and coil and a braided earth lead.

Item	Noise
Clock (analogue)	Regular ticking, even with ignition and engine switched off.
Windscreen wipers	Crackling sound when in use.
Heater fan motor	Crackling, as above, or a whine.
Windscreen/rear screen washer motor	Whine
Fuel pump	A fast irregular ticking, fast and then slow.
Coil/plug leads/plugs	A crackling sound which rises and falls with engine revs.
Alternator (or dynamo)	A whine in unison with the engine revs.

and put a probe to each end of the lead. The resistance should typically be about 10 ohms (consult your handbook or Haynes manual). If the reading is wildly different, replacement of them all is due.

Alternators and dynamos are a common cause of interference. Some alternators have capacitors already fitted, which should be visible close to the other electrical connections. Check that it is secure and the leads firmly attached. If you're not sure, your local specialist will be able to test it for you quite cheaply. Replacement is cheap and simple to effect.

Pull off the spark plug cap, push fit the suppressor into it and replace the whole lot on to the plug. Some plugs have in-built suppressors and have the letter 'R' as a prefix/suffix. Replacement/upgrading could solve your problems. The high tension lead to the coil can also be covered by using the in-line suppressor, which is fitted in the same way as the spark plugs.

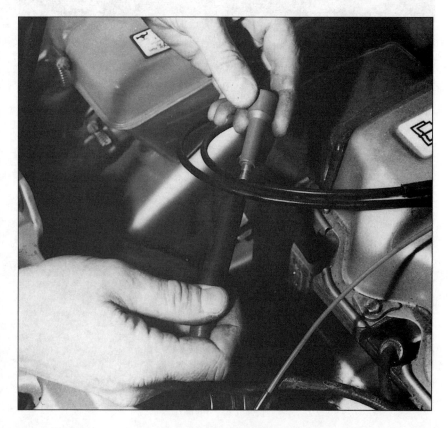

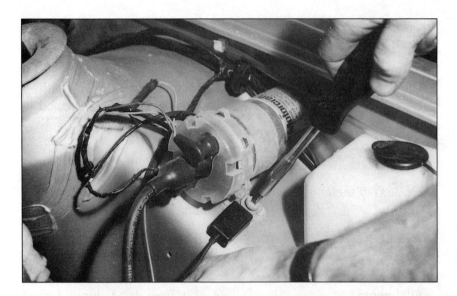

The coil suppressor should be securely earthed by its mounting bracket. For FM sets, use a 2.5 microfarad capacitor, for AM sets use 1 microfarad.

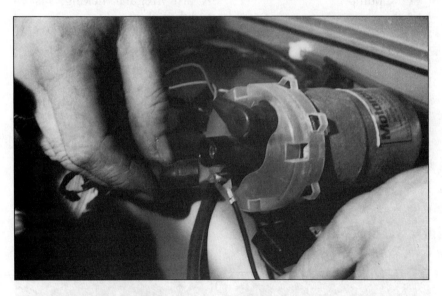

The suppressor lead then has to be connected to the ignition side of the coil.

Some cars have an earth connection fitted to the bonnet, as here. Where there isn't one, a braided connection will help enormously. Keep the terminals clean and treat with copper grease to prevent corrosion problems.

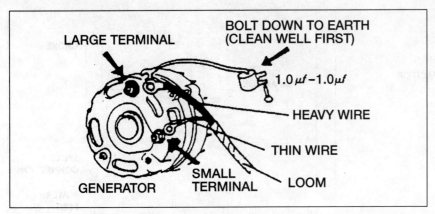

This diagram shows the correct way to install a suppressor on a typical dynamo – as ever, ensure there is a very good earth connection. If you can't use the original terminals, then you join into the nearest lead – either splice or use a screw-type terminal barrier block. Loosen the nearest mounting bolt and slide the 1–3 microfarad capacitor under it.

Suppression of motors

Ensure that motors are earthed correctly – remove the motor and clean up its earthing point bodywork with fine emery cloth. Alternatively, run a separate earth wire from the motor to a known good earth. If the problem persists, fit either a 1 microfarad capacitor, a 7 amp in-line choke, or both.

Interference could also be *re-radiation* where the problem is picked up by, say, the steering column, gear lever or exhaust, and transmitted around the car. Check by fitting an earthing strap to the various parts and then checking again for interference.

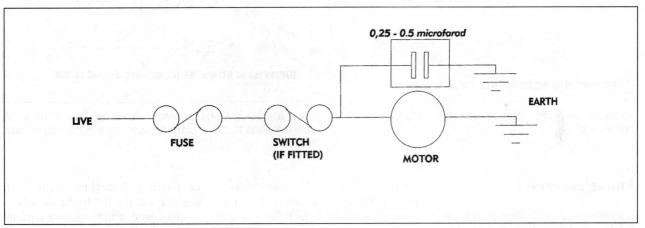

Connect the capacitor lead into the motor power lead. Use a 'piggy back' spade connector or the splice method. Tighten the capacitor to a nearby earthing point.

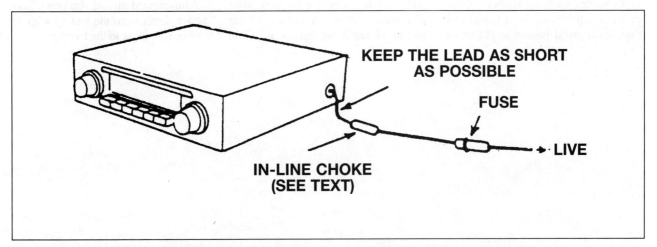

An in-line choke is a small coil of wire which produces a magnetic field when fitted in the supply lead of a component. This effectively cancels out interference. It should be sited as close as possible to the component and fitted as described previously.

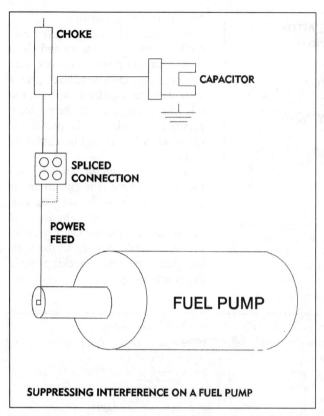

SUPPRESSING INTERFERENCE ON A FUEL PUMP

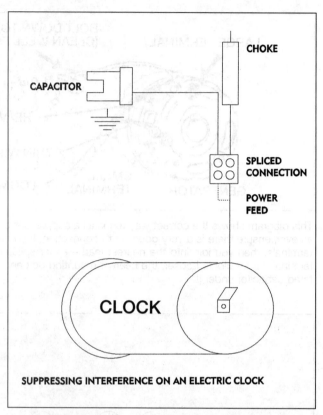

SUPPRESSING INTERFERENCE ON AN ELECTRIC CLOCK

A fuel pump should be suppressed with a capacitor and/or a choke, and . . .

. . . a clock can be treated in a similar way. Protect all connections from the extreme conditions in the engine bay.

Fibreglass cars

Owners of cars with fibreglass body-work will know that dealing with interference without the aid of a metal body is difficult. The fibre-glass makes earthing (either aerials or audio equipment) hard work, and there's no metal bonnet to act as an interference screen. You can counter this by fitting a special foil to the underside of the bonnet, and some screening against interference will be gained. Use specially perforated metal from your ICE specialist, NOT the foil you use to cook your Christmas turkey – it will cook your engine in much the same way! Glue or possibly fibreglass resin it in place. Earth the foil to the chassis.

Get a good earth by taking a separate braided lead directly to the chassis. Mount the aerial away from the engine bay – if possible, mount it at the rear of a front-engined car and visa versa. Take power direct from the battery with an in-line fuse close to the terminal.

Chapter 14

Classic security

The main problem with classic car security is that the cars were made at a time when car-theft was extremely unusual, unlike today's epidemic. Many classics don't even have door locks, which makes securing the car difficult, to say the least! A 'layered' approach should be taken, presenting a number of different hurdles for the thief to overcome. The thief's main enemy is time, and the longer it takes to steal a car, the less likely he is to continue with the attempt.

SAFETY NOTE: Do NOT try to fit any kind of vehicle immobilisation unless you are competent. Poor-installation could result in failure whilst the car is in motion, and this could be disastrous.

Wiring wisdom

A thief works quickly and will look for signs of recent work and bright pieces of wire strung in an amateur manner around the engine bay. Try the following:

● Use the same kind of wire as the vehicle.
● Use all-black wiring, to make identification difficult.
● Smear wiring with dust/oil to make it blend in.
● Slide wiring inside original looms or . . .
● Route wiring behind original looms within original cable clips.

Remember – the longer it takes you, the longer it will take the thief.

Old tricks

Simple but effective ways of protecting your classic include removing the distributor rotor arm – no sparks, no go – or fitting a simple interrupt switch. Typically, you'd do this on the fuel pump as here, or . . .

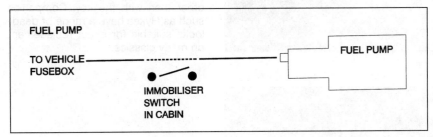

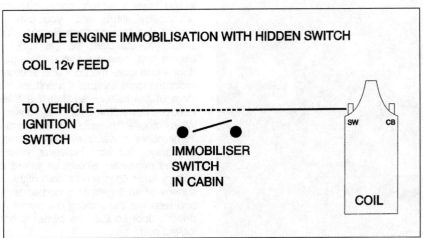

. . . the 12V feed to the coil. However, most thieves can 'hot-wire' around both these, so a more cunning way is to . . .

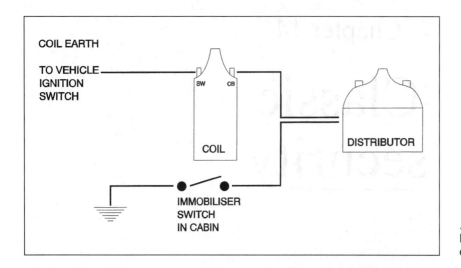

COIL EARTH

TO VEHICLE
IGNITION
SWITCH

SW   CB

COIL

DISTRIBUTOR

IMMOBILISER
SWITCH
IN CABIN

. . . interrupt the earth side of the coil. Make sure it can't accidentally be operated while the car is moving.

Locking doors and windows is essential, but they can easily be forced or broken – unless they are deadlocked, in which case they cannot be opened other than with the key. Companies such as Hykee have a range of deadlocks suitable for direct replacement on many classics.

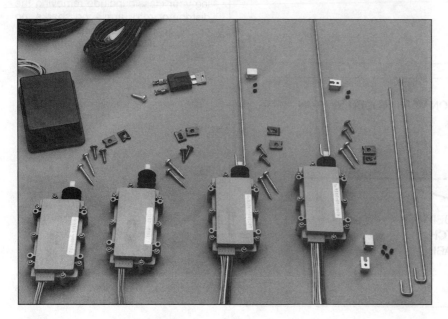

If you have a remote control device (immobiliser/alarm, etc.) you can fit central deadlocking from Sempal. It's similar to standard central locking except that there are two motors per door – one locks the door and another locks the lock! It's 'brain' monitors the state of the battery, so that if a thief removes power, the doors stay locked. When power is replaced, the brain 'remembers' it was previously locked, and stays that way. However, where voltage decreases slowly, as where a battery loses charge on a cold night, it senses when it gets to a certain level and removes the locking pin from the driver's door so that the owner is not locked out!

General hints and tips

● Park sensibly, in a garage where possible.

● ALWAYS lock your car, including the boot.

● If you have a security product, fit or arm it every time you leave the car.

● 55 per cent of thefts occur at or near the owner's home/driveway – you can never relax!

Alarms

Most alarms add more features to an immobiliser, such as a loud siren, pin switches on door, boot and bonnet and interior sensors. Of these, ultrasonic is the most common and microwave is better for convertibles, being unaffected by wind pressure. A shock/tilt sensor guards against someone jacking the car up to either remove the wheels or tow the car away. Interior glass sensors have become popular lately – these 'listen' for the high-pitched frequency of glass being struck (not necessarily broken). A battery back-up siren is recommended, as this will continue to sound even if the power is cut.

Most early-morning alarm problems relate to poor installation and/or incorrect setting-up. Take care with both to avoid upsetting your neighbours and pleasing the crooks – you want to do it the other way round!

No sense sensor

Voltage sensing is universally hated by alarm installers, customers and many unfortunate neighbours. It triggers the alarm if it detects a difference in battery voltage but it can't distinguish between a thief opening a door (and triggering the interior lamp) and a cold night. Most alarms so-fitted have the option to delete it – that's the best advice.

Electronic immobilisers

The Richfield Dis-car-nect replaces the battery power terminal with one which includes a simple screw out knob. When this is removed, it disconnects power from the car except for a trickle in order to keep a clock going or radio memory going. If an attempt is made to start the car, the in-line fuse blows. Though it is relatively simple to overcome by a thief, it does demand some effort. In addition, it's a useful device for classics where regular usage is not the norm, as it prevents excessive battery drain.

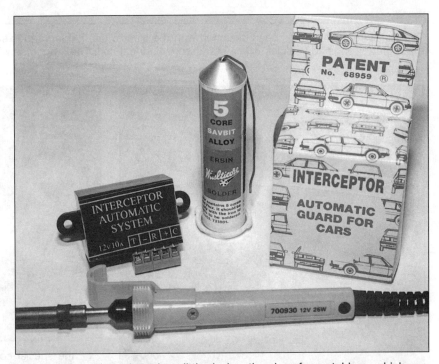

The Interceptor is an ingenious little device, the size of a matchbox, which can be used to isolate one circuit. It arms automatically and is disarmed by switching on the ignition and touching a metal fastener (you choose) at the same time. A neat and compact idea and easy to fit.

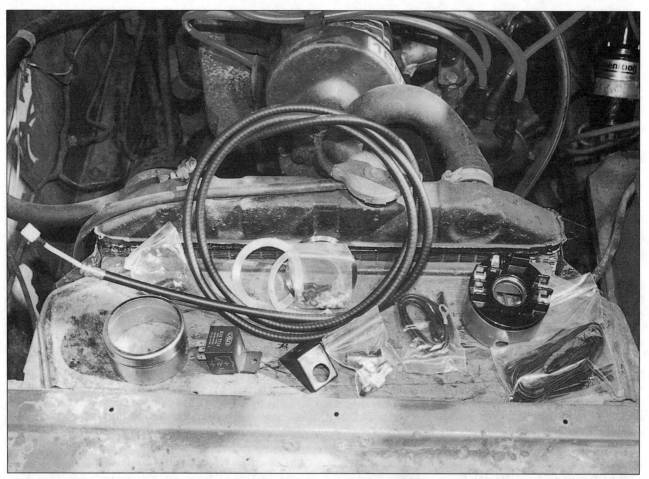

The Turret immobiliser has been designed with the classic car in mind and is suitable for all 12V (negative or positive earth) petrol-engined vehicles with a standard cylindrical coil. The kit comes with comprehensive instructions . . .

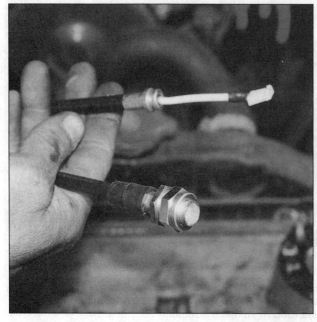

. . . the special cover which fits over the top of the coil. Because of its design, once fitted it can't be removed. Within the cover is an electronic circuit which controls the immobiliser. The normal coil connectors fit directly on to the terminal block, which is on top of the coil cover, and . . .

. . . plenty of armoured cable, switching, wiring, relay and . . .

. . . the armoured cable simply plugs in like this.

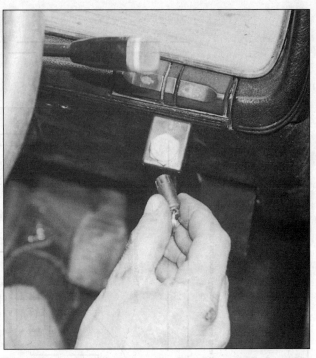

The other end of the cable goes to the car where the fixed plug (with built-in flashing LED) is fitted. This can be in the dash or the switch holder provided. Importantly, it's easy to use – where security is hard work, owners tend not to bother. The system immobilises automatically and the red LED flashes. Insert the key-plug in the socket and start the car within 30 seconds. Easy.

The lower section of the cover is fitted and locked into position.

If required, an optional powerful siren can be connected to warn of possible theft attempts.

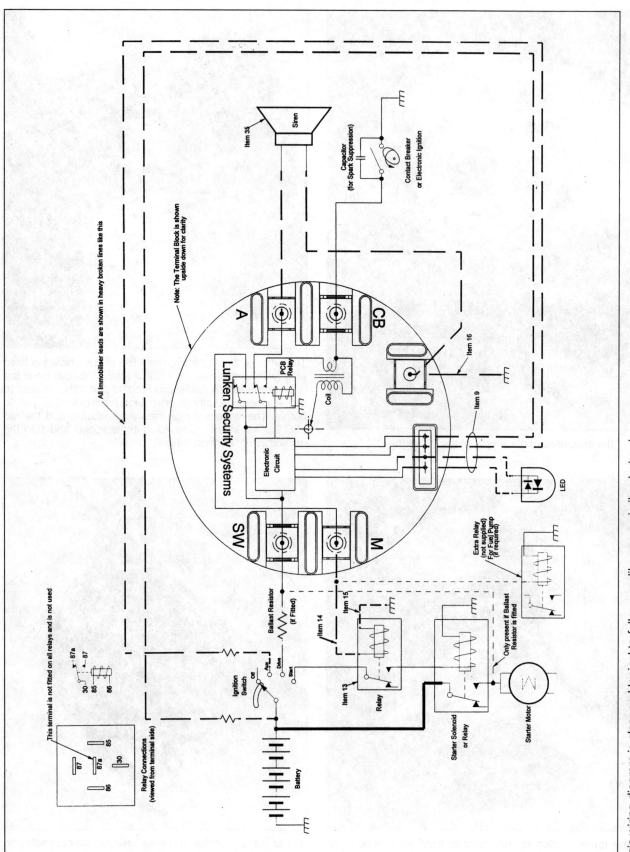

This wiring diagram is clear and logical to follow – unlike some similar devices!

Chapter 15

The wiring loom

Maintenance

How on earth can you maintain a wiring loom? On the face of it, there isn't much you can do when it comes to service time, but appearances can be deceptive, because you make plenty of checks that could be more than useful. As with virtually every other part of your car's electrical system, the loom is largely ignored until something goes wrong. However, if your battery fails to start one morning, it's not likely to be car- or even life-threatening. It's bound to be inconvenient and very annoying, but that's about it. However, a loom with faulty terminals, poor connections and trapped wiring could spell overheating and a fire that could put paid to your car, and maybe to you, too!

As such, it makes a great deal of sense to have a good nose around your car from time to time, checking under the dash, behind bits of trim and all those places you don't usually get to. Look hard at the wiring, how its routed and the condition of the various connections. Check out the following:

● All connections – wiggle them to ensure that they are not loose or about to come adrift.
● All wiring passing through holes should be protected by a grommet.
● Any clips, tapes or other fasteners that aren't doing their job.
● Leaks – most classics have either

Ooh, nasty – it's fair to say that this particular loom was just about ready for some attention! Incredibly, this car was still a runner. If your car's wiring looks like this, I'll have to take a rain check on that lift you offered!

leaking seals or poor bodywork seals. Make sure that wires/connections aren't laying in pools of water.
● Oil-leaks can affect older sheathing and leave cables unprotected.

But despite your best efforts at maintenance, there comes a time in every classic's life when enough is enough and the wiring just can't stand any more. Even a car which has retained its wiring intact, safe from the ministrations of the boy-racer and 'let's fit a host of electrical

accessories' brigade, it could still require re-wiring. Like its drivers, wiring gets old and worn out, but unlike the nut at the wheel, wiring looms can be replaced in part or in total for what is a relatively small outlay. Moreover, by using a company such as Auto Sparks, you can have a loom which not only looks like original, but which is also made from and to the same standards as the original. If only the NHS could manage something like that for the rest of us!

Over a period of many years, Auto Sparks has amassed a huge collection of classic wiring diagrams, plans and drawings and they certainly cover all popular classics I could think of. However, when a customer needs a loom for a car that isn't covered, as long as the original is supplied, a replica can still be recreated. This is how the original loom usually arrives. If this looks bad . . .

. . . take a look at this lot! As its from a Delahaye (and there aren't many of them to the pound) it's not surprising that Auto Sparks didn't have the diagram. However, once this has been completed, they will have.

I spent a day at Auto Sparks' Sandiacre factory where they produce wiring, looms, part looms, braided wiring and, in fact, just about everything required to link your classic's components in the way they were when originally built. My thanks to owner Roger Davis and general manager Martin Ethelston, for their time.

The company can provide just about all electrical and wiring requirements from a complete loom to a multi-plug or a grommet. Looms for popular classics are very much off-the-shelf, and if you've an unusual classic, they will make up a specific loom from the hundreds of diagrams and details they have amassed over the years. However, as Roger points out, when you have a real rarity that they haven't come across before, the wiring diagram isn't sufficient – they need to know such things as the lengths of specific sections of cabling, exactly where the wiring passes through holes in the trim and bodywork and what connectors are used and where. Therefore, it's important they get the complete original loom, regardless of how tatty it is, to use as a template. As a general rule, Auto Sparks produce looms in exactly the same way and with the same colouring, etc., as the original. This is vital for concours and even for a practical classic, it still looks good to be as the factory intended. However, if a customer wants to deviate from this, anything is possible. There are very often requests from customers to build in wiring for accessories, such as fog lamps, to neaten up the wiring and save having yards of loose extra cable running around the car.

It's essential that for one-offs, such as this one, every single wire is clearly marked. It's an unenviable task but this particular owner has been meticulous in the extreme, despite the rather tatty state of the loom. It's the sort of job you'd offer your worst enemy's more obnoxious brother!

THE WIRING LOOM

Auto Sparks can, if required, supply everything required for an owner to create his own classic loom. Without the full factory facilities, this is a massive amount of time-consuming hard work, but some owners insist that their rebuild should be just that – even down to the wiring! Personally, I reckon there are limits, and with prices of ready-made looms for popular classics being so reasonable, I'd probably pass this one up.

3 Getting hold of braid is, not surprisingly, very difficult, with more modern and efficient materials having replaced it long ago. However, in order to keep things as original as possible, Auto Sparks have taken the unusual step of making their own braid. They've invested huge amounts of capital in machinery to produce braid exactly as it would have been in the 1950s and '60s. This one looms the cotton from the large bobbins into triple strands which is then . . .

1 The Auto Sparks factory is laid out in logical order, starting with the wiring, job sheets, basic looms, fitting the terminals and finally packaging. Regardless of type, colour, thickness, covering, amp rating and anything else you can think of, it's hard to believe it won't be somewhere on these shelves.

2 The company uses the three basic types of wire which have been used in car-making, shown here from left to right – braided, PVC and thin wall. Braided was used from when the first wiring harness was introduced in 1930 up to around 1960. Largely because

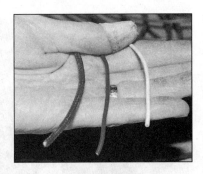

there was no way of colour-coding the rubber/plastic inners. As the '60s progressed, it became possible and ever easier to colour code PVC cable, but braided was still used to some extent, in many cases just to use up the old stocks. As electrics got more and more complicated, the '80s saw the introduction of thin wall (which is literally thinner, but with the same electrical qualities) cable which allows more wire per loom, with better heat resistance.

4 . . . transferred to these machines, unnervingly reminiscent of the Lancashire cotton mills of old, which create the braid from the strands. Despite the safety precautions and need for everyone to wear ear defenders, it is hard not to think of Les Dawson! Following this process, the braiding is then transferred to another machine for lacquering to complete the 'just as it was made originally' procedure.

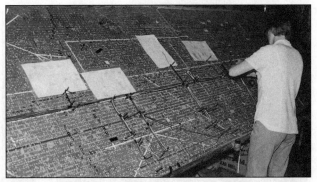

5 No, it's not a working diagram of the London Underground! The looms are planned out on huge sections of peg board, and the operator is supplied with a basket of wire pieces of the right colours and lengths to make the loom in question. As sections are completed, they are tagged together using electrician's tape prior to the final looming process.

6 This is where the loom can go to one of two basic work areas. Older looms (or even newer looms – it's all down to individual choice) go to the braiding area. With over a dozen bobbins feeding braid to the loom at a fast rate, there's no shortage of skill in producing a good braided loom. The various sections of the loom are individually braided before being completed; as Martin said, it's like a tree, with the twigs and branches being braided first, followed by the trunk.

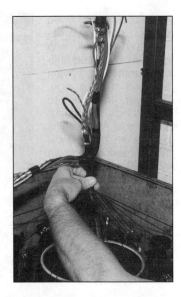

9 . . . it is being loomed using blue tape. For whatever reason, USA MGs of the period used blue instead of the black or grey tape favoured by the UK.

7 All in a day's work, yet another pile of braided looms ready for classic car-dom. Though it's mostly older classics that use braided looms, Martin pointed out that some cars originally produced in the '60s, continued to use it throughout their production lives – the Jaguar XJ6 being a prime example.

10 Though it looks like the wanderings of an ink-stained, nomadic spider, this is yet another 'underground map', absolutely essential for maintaining the originality of the loom. Its purpose is to aid the terminal fitter, who has to know the right terminal to put on the right wire at the right point.

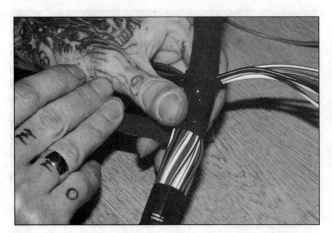

8 While older cars are braided (if their owners want it), more modern classics are loomed in an equally suitable manner. This is part of a loom for a '60s MGB, but because it is for an American specification vehicle . . .

11 The connectors are always fitted to the wires in the same way as the originals were – so, if they were crimped, Auto Sparks crimp them, as here.

12 Four sizes of crimp-on terminal are used. Crimp terminals can be recognised from their soldered cousins by the fact that they have straight 'shoulders'. From the left, the first four are crimp terminals being suitable for 9/0.30, 14/0.30, 28/0.30, 44/0.30 wire sizes respectively. On the far right is a solder type terminal suitable for 28/0.30. (As listed in Chapter 3, wire sizes are denoted first by the number of strands and then by the thickness of each strand; consequently, 28/0.30 means 28 strands of wire, each 0.30mm thick.)

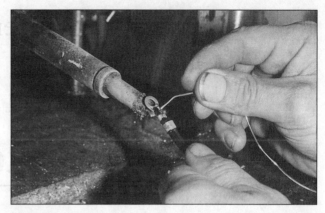

15 Some terminals have to be soldered. This huge soldering iron is fixed in position, allowing the operator two hands to produce perfect solder joins – note that the terminal is being heated and then the solder applied to run into the join.

13 Fitting Lucar terminals is easier, because there's a machine purely for that task. The bared end of the wire is pushed through this Perspex hole and . . .

16 Rubber multipin connectors like this are long out of production at the original factories. The answer for Auto Sparks was to have them specially made to original specification. Because this particular plug has the terminals moulded into the housing, all connections are made by the moulding company.

14 . . . when it comes out, the job is complete. The actual crimping is achieved by an automatic mechanism which comes down with considerable force – hence the clear screen which prevents errant fingers getting crimped by mistake. Martin reckons that this kind of terminal with a separate insulator is much better than those where the insulator is all of a piece with the terminal.

17 The finished product is then heat sealed in its bag ready for collection or mail order despatch.

Appendix I

Useful names and addresses

To keep in line with the latest in technology, the electronic contact details have also been included where known and/or available. The numbers given after the address are; telephone number, E-mail address and web site. It is important that this address is entered exactly, otherwise the connection will not be made. E-mail is an electronic address for writing letters, sending orders, etc., and the web site is effectively an electronic catalogue for the company, enabling them to give you up-to-date details of products and services. In many cases, orders can be placed electronically – if so, it is important to recognise the importance of having a secure connection, to prevent your credit card details falling into nefarious hands.

AG Products
PO Box 575
Ascot, Berks. SL5 9XS
Distributors of the Battery Sava, a battery trickle charging device which prevents a battery discharging completely during the winter or long lay-ups.
01344 24131

Alpine Electronics of UK
13 Tanners Drive,
Milton Keynes, Bucks. MK14 5DU
All types of ICE equipment.
01908 611556

P & J Autos
Unit 6, Grove Park Road,
Rainham, Essex. RM13 7BX
Specialists in remanufacture and repair of classic, veteran and vintage car electrics. Instrumental in producing several chapters of this book.
01708 500010

Autocar Electrical Equipment Company Ltd
49/51 Tiverton Street,
London. SE1 6NZ.
Lumenition electronic ignition conversion kits and uprated HT leads.
0171 403 4334
autocar@denaploy.co.uk
http://www.denaploy.co.uk/autocar

Becker
See Hirschmann

Bosch, Robert Ltd
PO Box 98, Broadwater Park,
North Orbital Road,
Denham, Uxbridge, Middx. UB9 5HJ.
All kinds of automotive electrical systems and products including Blaupunkt in-car entertainment and Bosch spark plugs and test equipment.
01895 838547

Champion
Arrowbrooke Road,
Upton, Wirral, Merseyside. L49 0UQ
Spark plugs, wiper blades, ignition components.
0151 678 7070

Cibié
See Ring Automotive

Clarke International
Hemnal Street,
Epping, Essex. CM16 4LG
A wide range of hand and power tools, including jacks, axle stands, pneumatic tools and parts washers.
01992 565300

Draper Tools Limited
Hursley Road,
Chandlers Ford, Eastleigh, Hants.
SO53 1YF
Suppliers of high-quality tools and Metabo power drills, etc.
01703 266355.
Sales@draper.co.uk
http://www.draper.co.uk

Enterprise Europe
2033 Battlebridge, Essex. S11 8RU
Suppliers of the Interceptor immobiliser.
0181 249 3576

Fluke (UK) Ltd
Colonial Way, Watford, Herts.
WD2 4TT
High-quality professional-standard multimeters and associated accessories.
01923 216400

Gunson Limited
Coppen Road, Dagenham, Essex.
RM8 1NU
DIY and professional electrical and electronic test equipment.
0181 984 8855

Halfords Ltd
A wide range of tools, electrical
components and spares for classic
cars.
0345 626625 for nearest store

Hella Ltd (Beru)
Wildmere Industrial Estate,
Banbury, Oxon. OX16 7JU
Sparking plugs, electronic test
equipment (Optilux), alternators,
lighting equipment, drive belts, etc.
01295 272233

**Richard Hirschmann Electronics
UK Ltd**
St Martins Way,
St Martins Business Centre, Bedford.
MK42 0LF
High-quality in-car electronics
including Hirschmann aerials and
Becker sound equipment.
01234 345999

Hykee
100 High Street,
Broadstairs, Kent. CT10 1JB
Deadlocking replacements for many
classic cars.
01843 862952

Indespension
Belmont Road,
Bolton, Lancs. BL1 7AQ
Complete and kit-form trailers, all
manner of parts, accessories and
security items for towing and trailers
generally, trailer rental.
0800 720720 (for nearest stockist)

JVC UK Ltd
12 Priestley Way,
Eldon Wall Trading Estate, London.
NW2 7BA
All kinds of ICE equipment.
0181 450 3282

Kenwood Ltd
Dwight Road,
Watford, Herts. WD1 8EB.
All kinds of ICE equipment.
01923 816444

Lucas Aftermarket Operations
Great Hampton Street,
Birmingham. B18 6AU
All kinds of classic automotive
electrical systems and products
including lighting, ignition and a
range of remanufactured starter
motors, alternators, etc.
0121 236 5050

Lunken Security Systems
The Larches, Blackpond Lane,
Farnham Royal, Slough. SL2 3ED
Manufacturers of the Turret electronic
immobiliser, ideal for classic cars.
01753 644040
101362.1507@compuserve.com
http://www.hartlana.co.uk/turret

Moss International Limited
Victoria Villas,
Richmond, Surrey. TW9 2JX
A supplier of classic spares for many
models.
0181 948 8888

Mr Fastner
Units 6/12,
Warwick House Industrial Park,
Banbury Road, Southam, Warwicks.
CV33 0PS
A massive range of standard and
exotic fasteners, including Torx,
Allen, anodised, stainless and thread
repair kits.
01926 817207

NGK Spark Plugs (UK) Ltd
7-9 Garrick Industrial Centre,
Hendon, London. NW9 6AQ
Spark plugs, plug covers and technical
ceramics (sensors).
0181 202 2151

Omega Trolley Jacks
See SIP.

Radiomobile
19 Fairways,
New River Trading Estate,
Cheshunt, Herts. EN8 0NL
All kinds of ICE equipment.
01992 634428

Ring Automotive
Gelderd Road,
Leeds. LS12 6NB
Major supplier of all types of electrical
products including Ring and Cibié
lighting, workshop lighting, halogen/
xenon bulbs, trailer equipment,
cables, fuses and all ancillaries.
01532 791791

Sempal Limited
The Commercial Centre, Sherrif Street,
Worcester. WR4 9AB
Electric windows and the only
aftermarket central deadlocking kit
available.
01905 617544

SIP (Industrial Products Ltd)
Gelders Hall Road,
Shepshed, Loughborough, Leics.
LE12 9NH
High-quality DIY equipment,
including Omega hydraulic trolley
jacks, axle stands and power tools.
01509 503141

**SJAB (St John Ambulance
Brigade) head office**
1 Grosvenor Street,
London. SW1X 7EF.
National first-aid society offering
training courses via its regional
training centres and sales of first-aid
kits designed for many specific uses
including in-car.
(See under St John Ambulance
Brigade in your local directory or
ring 0171 251 0004 for sales
enquiries.)

Sony UK Ltd
The Heights,
Brooklands, Weybridge, Surrey.
KT13 0XW
All kinds of ICE equipment.
01923 816000

Sykes Pickavant Ltd
Kilnhouse Lane,
Lytham St Annes, Lancs. FY8 3DU
All kinds of electronic test and
diagnostic equipment, including
multimeters.
01253 721291

Turret Immobiliser
See Lunken Security Systems.

Thatcham (Motor Insurance Repair Research Centre)
Colthrop Lane,
Thatcham, Newbury, Berks.
RG19 4NP
The insurance testing agency for security products. A list of approved immobilisers/alarms is available on request from the ABI, 51 Gresham Street, London. EC2V 7HQ or on faxback (49p per minute) 0660 666680.
01635 868855

Vehicle wiring/accessories/terminals/tools, etc.

Auto Sparks
80–88 Derby Road,
Sandiacre, Nottinghamshire.
NG10 5HU
Extensive range of custom-made wiring harnesses covering most vehicles from 1930 to 1980.
Comprehensive catalogue of cables, terminals and sundries.
0115 949 7211
Sales@autosparks.co.uk

Blue Beehive
152 Church Lane,
Tooting, London, SW17 9PU
A wide range of electrical terminals, fuses, connectors and other accessories for the DIY motorist, available cheaply in bulk.
0181 767 0057

Holden Vintage & Classic
Linton Trading Estate,
Bromyard, Herefordshire. HR7 4QT
A vast range of classic car electrical items; one of the biggest stocks in the country of guaranteed rebuilt distributors.
01885 488000
holden@holden.co.uk
http://www.holden.co.uk

VWP (Vehicle Wiring Products)
9 Buxton Court,
Manners Industrial Estate,
Ilkeston, Derbyshire. DE7 8EF
Mail order supplier of electrical cables, connectors, tools and accessories, all parts required for complete rewire or modification. Phone/write for free illustrated catalogue.
0115 930 5454

Batteries

Manufacturers and restorers of new classic batteries.

Autolux Batteries
The Boathouse, Timsway,
Chertsey Lane,
Staines, Middx. TW18 3JY
01784 462944

Classic Batteries
Home Farm,
Middlezoy, Somerset. TA7 0PD
01823 698437

Lincoln Batteries
Arterial Road,
Leigh-on-Sea, Essex. SS9 4EG
01702 525374

Shepherd Batteries 1928
6 Chapel Street,
Salford, Manchester. M3 7WJ
0161 834 8589

Stanford Battery Service
Stanford Road,
Norbury, London. SW16
0181 679 3962

Radios, in-car entertainment, sales, repair and spares services

Car Radio Repair & Restoration Service
10 West View,
Paulton, Bristol, Avon. BS18 5XJ
01761 413933.

Moon, Lester
Winterbourne, Bristol
01454 772814

Radiocraft
56 Main Street,
Sedgeberrow, Herefordshire.
WR11 6UF
01386 200436

Vintage Wireless
174 Cross Street,
Sale, Cheshire.
0161 973 0438

Appendix II

Glossary of commonly used terms and abbreviations

Alternating current (AC)
Electricity varying in polarity and voltage and reversing direction regularly. It is produced by an alternator. Abbreviated to AC.

Alternator
A device which generates alternating current and converts it to direct current for vehicle use. Compared with its predecessor, the dynamo, it is more efficient, particularly at lower engine speeds.

Ammeter
A gauge which shows charge being put into the battery by the dynamo and how much is being taken out by vehicle components. It shows as a + (charge) or – (discharge).

Amps
Abbreviation of amperes, a measurement of the rate of current flow in an electrical circuit.

Amp hour (AH)
A measurement of battery performance, used less frequently as time goes by.

Anode
The positive pole in a direct current system (see also cathode).

Armature
The part of an electrical device which comprises the electrical windings in which a current flows or a

magnetic field is generated or excited (for example, dynamo or solenoid).

Automatic advance
See centrifugal advance.

Arcing
When an electrical spark jumps through air, such as between contact breaker points or spark plug electrodes.

Ballast resistor
An electrical device which reduces the spark to the coil which is automatically cut-out of the circuit whilst the starter motor is operating to enable as much spark as possible to get to the engine.

Battery voltage
The voltage of the battery taken without load, typically 12V–14V (or 6V–8V on a 6V system).

Brushes
Pick-up brushes are used in electric motors of various types, such as dynamos and starter motors. They can pick up current or draw it from a commutator.

Capacitor
The correct name for a condenser, but usually one which has a larger capacity for holding electricity and able to perform a smoothing role in current generating where there is no battery.

Cathode
The negative pole in a direct current system (see also anode).

Centrifugal advance
A system of springs and bob weights within the distributor by which the spark can automatically be advanced as the engine speed rises.

Charging
The process of electrically boosting a battery after it has been partly or completely drained. This is either by a dynamo/alternator on the vehicle or a mains-powered battery charger off the car.

Coil
The cylindrical device in a petrol engine ignition system which boosts the car's 12V (or 6V) up to the extremely high voltage required for the spark plugs.

Commutator
The part of an armature (in a dynamo or starter motor) against which the brushes rub.

Condenser
Another name for a capacitor. A device which can store electricity and then release it quickly as required.

Contact breaker
Part of the distributor which alternately makes and breaks a connection whereby the current from the coil is fed to the various spark plugs.

Crimper
A scissor-like device which enables strong wire-to-terminal joins to be made without soldering.

Diode
An electrical component which allows electrical current to flow in one direction only, in the same way as a one-way valve in a water system.

Direct current (DC)
Electricity of constant polarity which may or may not change its voltage. Produced by a dynamo and abbreviated to DC.

Distributor
The device on a petrol engine which distributes the high voltage from the coil to the spark plugs.

Dynamo
A generator of direct current, driven by an engine pulley, used to produce electricity to run vehicle electrical components and charge the battery.

Earth
The pole of the battery which is connected to the vehicle body and/or chassis. Can be positive or negative.

Electrolyte
The liquid contained in the battery case, usually a dilution of sulphuric acid.

Electromagnet
A magnet which becomes magnetic when excited by an electric current but which loses its magnetism almost as soon as the current is removed.

Feeler gauges
Very thin strips of hardened steel produced to high tolerances and uniform thickness, used to measure very small gaps, such as contact breaker points and spark plugs.

Generator
A device which makes, or generates electricity – see dynamo and alternator.

Heat shrink tubing
Ingenious rubber-like tube which can be used to loom wiring and which shrinks around the wires when heat is applied.

Hydrometer
A device looking like a large syringe, used to suck up electrolyte from a battery and which gives a specific gravity reading. This in turn indicates the state of battery charge.

HT (High tension)
High-tension, a term used for the high-voltage side of the ignition system, typically around 20,000V, after the 12V input has been boosted by the coil.

Insulator
Any substance which prevents the flow of electricity.

Lambda sensor
Not common on classics, and used only where a catalytic exhaust is fitted. This device is fitted into the down-pipe near the engine and measures the exhaust content, electrically triggering an increase or decrease in fuel mixture.

LT (low tension)
Low-tension, a term used for the low-voltage side of the ignition system, which is at battery voltage (12V–1 4V, or 6V–8V).

Multimeter
A modern version of the original volt-meter which measures a variety of electrical units (volts, ohms, etc.).

Negative earth
A vehicle electrical system where the negative terminal of the battery is connected to the chassis/body (earth).

Ohms
A measurement of electrical resistance.

Permanent magnet
A magnet which retains its magnetism extremely well.

Petroleum jelly
A very useful substance, usually referred to by its trade name of Vaseline. A semi-solid made from wax with a high oil content, it is useful for preventing the ingress of moisture and water.

Plug cap
The insulated cover fitted to the top of the spark plug. It protects the electrical connection and includes a legally-required suppressor.

Plug lead
The HT (high tension) lead from the distributor cap to the spark plug. Once always made with a thick copper inner, but latterly produced using silicone for better electrical transmission and less interference. Always highly insulated.

Positive earth
A vehicle electrical system where the positive terminal of the battery is connected to the chassis/body (earth).

Pre-ignition
A situation where the spark and subsequent explosion in the cylinder head occurs before it should. Very damaging to the engine.

Primary current
The low voltage current in the ignition circuit, often called low tension and abbreviated to LT.

Primary Winding
The winding inside the ignition coil which runs at battery voltage (occasionally less).

Rectifier
A device which converts AC current to DC current.

Relay
An electro-magnetic switch used to allow a heavy current device to be operated by a smaller current switch and its wiring.

Rheostat
A variable resistance which varies the amount of current used by a component, e.g. a panel light dimmer.

Rotor arm
Fixed to the distributor cam, it is made from non-conductive material with a metal (brass) tip. As the cam turns, the tip of the rotor makes contact with the connections in the distributor cap for the HT spark plug leads.

Solenoid
A remote operating switch which is able to physically push or pull on a mechanism.

Spark plug
A device which arcs an electric current between two electrodes which are inserted into the combustion space. The spark created is used to trigger the fuel air mixture.

Spiral binding
Flexible plastic apple peel method of looming separate wires.

Suppressor
A small component designed to produce a resistance in order to reduce interference by an engine with the in-car radio, but also with domestic electrical equipment. Fitted to the HT side of the ignition system the values are typically 5 ohms–15,000 ohms. Much lower rated suppressors (typically 1 ohm) are used on the LT side of the ignition system to kill the interference from such items as a dynamo, clock, wiper motor, etc.

Stroboscope
Used in vehicle timing lights. Produces one flash per revolution of the engine crankshaft.

Tachometer
The proper name for a rev counter. Can be electrical (counting the sparks from the coil) or mechanically driven by cable.

Tell-tale
A small warning light in the car within the driver's vision to indicate that some electrical function is operating (typically used for rear fog lamps).

Terminal
The metal fitting to which an electrical connection is made. Can be fixed to an electrical component – e.g. the battery – or to the end(s) of a wire to enable connection to be made.

Transistor
A small electrical device which boosts a small input to a much larger one. Used in ignition systems and radios, etc.

Trickle charging
When a battery is being charged off the vehicle, some chargers are capable of working at a very low rate – typically between 1/2A and 2A. This is referred to as a trickle and is generally better for the battery than a faster charge, although clearly it takes longer to complete.

Volts
A measurement of electrical force.

Watts
A measurement of electrical power.

Appendix III

Useful information

Typical power requirements

Power is quoted in watts (see Chapter 2) and the table here quotes the typical power requirements for various components on your classic. They have been rated relating to the length of time the power is required, ranging from continuous for all the time the car is running to those lasting just a few seconds at a time. Possibly the most informative for most owners is the massive power required by the starter motor – there's no wonder that you need a well-charged battery to start a cold engine!

Basic trouble-shooting

Check the obvious

The over-riding message when checking the electrics on your classic is simple – don't forget to CHECK THE OBVIOUS. Just as many a motorist has spent hours trying to start a car with an empty petrol tank (been there, done that!) just as many have spent hours looking for a complicated electrical fault only to find a fuse has blown or that the ignition was not switched on!

Assume nothing

Which brings us to lesson 2. As that great sage, Benny Hill, once said: 'to assume makes an ASS out of U and ME.' Electrics can be complicated, but there's still nothing to stop a problem being caused by something simple and obvious. So, assume nothing, and when you have a fault, whatever it is, work through the set procedure start to finish; skipping bits is a recipe for wasting lots of your valuable time.

Short circuits

The most obvious clue that there's a short circuit is the harsh 'snap' of a blown fuse, followed by a moment

Watts	Circuit	Time
2W	Panel lamps (each)	Long term
5W	Sidelamps (each)	Long term
5W	Rear lamps (each)	Long term
5W	Interior lamp	Short term
10W	Number plate lamp	Long term
15W	Radio/cassette	Long term
20W	Ignition	Constant
21W	Stop lamps (each)	Short term
21W	Indicator lamps (each)	Short term
30-90W	Windscreen wiper	Long term
40W	Horn	Short term
55W	Electric fuel pump	Constant
55W	Fog/spot lamps (each)	Long term
60W	Headlamps (each)	Long term
60W	Heater motor	Long term
60W	Rear wiper	Short term
60W	Headlamp wash/wipe	Short term
90W	Fuel Injection	Constant
100W	Cigarette lighter	Short term
130W	Heated rear window	Long term
150W	Electric windows	Short term
200W	Radiator fan	Short term
800-2500W	Starter motor	Short term

(Refer to Chapter 2 for more details on power consumption and equations.)

of panic as you jump back in shock! Often the cause of the problem is obvious – if you've just fitted a radio and the fuse blows when you first switch it on, the odds are that the radio is the cause. However, it's seldom quite as simple, and most vehicle fuses control several items.

Set your meter to: '12V/DC'

Locate the fuse that has blown and switch off all items controlled by it. Remove the fuse and connect the leads to the fuse terminals – there should be no reading at all. One at a time, switch on the fused items, and when you get a reading, that is the problem circuit. It is then a question of following the wiring for that particular item to check for faults. Leave the meter connected so that when you disconnect any plugs or remove any connections you can keep an eye on the reading. When it goes to zero, then you have isolated the problem. Look for plugs that have developed internal corrosion, poor earth connections and chafed and split wiring.

Switch trouble

Switches can often develop their own internal problems, which can lead to non-existent or intermittent operation. As a switch does its job (carrying current) heat is generated and the first upshot of this is that, over a period of years, the contact surfaces inside the switch start to burn and degrade – like contact breaker points in a distributor. The other heat-related problem is that hot terminals can actually 'sink' into the (usually) plastic casing of the switch. When this happens, though their surfaces may be fine, the terminals could actually end up being too far away to make contact at all. This kind of problem can only be solved by physically opening the switch, where possible, and looking inside.

If you do this, take great care, because most are fitted with tiny springs and ball bearings, which can hurtle out at a rate of knots. They're unlikely to do you much harm, other than to your sanity as you search for them on a dirty garage floor!

Useful conversions

When working on your classic, you'll often find that you are working in imperial sizes and need to convert them to metric – or visa versa. This table should help make life easier.

To convert	To	Multiply by
Inches	Millimetres	25.4
Millimetres	Inches	0.0394
Feet	Metres	0.305
Metres	Feet	3.281
Miles	Kilometres	1.609
Kilometres	Miles	0.621
Miles per hour	Kilometres per hour	1.609
Kilometres per hour	Miles per hour	0.621
Ounces	Grams	28.35
Grams	Ounces	0.035
Pounds	Kilograms	0.454
Kilograms	Pounds	2.205
US gallons	Litres	3.785
Litres	US gallons	0.2642
UK gallons	Litres	4.546
Litres	UK gallons	0.22
UK gallons	US gallons	1.20095
US gallons	UK gallons	0.832674
Miles per UK gallon	Kilometres per litre	0.354
Kilometres per litre	Miles per UK gallon	2.825
Miles per US gallon	Kilometres per litre	0.425
Kilometres per litre	Miles per US gallon	2.352
Pounds feet	Newton Metres	1.356
Newton Metres	Pounds feet	0.738
Pounds feet	Kilogram metres	0.138
Kilogram metres	Pounds feet	7.233
Cubic inches	Cubic centimetres	16.387
Cubic centimetres	Cubic inches	0.061
Fahrenheit	Celsius (centigrade)	(subtract 32) 0.5555
Celsius	Fahrenheit	1.8 (plus 32)

Other titles of interest